Emergency?
Fix It Yourself With
THE NEW PRACTICAL HOME REPAIR FOR WOMEN

"The preface to this admirable ready-reference book says with sad truth that the demand for the expert handyman's services has increased so greatly it is practically impossible to hire him at any price. And the man of the house, overwhelmed with commuting, working and travelling on the job is never around when he is needed for that important chore.

Many women are the heads of households—and for sure, they're the ones who are around when pipes burst, light bulbs explode and things go pop all around."
— *Detroit Free Press*

Here is the new, updated version of an extremely popular book—the first complete, illustrated handbook for do-it-yourself home repair written especially for women by Bruce Cassiday, Home Maintenance Editor of ***Argosy Magazine***.

THE NEW PRACTICAL HOME REPAIR FOR WOMEN

Your Questions Answered
BRUCE CASSIDAY

LANCER BOOKS NEW YORK

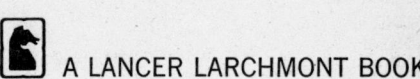 A LANCER LARCHMONT BOOK

THE NEW PRACTICAL HOME REPAIR FOR WOMEN

Copyright © 1966, 1972 by Bruce Cassiday
All rights reserved
Printed in the U.S.A.

This book was published by arrangement with Taplinger Publishing Company, Inc. Its large sale in the hardcover edition makes possible this inexpensive reprint.

LANCER BOOKS, INC. • 1560 BROADWAY
NEW YORK, N.Y. 10036

To Doris
The Heroine of the Book

FOREWORD

It was a bitter cold morning. The temperature had dropped to ten degrees below zero in the night. After the children had set off for school and my husband for the office, I began my morning chores.

While I cleared the kitchen table I could hear water dripping, as if someone had left a tap open. I turned to look at the faucet in the kitchen sink, but it seemed to be off. The dripping stopped, to be replaced by the sound of a waterfall. In a moment, I not only heard rushing water, but I felt it around my feet. It was flowing rapidly out of the wall behind the sink.

Something had to be done quickly—but what?

I thought immediately of two things to do, but, as I learned later, the simplest and most logical move eluded me.

I called the plumber, reporting the flood in my kitchen. Then I ran for a mop and bucket to soak up the water before it could damage the floor and furniture. I mopped as I had never mopped before, but it did no good. The water simply kept coming.

When the plumber arrived, he naturally closed the main supply valve, and the flow of water gradually subsided. If I had been able to refer to my husband's book, PRACTICAL HOME REPAIR FOR WOMEN, when our pipes froze and burst, I would have known exactly what to do: turn off the water supply.

At that time, unfortunately, the book was not yet written. Now that it is, I wholeheartedly recommend it to any woman who wants to know the how, when, and why of home repair and maintenance.

Doris Cassiday
(Mrs. Bruce Cassiday)

PREFACE

When I appeared on "To Tell The Truth" to promote the first edition of this book, I was questioned most intently by Kitty Carlisle as to why I thought women could do home repair work. "If women have enough mechanical aptitude to do home repairs," she asked, "why aren't there more women famous in the field of construction and building?"

"Perhaps because they never tried," I said honestly, thus unmasking myself as the real author of "Practical Home Repair for Women" and losing the prize money.

Who can say how many famous women might not now be in construction and building if they had really been given the opportunity to be architects and engineers?

This book was published before women had decided that they *could* be astronauts, football players, longshoremen, and many other things they have been conditioned *not* to be over the centuries.

Since there is now no stigma attached to a woman who does her own thing, even if it isn't the conventional "feminine" thing to do, this book today will serve an even greater purpose than it did when it was originally published.

The helpless, hand-fluttering, faint-hearted female of yesterday who swooned at the sight of a hammer and nail no longer exists. Even though sewing and cooking may be more to her liking—because of conditioning from birth or natural inclination—she can nevertheless grab up a screwdriver or wrench and tackle a plumbing emergency without dissolving into tears and hysteria.

It is to this valiant, no-nonsense individual—the woman of today

—that the second edition of this book is dedicated, and it is dedicated to her for her own enlightenment, inspiration, and, I hope, genuine pleasure in accomplishment.

Bruce Cassiday

[1972]

ACKNOWLEDGMENTS

I want to extend my thanks to the following people, without whose technical assistance it would have been impossible to prepare this book:

Warren Phillips of the Aluminum Council; Elizabeth M. Rich of American Iron and Steel Institute; Tony Mancino of Hill and Knowlton, Inc.; Thomas O. McCarthy, Charles Custer, and David Strong of the American Plywood Association; John R. Hays and Lee Rappleyea of the California Redwood Association; Martin C. Powers and Neil B. Garlock of the National Paint, Varnish and Lacquer Association; Richard G. Knox of the Portland Cement Association; Edward C. Benfield of the Stanley Tool Division of the Stanley Works; Sam K. Wilson of the Sprayit Division of Thomas Industries Inc.

I would like to express my appreciation to Doris Cassiday, my wife, for her untiring editorial and clerical assistance, as well as her criticisms and suggestions on the wording and structure of the book.

In addition to the above, I would like to thank the following associations, corporations, and government departments for their invaluable aid and assistance: Alcoa Aluminum, American Brush Manufacturers Association, American Home Lighting Institute, American Machine and Foundry, Arco Tools, Bernz-O-Matic Company, Black and Decker, Bostitch Corporation, E. L. Bruce Company, Inc., Bureau of Naval Personnel, Celotex Corporation, Departments of the Army and the Air Force, Devcon Corporation, Dow Corning, Fastener Division of U. S. Machinery Corporation, Fiberglas Screen Cloth, Fire Grille Company, General Electric,

Georgia-Pacific Corporation, Gering Plastics Company, Housing and Home Finance Agency, Masonite Corporation, Metal Lath Association, Millers Falls Company, Minnesota Mining Corporation, Mystik Tape, National Electrical Manufacturers Association, National Lumber Manufacturers Association, National Mineral Wool Insulation Association, National Wiring Bureau, Nicholson File Company, O'Malley Valve Company, Porter-Cable Division of Rockwell Corporation, Public Housing Administration, Rain Drain, Ramset, Winchester-Western Division of Olin, Rural Electrification Administration, Sears, Roebuck and Company, Skil Corporation, Smith-Gates Corporation, Stylon Corporation, U. S. Department of Agriculture, U S. Department of Agriculture Forest Service, U. S. Department of Commerce, U. S. Department of Health, Education and Welfare, U. S. Post Office Department, U. S. War Department, Union Carbon and Carbide, Uvalde Rock Asphalt Company.

ART CREDITS

Art credits as follows:
Pages 6, 7, 53, 85—Drawn by Tony Mancino, Hill & Knowlton, Inc.; Pages 109, 125, 126, 129—Courtesy American Plywood Association; Page 56—Courtesy California Redwood Association; Pages 96, 98, 99—Courtesy National Electrical Manufacturers Association; Pages 18, 21, 24—Courtesy National Paint, Varnish and Lacquer Association; Pages 175, 176—Courtesy Portland Cement Association; Pages 37, 38—Courtesy Sprayit Division of Thomas Industries, Inc.; Pages 41, 42, 44, 44, 46, 47, 48, 49—Courtesy Stanley Tool Division of the Stanley Works; Pages 9, 71, 111, 112, 124, 134, 157—Drawn by the Author.

CONTENTS

1. Emergency!	1
2. Painting	13
3. Tools and Fasteners	39
4. Wood	66
5. Plumbing	77
6. Heating	84
7. Electricity	90
8. Floors	108
9. Outside Walls	123
10. Inside Walls	133
11. Doors	148
12. Windows	156
13. Concrete	170
14. Masonry	182
15. Insulation	190
16. Air Conditioning	198
17. Sound Conditioning	205
18. New Developments in Home Repair	214
Index	227

The New Practical Home Repair for Women
YOUR QUESTIONS ANSWERED

Emergency!

unsure of its condition, remove a good bulb which lights, insert the questionable bulb, and see whether or not it works.

¶ How do you go about repairing a wall switch which has broken?

You start first by removing the fuse in the fuse box which controls the circuit. If you are not sure to which circuit the switch is attached, take out all the fuses. Then remove the outer switch plate by unscrewing the two screws which attach the plate to the box in the wall. You will see that the toggle, or on-and-off switch, is mounted on a metal strip attached to a box crammed with wires. Unscrew the toggle strip, and pull it away from the wall until you can see the screws in back which attach the power wires to the toggle strip. Unfasten these wires, carefully noting the connections. Replace the broken toggle mounting with a new one, and refasten the power wires. Be sure the ends (or "leads") of the wires curve around the screw in the same direction as you turn the screw to fasten it. Push the toggle strip back onto the box, working the wires in behind. Refasten the toggle strip, put on the outer plate, and fasten the screws.

¶ What is wrong with an electric appliance when it suddenly won't work after giving good service?

There may be many things wrong. Your first move is to make sure that the cord is properly plugged into the convenience outlet. If this is not the problem, check the cord for breaks. Repair them. Make sure the cord has not pulled out where it enters the appliance. If it has, secure it. After you have thoroughly checked the cord and plug, see instructions under the specific appliance in Chapter Seven on Electricity.

¶ Why does a fluorescent lamp fail to light at once, or blink for some time before lighting?

You need a new starter, a small activator which plugs into the fixture at one end. The gas in a fluorescent lamp must be heated to 50 degrees before it will transmit electricity; the starter does the job instantaneously. When one burns out, replace it with a new one.

¶ How do you fix a front doorbell which will no longer ring?

If your bell (or chimes) is operated by batteries, check first to see if the batteries need replacing. If your bell is operated by your regular electric circuit, take out the fuse in the bell circuit; remove the cover of the bellbox; and go over all the electrical connections to make sure they are clean, and tightly attached. You will probably find your trouble in a loose wire in the bell itself.

❡ *What is the matter when a lot of lights or appliances go out at once?*

If the trouble is confined to a specific area of your home, you have burned out a fuse. Check your fuse box. A fuse has a transparent cover through which a strip of bright metal is visible. If the metal is intact, the fuse is functioning. If the metal is broken, the fuse has burned out. You have overloaded the circuit, either by a "short" somewhere, or by running too many appliances at once. See Chapter Seven on Electricity for a fuller discussion.

❡ *When a fuse blows out or a circuit breaker goes out, what should you do?*

(1) Disconnect all the lamps and appliances in use when the circuit went out.

(2) Open the Main Switch, or pull out the section of the panel labeled "Main" in the Service Entrance. This will cut off the current while you go to work at the Branch Circuit Box.

(3) Replace the blown fuse in the Branch Circuit Box with a new one of the proper size. They screw in and out just like light bulbs. Make sure your hands are dry, and that you are standing on a dry board while doing this.

(4) Close the Main Switch, or replace the pull-out section to restore service.

(5) Throw away the blown fuse.

❡ *How do you repair a lamp which flickers on and off?*

Unplug the lamp, making sure it is not attached to current. Unscrew the bulb, and put it in a properly functioning lamp first. If it is all right, remove the bulb socket from the flickering lamp by loosening the screws which attach it to the frame. Pull the socket free and examine the connections, making sure no loose strands of wire can cause a short. Then examine the length of the cord inside the fixture to see if there is frayed cord. Tape up all bare spots. Trace along the wire all the way to the plug, and make sure there are no loose connections. Then reassemble. The lamp should work.

Emergency!

❦ How do you fix a toilet which will not flush?

Remove the top from the tank at the rear. You will see that a floating metal "ball" operates the valve which fills the tank with water. If the hollow ball has a leak, it will not rise when the water flows in; the cut-off mechanism will not operate properly. If this is the trouble, replace the ball with a new one. If this is not the trouble, look at the valve washer to see if it is worn. If it is, replace it with a new one. If the trouble is not corrected yet, find the flush valve. This mechanism is operated by a rubber ball which drops over the opening at the bottom of the tank when it has been emptied, allowing water to flow in and refill the tank. Sometimes this ball rots away; water will run out through it. If the ball is defective, replace it. Sometimes, the various wires and arms which hold the floats become bent or stuck; twist them a bit or work them free. By watching the mechanism in operation, you can frequently spot the trouble and correct it.

❦ If there is a sudden flooding of the house from a leak in the plumbing, is there any immediate remedy or course of action?

Yes. Turn off the main supply valve which lets the water into your house. (You should locate this valve, and know where it is, when you first move in.) When the valve is turned off, water will no longer flow in from its outside source. Then you can go ahead and try to find the reason for the flooding. It is always best to get in a plumber, once you have handled the emergency of the overflow.

❦ How do you repair a leaky faucet?

Usually the reason a faucet leaks is a faulty or deteriorated washer. To replace a worn washer, locate the shut-off valve on the pipe which supplies water to your system. Turn it off. Now locate the packing nut, a hexagonal nut to which the faucet handle is attached. Unscrew the packing nut from the faucet with a wrench. Turn the faucet handle to the "turn-on" direction, and keep turning it until you can lift out the handle, the loosened packing nut, and the valve stem from the body of the faucet. The valve stem is a smooth stem at the top, with strong wide threads at the bottom. Unscrew the set screw at the bottom of the threaded stem, and remove the valve washer. If it won't come out, try a few drops of kerosene to unstick it. If the groove in the screw head has corroded

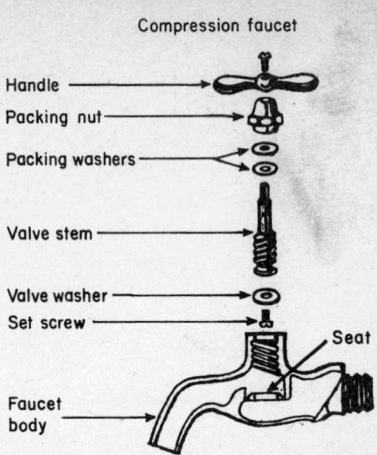

Compression faucet

over, make a new groove with a file or hacksaw, and replace it with a new set screw. Pry off the old washer after removing the set screw. Screw in the new washer at the end of the valve stem. Replace the stem, the packing nut, and the handle in the faucet, and turn it back to the "turn-off" direction. Continue until the stem is screwed most of the way in. Turn the packing nut back onto the faucet body, and tighten with a wrench. Turn on the water, and test it out.

([*How do you unstick a drainage pipe?*

First, try a rubber plunger; then try solvents; if these methods fail, use a wire, a closet auger, or remove the "trap."

(1) A plunger is a rubber suction cup screwed onto the end of a long pole. To clean out a trap, stick the mouth of the cup over the clogged drain. Let about 3 or 4 inches of water cover the cup of the plunger. Add water if there isn't enough. Pump the handle up and down at least a dozen times. If the plunger doesn't bring up refuse from the pipe and free it, try solvents.

(2) Plumbing solvents are used to dissolve or disintegrate obstructions and are usually formed by combinations of caustic potash. Potash lye may be used, but it does not cut grease well. It will also attack aluminum and enamel fixtures. You can buy commercial mixtures at any market. Read and follow the directions carefully, observing all precautions.

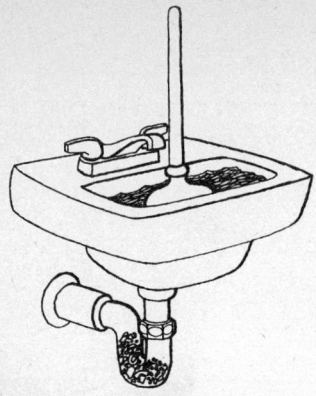

Agitate plunger up and down

(3) If both plunger and solvents fail, examine the fixture to see if the trap has a cleanout plug. The trap is the loop of pipe under the bowl or sink which connects the sink with the drainpipe. The trap is there to prevent large objects from jamming the drainpipe further on and causing serious damage. Most traps have cleanout plugs. To use the plug, draw as much water as you can from the trap into the sink with a suction pump or siphon hose. Now place a bucket beneath the trap. Remove the trap plug with a wrench. Insert a short stiff wire or auger into the trap plug and rake out as much waste as you can. Flush boiling water through the fixture into the trap, and then replace the plug. If the trap has no plug, place a bucket under it to catch water after it is removed. With a wrench, unscrew the "slip-and-union" fittings which hold the trap in place below the fixture. Remove the trap, and scour it in hot soapy water with a wire brush.

《 What is the best way to repair a leak in a garden hose?

You can always wrap friction tape around the hole. A better and more satisfactory way is to cut out the bad portion of the hose, and connect the good ends with a metal splicer, which you can get at a hardware store.

《 Is it possible to empty an expansion tank in a hot-water heating system, if the tank has become too full?

Yes. Simply fasten a hose to the connection, and drain out the water through the hose. An expansion tank functions best when it is two-thirds full.

❧ Is it possible to mend a leaky plumbing pipe?

Pipes usually leak at connections and joints. With a wrench, tighten each joint. Often, this will completely stop the leakage. If the leak is in a length of pipe, you can always close the hole quickly for emergency repair by pressing a wad of chewing gum into the hole and securing it there with friction tape. If the crack has developed in a cast-iron water pipe, use the new convenient iron cement, plastic aluminum, or steel cement.

❧ How do you unstick a window sash which is completely jammed in the frame?

There are four reasons why a window sash sticks in the frame. It may be jammed, because it is paint-frozen; it may be binding because of swelling; it may be sticking, because the stop is too close to the sash; or the sash itself may be too big.

(1) To unstick a paint-frozen sash, first run the point of a sharp knife between the sash and the stops all the way up and down both sides. Scrape away any extra paint. If the paint is not too thickly spread between the sash and the stops, this may unfreeze it. If not, remove the stop completely. Clean the stop with a file or knife. Replace the stop.

(2) To fix a sash which binds due to swelling, locate the point where it binds, and with a jack-knife, force beeswax into the joint between the sash and the stop. If the sash will still not move, remove it. Plane down the area of the sash where it binds.

(3) To unstick a sash pinned by a too-close stop, pry off the stop and renail it 1/8 to 1/4 inch away from the sash. Be sure you do not move the lower half of the vertical stops more than 1/8 inch from the bottom of the sash, or you will lose your weather-tightness.

(4) To fix a sash which binds because it is too wide, remove the sash, and plane the edge where the binding occurs. Coat the sash with linseed oil. Wax it completely when it is dry. Replace the sash. It should work smoothly now.

❧ What is the easiest way to unstick metal storm windows or metal screens, and keep them in working order?

You'll have to jimmy the windows or screens until you get

them sliding up and down. Then apply graphite or jellied silicone compound to the groove in the window frame.

❰ *How do you replace a broken pane of glass in a window?*

You will see that a pane of glass is held in the frame on one side by wood, called a "rabbet" cut, and on the opposite by putty. Remove the putty from the glass left in the frame. You'll find tiny

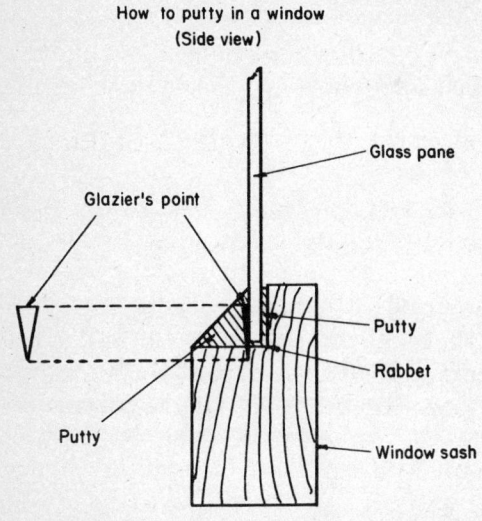

How to putty in a window (Side view)

metal wedges, called glaziers points, which hold the glass in the wood. Remove them. Scrape the wood clean. Measure the area to be covered by the glass pane. Deduct 1/16 inch from the measurement to allow for wood expansion. Buy a piece of glass, cut to the proper measurement. Store-cut glass will be more accurate than home-cut. Now you're ready to put in the new pane. First paint the rabbet—the L-shaped seat in which the pane fits—with linseed oil. Soften a mound of putty with linseed oil. Spread a putty bed 1/16 inch thick on the sash rabbet. Make the bed very even, so there are no gaps. Turn the pane of glass sideways, and sight along it. You'll find that the glass curves. Put the pane against the putty, with the concave side in. Press it firmly. With a screwdriver, insert the glaziers points on each side of the pane of glass to hold it there. If the glass does not tighten to the sash, remove the points, press the glass more firmly against the putty, and replace the points. Roll a small piece of putty in your hands until it is pencil-shaped. Lay putty rolls along one side of the glass pane. Press the putty knife on the putty, moving it along the end of the glass where it touches the muntin—the middle rail or piece of wood which crosses the sash and divides it into sections. Form a smooth bevel in the putty, and let it dry; then paint it.

❡ *What's the best way to repair a window which leaks around the joints?*

Find the spot where the window leaks by placing your hand in various positions around the edge during a high wind. With window caulking compound, seal up the loose spaces for a tight fit.

❡ *How do you mend window or door screens which have pulled out of their frames?*

First of all, remove the outer molding which covers the place where the screen is attached to the frame. You'll notice there is a tight groove in the inner frame into which the screening fits. Pulling hard on the screening to take the wrinkles out of it, tuck the end into the groove. Now, with a staple gun pushed against it, hold the screening firmly in position, and squeeze the trigger. Each staple will span several strands of wire and fasten the screen securely, without splitting the wood. When you've stapled all along the loose part, put back your cover molding.

❡ *How do you keep a door from sticking on the floor when it swings open?*

A door is hung either by two hinges, or by three. If the door scrapes on the floor, check the hinge at the top. Quite frequently, the top hinge, which supports most of the weight of the door, has become loosened in the door frame. Tighten the screws, making sure the hinges are solidly secured. If this does not solve your problem, you may have to remove the door from the frame and trim along the bottom edge. See Chapter Eleven on Doors.

❡ *What is wrong if the heating plant in a house does not keep it warm enough?*

Before calling in a repairman, check your thermostat. Someone may have accidentally set it too low. If the thermostat is located in a very warm spot in the house, set it a bit higher than you ordinarily would.

Emergency!

❨ How do you locate a leak in the roof?

This may take some detective work. First, find the spot where the water comes in through the ceiling or wall. Locate that spot outside by measuring from the walls, and trace up from there to the peak of the roof. Somewhere in between, you should find evidence of trouble—possibly a broken or missing shingle, or a tear in the roofing paper. If you need to call in a repairman, it is best to mark with chalk the exact spot where the leak occurred.

❨ How do you keep nails from popping out of a ceiling?

Popping nails are usually caused by vibrations or pressure from above. You'll notice that such a situation occurs in a room directly downstairs from a hallway or room which sustains a great deal of movement or activity. Don't worry about the ceiling; it won't fall down. You can buy non-slip nails at your hardware store. Pull out the protruding nails, and replace them with non-slip nails, or annular-ringed nails.

❨ How do you get rid of wet paint dripped on an already-painted surface?

Wipe it off immediately with a clean rag.

❨ What's the best way to get paint off your hands?

Oil your hands with linseed oil, or any fatty oil; then wash them thoroughly with soap. Turpentine will chap your hands.

❨ How do you hang a picture on a wall which is made of gypsum board?

(1) If the picture is fairly small, use a special picture-hanging clip which points a nail diagonally into the gypsum board. If the nail tears out, you'll have to locate the stud, and nail directly into that.

(2) To locate a stud in a wall covered by gypsum board, plasterboard, or veneer paneling, you'll have to do some guessing and testing. Start at one end of the wall. Assume there is a stud at the end where the walls meet. Since most studs are 16 inches apart in interior walls, simply measure 16 inches in from the corner. Drive a nail through the plaster to see if the stud is there. If it isn't, try tapping around the area with a hammer. Although it is

extremely difficult for the ear to tell the difference between a hollow space behind plaster and a solid stud, you may be able to tell with practice. Try another nail. If this one hits the mark, measure 16 inches from that spot to the next stud; it should be there. Mark each stud with a vertical line from ceiling to floor on your wall. Remember, however, that some studs may have warped out of line. There is a gadget on the market containing a swinging magnetic bar. As you pass this over the surface of a wall, the magnetic bar will turn when it is attracted by a nail. The presence of the nail indicates a stud. When you have found your stud, nail your picture hanger directly into it.

❕ *How do you sharpen dull scissors?*

Open the scissors, and draw the cutting edge back and forth on a piece of glass. Or, simply cut a piece of sandpaper with the scissors.

❕ *How do you extinguish a fat fire in the oven?*

Throw salt on burning fat until the flames go out. Never use water!

❕ *Which way do you turn a screw or nut to loosen it?*

Most screws or nuts have right-hand threads. Think of the head as the face of a clock. To tighten, you rotate the screwdriver or wrench in the same direction as the clock hands move. To unscrew, or loosen, you turn the tool from right to left (counter-clockwise).

❕ *How do you remove scorched spots in cloth?*

Wet the scorched spot with water. Apply a thick paste made of lump starch, adding just enough water to make it stick well. Use this paste freely, and let it dry. Then, rinse out all the starch with water, press, and place in the sun to dry.

❕ *How do you keep dogs out of your garbage can?*

Use clip-on springs, which hold the lid tightly to the can. When you want to open the lid, you simply slip the cover off at an angle. Such devices are available at any hardware store or supermarket.

2
Painting

No improvement in your home can bring you more personal satisfaction and psychological uplift than a well-done paint job. The effect of a fresh coat of covering on a dull wall is dramatic and immediately rewarding. With the many new improvements in paint manufacture, you can now do the work with a minimum of time and effort.

Aside from its strictly esthetic value, paint is vitally important to the future and upkeep of your home. Any surface will eventually wear out from constant usage or from exposure to weather. Paint is the protective cover which will arrest such deterioration. If not properly painted, wood will rot and metal will rust.

One of the most important rules for keeping your home bright and safe is to be sure all painted surfaces are freshly coated. Woodwork should be shining and exterior siding should be refinished regularly.

With paint, the most important thing for you to know is the proper covering for every different surface. Otherwise, the variety of paints available on the market will simply bewilder you.

The questions and answers in this chapter have been prepared to inform you as much as possible about paint facts: what types of paints there are, what they are used for, the methods of applying them, and the proper use and care of brushes and rollers.

Q & A

PAINT COMPONENTS

❦ What is paint?

Paint is a white or colored liquid applied to wood, plaster, metal, masonry, or composition surfaces. It dries by oxidation or evaporation to become a solid, durable film.

❦ What are the three main kinds of surfaces which paints provide?

You can get glossy surfaces, semigloss surfaces, or flat surfaces. Glossy surfaces are usually good for trims, molding, and woodwork in general. Flat or semigloss surfaces are preferable on walls, ceilings, and so on.

❦ Of what are most paints made?

Four basic ingredients make up paint: pigment, binder or vehicle, thinner or solvent, and a drier.

❦ What kinds of pigments are there?

Pigments are divided into several groups. The most important group is the opaque type. Opacity gives paint the ability to hide and color a surface. Pigments without opacity are known as inerts, fillers, and extenders.

❦ What kinds of binders or vehicles are there?

Binders or vehicles are liquid mediums which bind the pigment particles together and give a paint spreadability. Vehicles may be oil, resin, varnish, or resin emulsion. Oil-based paints use oil, usually linseed oil; enamels use varnish; water-based paints use resin emulsion-and-water as a vehicle.

❦ What are thinners or solvents?

Thinners work on the oil and pigment to improve the flowing quality of a paint and make it easier to apply. Gum turpentine, wood-distilled turpentine, and mineral spirits are used. Mineral spirits is a petroleum solvent used like turpentine.

❊ What are driers?

Driers are specially compounded materials designed to quicken the drying of a paint.

PAINT TYPES
❊ What are the main types of painting mixtures?

Oil paint; alkyd resin paint; emulsion paint, including latex paint; water-thinned paint; casein paint; calcimine; enamel; varnish; shellac; lacquer; and paints made to cover specific surfaces.

(1) *Oil paint* contains linseed, china wood, soybean, fish, or any other kind of natural oil. Exterior house paints, wall paints, floor paints, primers and so on, are oil paints, although some may be classed as alkyds.

House paint contains lead, zinc, or titanium pigment; its vehicle is linseed oil; it has a drying agent, and solvents like turpentine or mineral spirits. It dries with a gloss, is resistant to water, and is not affected by temperature changes.

House-paint undercoat, also called *primer*, is used to sink into the surface of wood to seal it. It covers previous coats of paint and will give a thick first paint layer at less cost.

Inside flat paint contains zinc or titanium, or a combination; its vehicle is turpentine; it also has mineral spirits, or a "flatting" oil which dries without a gloss.

(2) *Alkyd resin paint* contains a synthetic resin which replaces part or all of oil as the vehicle; alkyds and acrylics give it tougher coating properties. Alkyds are usually used with enamel or wall paint; acrylics or alkyds are used with exterior paint.

(3) *Latex paint* is actually *emulsion paint*; the emulsion, which is the vehicle, simply looks like rubber latex. Certain oils, resins, or mixtures are emulsified so that they can be thinned with water. Emulsion paint is quick drying and odorless; it is easy to work with. You can clean brushes, rollers, and equipment with soap and warm water. It can be used as a primer on uncured plaster, is alkali-proof, and porous to water vapor. It can be applied to wood, plaster, metal, or wallpaper. It has good hiding, especially when applied with a roller. It can be recoated in one-half to one hour. It usually dries to a flat or semigloss finish.

Polyvinyl-acetate (vinyl) paint, acrylic paint, butadiene styrene paint, alkyd paint, and others are all emulsion paints.

(4) *Dripless paint* contains pigment particles which have been homogenized and suspended; it does not need to be stirred. The paint flows on without dripping—excellent for use on ceilings.

(5) *Water-thinned paint* is simply paint which can be thinned with water instead of with turpentine or mineral spirits.

Whitewash is made of slaked lime and water, but it flakes off quickly when dry. It is used to cover temporary structures.

Texture paint is applied as a thick paste, "textured" or troweled on; it is useful in filling cracks or irregularities in surfaces. It gives you a plastered effect.

Calcimine, made of powdered chalk or whiting mixed with glue and pigment, is used for ceilings and other plastered areas. It can be washed off with warm water; but it also rubs off, flakes, and waterspots.

(6) *Casein paint,* made of skim milk and whiting, to which pigments, water, and protein binders are added, dries with a dull finish and will stand moderate wear; but it may mildew.

(7) *Varnish* is made of gum or resin, usually carried in a linseed or tung oil vehicle; it is thinned with turpentine or other solvent. Varnish provides a hard, tough film when dried. It may be clear or amber-colored. Wood grains show up nicely through its high or low gloss. Varnish gives wooden floors good resistance to wear.

Sealer is a varnish made of resinous materials which bond with the fibers of hardwood to make a tough, abrasion-resistant surface impervious to wear until the wood itself goes. Sealer usually doesn't penetrate more than 1/16 inch; it is unaffected by alcohol, alkalies, water, and most household staining agents.

Shellac is a spirit varnish, widely used on floors; but it does not resist water or alcohol, nor excessively heavy traffic or abrasions. It is best used as an undercoat or sealer for raw wood, or to cover knots or resinous areas in order to prevent bleeding through paint.

Lacquer is composed of nitrocellulose—cotton fibers treated with nitric and sulphuric acids—mixed with solvents, gums, and pigments. A special resin varnish, lacquer is hard, tough, and has a high luster. It is excellent for furniture finishing; sanded smooth, it has a hard glossy surface like glass.

Enamel is varnish carrying a pigment. It comes in flat, eggshell, and semigloss finish. Some enamel employs alkyd resin as its vehicle. *Interior enamel* takes 8 hours to dry, is washable, and has good hiding power; it comes in high gloss, semigloss, and flat. *Exterior enamel* is used for trim, window frame, door frame, porch railing, and so on. *Enamel undercoat* is not really enamel, but flat oil or resin-based paint; it is used to seal the surface at reduced cost. *Screening enamel* is especially made to stick to galvanized iron, brass, or copper screening; thin, and highly glossed, it flows on without clogging the openings.

(8) *Masonry paint* includes cement water, rubber, waterproof sealer, basement waterproofer, and epoxy resin. Made up of Portland cement, it can be used on any type of masonry—brick, stucco, concrete, stone, and cinder block. It can be used either as a waterproofing compound or a cover for cracked cement surfaces.

(9) *Rubber paint* is especially made for outside masonry and for interior concrete floors. Exterior rubber paint is flat; indoor rubber paint is glossy enamel.

(10) *Waterproofing sealer*, containing silicones, synthetic resin or varnish, penetrates the surface of masonry to form a water-shedding protection. It is used on exterior surfaces, never in basements.

(11) *Epoxy resin* waterproofs basements. It is applied to clean, dry concrete, on the side through which there is water penetration. It will stop leaks or seepage. It bonds firmly to any type of surface, and will hold back water even under pressure.

GENERAL INTERIOR PAINTING

❪ How do you go about choosing a paint to use inside your home?

Be sure you use an interior paint, and not an exterior paint. This is a must.

❪ What kind of paint do you use to cover plaster walls and ceilings?

For repainting, use any quality flat paint with an alkyd or latex base. For bathrooms and kitchens, use semigloss or gloss enamel: it has greater washability, resistance to moisture, steam, and grease. If you use an alkyd paint, prime any patches. Latex paints prime themselves.

PRACTICAL HOME REPAIR FOR WOMEN　　　　[18

INTERIOR PAINTS

WHAT PAINT TO USE & WHERE

	Flat Paint	Semi-Gloss Paint	Enamel	Rubber Base Paint	Emulsion Paint	Casein	Interior Varnish	Shellac	Wax (Liquid or Paste)	Wax (Emulsion)	Stain	Wood Sealer	Floor Varnish	Floor Paint or Enamel	Cement Base Paint	Aluminum Paint	Sealer or Undercoater	Metal Primer
Plaster Walls & Ceiling	✓	✓		✓	✓	✓											✓	
Wall Board	✓	✓		✓	✓	✓											✓	
Wood Paneling	✓	✓		✓	✓		✓	✓	✓		✓	✓						
Kitchen & Bathroom Walls		✓	✓	✓	✓												✓	
Wood Floors							✓	✓	✓	✓	✓	✓	✓					
Concrete Floors									✓	✓	✓			✓				
Vinyl & Rubber Tile Floors									✓	✓								
Asphalt Tile Floors									✓									
Linoleum							✓	✓	✓				✓	✓				
Stair Treads							✓				✓	✓	✓	✓				
Stair Risers	✓	✓	✓	✓			✓	✓			✓	✓						
Wood Trim	✓	✓	✓	✓	✓		✓	✓	✓		✓						✓	
Steel Windows	✓	✓	✓	✓													✓	✓
Aluminum Windows	✓	✓	✓	✓													✓	✓
Window Sills			✓				✓											
Steel Cabinets	✓	✓	✓	✓														✓
Heating Ducts	✓	✓	✓	✓												✓		✓
Radiators & Heating Pipes	✓	✓	✓	✓												✓		✓
Old Masonry	✓	✓	✓	✓	✓	✓									✓	✓	✓	
New Masonry	✓	✓	✓	✓	✓										✓			

Black dot indicates that a primer or sealer may be necessary before the finishing coat (unless surface has been previously finished.)

These recommendations through the courtesy of the National Paint, Varnish & Lacquer Association.

❲ What kind of paint do you use on drywall construction?

Drywall construction refers to insulation board, plasterboard, fiber board, or the like. You should seal wallboard first with a primer sealer, and then follow with any interior wall paint.

❲ How do you paint over vinyl wall coverings?

(1) If the vinyl wall covering is smooth fabric without design,

prime with an alkyd flat wall paint the same color as the final coat. You can use either latex or alkyd.

(2) If the vinyl wall covering is smooth fabric with design, use a latex primer sealer only. You can use either a latex or an alkyd finish coat.

(3) If the vinyl wall covering is textured fabric, use an oil primer sealer, or an alkyd flat wall paint. Use alkyd paint or enamel for the top coat.

(4) If the vinyl wall covering is flexible installation, do not paint it at all.

¶ *What kind of paint should go on inside moldings, baseboards, trims, and so on?*

Use semigloss enamel the same color as the walls. In the kitchen and bathroom, use full gloss. For new wood or bare wood, use an enamel undercoater, plus a suitable topcoat.

¶ *How do you prepare an oil paint for use?*

Shake the can. Open it, and pour the liquid into another bucket. Stir the remainder of the material in the can thoroughly, pouring back small amounts of liquid from time to time. Pour the mixed material from container to container several times. Add thinner if required, and stir. Pour the paint from container to container once more. Add thinner if the paint does not flow on easily.

¶ *How do you prepare enamel for painting?*

Proceed the same as for oil paint, but do not shake the can.

¶ *How do you prepare varnish for painting?*

Varnish needs no stirring and should not be shaken.

¶ *How do you prepare water-thinned paints for painting?*

Every water paint manufactured must be handled differently. Study the directions and follow them carefully.

¶ *How can you remove lumpy particles of paint from the top of the can?*

Cut out a disk of window screening the same size as the can, and let it settle down in the mix. As the screen sinks, it will carry the lumpy particles to the bottom with it.

How do you finish radiators?

Use flat wall paint or enamel the same color as the walls. Do not use metallic paints; they hold back the heat.

With what do you paint basement walls?

Use Portland cement paint or latex paint made for masonry. If the previously painted surface was not Portland cement paint, do not follow it with Portland cement paint.

What kind of paint is made for basement floors?

Use floor enamel designed for concrete. Do not paint floors which are always damp.

What kind of finish should you use on interior wood floors?

You can re-varnish previously varnished floors, if they are in good condition. Remove all the wax and polish first. If the old varnish is in poor condition, sand it off. You can finish new floors, and floors from which old finish has been removed, with penetrating floor finish. If the wood is in hopeless condition, hide it with floor enamel.

How can you keep clean a can which is half full of paint?

Pour out the paint you need to use, and then wrap aluminum foil over the rim and the outside of the clean can. This will keep the rim from caking with paint. When the job is done, remove the foil, and seal the can tightly.

How can you prevent paint from splattering when you try to get a tight seal on a partly used can of paint?

Cover the lid with an old cloth before you hammer it down. The cloth will catch any paint that is squeezed out.

GENERAL EXTERIOR PAINTING

About how often is it necessary to paint your house?

A recent survey shows that the average homeowner paints his house every 5.3 years.

What is the average cost of painting a house?

An average breakdown recently showed that the cost of painting the average house comes to $410.

Painting [21

EXTERIOR PAINTS
WHAT PAINT TO USE & WHERE

	House Paint	Water Repellent	Cement Base Paint	Rubber-Base Paint	Emulsion Paint	Penetrating Sealer	Aluminum Paint	Wood Stain	Trim-and-Trellis Paint	Awning Paint	Spar Varnish	Porch-and-Deck Paint	Primer or Undercoater	Metal Primer
Wood Siding (Painted)	✓												✓	
Wood Siding (Natural)					✓		✓				✓			
Brick	✓	✓	✓	✓	✓								✓	
Cement & Cinder Block	✓	✓	✓	✓	✓								✓	
Asbestos Cement	✓			✓	✓								✓	
Stucco	✓	✓	✓	✓	✓								✓	
Stone	✓	✓	✓	✓	✓								✓	
Asphalt Shingle Siding	✓			✓			✓							
Metal Siding	✓						✓							✓
Wood Frame Windows	✓						✓						✓	
Steel Windows	✓						✓							✓
Aluminum Windows	✓						✓							✓
Shutters & Other Trim							✓						✓	
Cloth Awnings										✓				
Wood Shingle Roof						✓								
Wood Porch Floor												✓		
Cement Porch Floor				✓								✓		
Copper Surfaces											✓			
Galvanized Surfaces	✓						✓		✓				✓	✓
Iron Surfaces	✓						✓		✓					✓

Black dot indicates that a primer or sealer may be necessary before the finishing coat (unless surface has been previously finished.)

These recommendations through the courtesy of the National Paint, Varnish & Lacquer Association.

❡ What paint do you use to finish a wooden house?

Clapboard or vertical siding will take linseed oil paint, alkyd-based paint, or oil-modified alkyd paint. You can also use water-thinned latex house paint; use this only over the primer specified by the manufacturer, and apply it exactly in the manner designated.

❡ How many coats of paint should be used on a house?

Use three coats for new wood: one coat of the primer made by the manufacturer of the finish coat, and two finish coats to complete the job. For previously painted surfaces, you'll need only one coat to renew the brilliance. If the paint has worn thin, try two.

❮ **What do you use to get a natural wood finish on a ranch-type house?**

Use a transparent sealer or an exterior varnish. Special clear coatings are made for redwood and cedar.

❮ **How do you cover wooden shingles or shakes?**

You can use either regular house paint, or you can stain them with tinted preservatives.

❮ **How do you cover masonry?**

Use a special masonry paint. Do not use a regular house paint. The chalking process, which is part of its self-cleaning property, will disfigure the surface underneath.

❮ **How do you paint wood trim on the outside of a house?**

Use a bright exterior enamel or a "trim-and-trellis" paint. You can use house paints for these surfaces, but they will not have the same toughness and brightness as the exterior enamels.

❮ **What do you use to coat a porch floor?**

Use a tough, wear-resistant porch and deck enamel which is built to withstand leather and weather. You can get deck enamel in solvent-thinned or water-thinned latex formulations.

❮ **How do you prepare a new brick surface for paint?**

Apply boiled linseed oil and drier to seal the pores of the new brick. Use a special brick undercoat over this.

❮ **How do you prepare fresh plaster for paint?**

Wait three months after the fresh plaster has been applied before painting. Then put on a solution of zinc sulphate, ammonium carbonate, or carbonated water, to neutralize the alkali in the surface. Size all new plaster with flat oil paint or varnish.

❮ **How do you prepare old plaster for paint?**

Thoroughly wash with warm water and mild soap before sizing and painting. You should then coat all stains with shellac, varnish, or aluminum paint mixed with banana oil.

❮ **How do you prepare plaster walls which have been previously painted with calcimine?**

Wash off all the calcimine. Then paint.

❮ **What do you do with cracks, holes, and dents before painting?**

Touch up the patches with a sealing coat, or use a pigmented sealer, shellac, or white brushing lacquer. Sand the surface lightly. Then paint.

⁋ How do you prepare new unpainted wood for paint?

Dust it off. Remove mortar, cement, or plaster with a scraper. Fill all nail holes, and open joints with plastic wood filler or putty. Apply a thin coat of orange shellac, knot-sealer, or exterior aluminum paint to all pitchy places, including knots. With resinous wood, such as yellow pine, brush with turpentine immediately before painting.

⁋ How do you prepare painted wood for repainting?

If the paint has begun to scale or peel, scrape or brush it off with a wire brush. Smooth the surface with sandpaper. Remove loose or crumbly putty or filler from windows. Prime the sash, and apply new putty. Renail all loose boards, and prime nail heads with anti-corrosive primer. Rub varnished or enameled surfaces with fine sandpaper or steel wool to remove all gloss. Use varnish remover on marred surfaces, then smooth surface with steel wool or sandpaper. Wash off dirt or soot with warm water and soap. Wash off grease with a thinner. Spot-prime any brown stains caused by moisture in the wood with two coats of primer. Wash mildewed surfaces.

⁋ How do you remove mildew and fungus growths?

Mix a solution of sodium hypochlorite by adding one and one-half cups of full-strength Chlorox or Purex to a gallon of water. Brush this solution on the mildew, or spray it on, and allow it to remain about five minutes. Rinse the surface with clean water. If the growth is heavy, you may have to scrub with a bristle brush. Or, you can use such products as Soilax, Oakite, and Spic and Span. They contain trisodium phosphate, which is a good mildew cleaner.

⁋ How do you kill mildew?

Use a paint with a mildewcide mixed into it.

⁋ How do you make mildew paint?

Mix any proprietary mildewcide with your paint in a wooden or enamel container. Wear gloves when applying the paint, and thoroughly wash your hands afterwards.

⁋ How is it best to paint exterior siding?

Start at the top and move down. Cover one stretch and work

Cover power of paints

Surface and Product	Coverage Per Gallon in Square Feet		
	1st Coat	2nd Coat	3rd Coat
Frame Siding			
Exterior House Paint	468	540	630
Trim (Exterior)			
Exterior Trim Paint	850	900	972
Porch Floors and Steps			
Porch and Deck Paint	378	540	576
Asbestos Wall Shingles			
Exterior House Paint	180	400	
Shingle Siding			
Exterior House Paint	342	423	
Shingle Stain	150	225	
Shingle Roofs			
Exterior Oil Paint	150	250	
Shingle Stain	120	200	
Brick (Exterior)			
Exterior Oil Paint	200	400	
Cement Water Paint	100	150	
Cement Floors and Steps (Exterior)			
Porch and Deck Paint	450	600	600
Color Stain and Finish	510	480	
Medium Texture Stucco			
Exterior Oil Paint	153	360	360
Cement Water Paint	99	135	
Doors and Windows (Interior)			
Enamel	603	405	504
Floors, Hardwood (Interior)			
Oil Paint	540	450	
Shellac	540	675	765
Varnish	540	540	540
Linoleum			
Varnish	540	558	
Walls, Smooth Finish Plaster			
Flat Oil Paint	Primer 630	540	630
Gloss or Semi-Gloss Oil Paint	Primer 630	540	540
Calcimine	Size 720	240	
Casein Water Paint	540	700	

across to another. Thoroughly brush out the paint to a thin, even coating. Stroke up and down as well as across. After the entire surface within arm's reach has been covered, draw the empty brush lightly and smoothly across the entire length, from the edge of the unpainted surface toward the painted portion. Use a long stroke with the grain of the wood.

(*What is the best kind of weather in which to do exterior painting?*

The ideal weather to brush on outside paint is a clear, dry day, with the temperature 50 degrees or above. Don't paint if the temperature is above 90 in the direct sun. You'll find the paint dries too fast, and eventually will wrinkle.

(*What are the best seasons of the year for painting?*

Spring and fall are the best months because of the milder temperatures.

❬ What if the temperature drops unexpectedly below 50 degrees during a paint job?

Stop work early in the afternoon, and allow the paint to set before the colder temperatures of evening come on.

❬ Should you apply a second coat immediately over a first?

Generally speaking, no. Unless otherwise specifically instructed, it is best to wait for the first coat to dry completely.

❬ How do you finish knotty pine?

Apply two coats of floor sealer, buffing the last coat with #ooo steel wool.

❬ How do you stain knotty pine?

Apply a coat of oil stain of the desired color. When dry, sand it lightly. Apply a thin coat of white shellac. Finish with two coats of paste wax.

PAINTING A WALL

❬ What is the first step in painting an inside wall?

Choose your type of paint: water-thinned latex, or solvent-thinned alkyd resin paint.

❬ What are the advantages of a latex paint?

Called emulsion, plastic, or rubberized paint, a latex will dry in less than an hour. Latex is odor free. It does not show lap marks. It can be touched up later. You can use a brush, a roller, or a spray gun to apply it. A latex paint can be used on any previously painted surface, because it serves as its own primer on plaster and drywall and can be used as a prime for alkyd paint. Latex is usually flat, but you can get semigloss.

❬ What are the advantages of an alkyd paint?

It is available in flat, semigloss, and gloss, and is relatively odorless. It is tough and washable, and has great hiding power. It dries in three to four hours.

❬ What kind of paint is best for an inside wall?

You should use a flat paint for the wall and the ceiling of a living room, a dining room, and bedrooms.

❬ What kind of paint is best for inside woodwork?

Semigloss and gloss enamels.

❨ How should you prepare a wall for paint?

Remove all wax and polish. Scrape or sand away loose, cracked, or peeling paint. Sand down rough spots. Smooth rough areas. Fill cracks in plaster with patching compound; sand smooth when dry. Dust off the walls. Remove switch plates, and loosen wall or ceiling fixtures. Cover furniture and floor with drop cloths or newspapers. Then mix the paint. Apply the prime coat.

❨ When do you paint cover plates for light switches and electric outlets during a wall painting?

Before painting a wall, remove all the electric plates, and paint them separately. Let them dry before replacing them. This will eliminate the danger of chipping paint off later if you have to remove the plate.

❨ Exactly how do you paint a wall?

(1) Dip the brush one-third the length of the bristles into the can, and tap off the excess paint against the side of the container. Use rhythmical strokes back and forth. Lift the brush gradually at the end of each stroke, so as not to deposit too thick an edge on the wall. Always paint from a dry area into a wet one. Start at the upper right-hand corner and work down toward the floor. Cover an area only as wide as you can comfortably and safely reach from a ladder. To protect the ceiling from fresh paint, use shirt cardboard, a paint guard, or a special roller painter.

(2) If you are using a roller, pour the paint into the tray, covering about two-thirds of the bottom. Roll the applicator in the paint, coating it evenly. When painting a wall, first brush a narrow strip next to the ceiling, or use a special roller. Always roll the paint upwards from a dry surface into a wet one. After you have coated an area about two feet wide by three feet long with up-and-down strokes, go over it with back-and-forth strokes. Don't spin the roller at the end of the stroke, or it may splatter. When you reach the baseboard or woodwork, protect the surface as you did the ceiling. Always provide adequate ventilation, and avoid smoking when using solvent-thinned alkyd paints.

❨ If interrupted in a wall painting job, how do you continue when you get back?

Paint from a dry area into a wet area. Don't start a job, unless you know you can finish an entire surface.

PAINTING A CEILING

(What kind of paint do you use for a ceiling?

Flat paints are always best for ceilings. They reflect light evenly, and do not produce glare as gloss and semigloss finishes do. You can use either water-thinned latex paint or alkyd paint.

(Is a brush or a roller the easiest for painting a ceiling?

Use a long-handled roller for possibly the easiest way to paint a ceiling.

(How do you start a ceiling if you are using latex paint and a long-handled roller?

If the walls are going to be painted too, just roll the paint on the ceiling, with the first stroke going away from you. Paint across the width of the room. Always start a new stroke in a dry area, and paint toward a wet one. Finish up by making right angle or criss-cross strokes to be sure the surface is completely covered. Even though you're not worrying about getting paint on the walls, don't slop it all over, and don't smash your roller into the ceiling at a high speed.

(How do you paint a ceiling with alkyd paint?

Paint two-foot strips across the width of the room so that you'll have a still-wet edge to paint into when you make the next trip across.

(How do you protect the walls if you don't intend to paint them, too?

When using latex, paint a narrow band all around the perimeter of the ceiling, protecting the walls with the metal strip known as a painter's time saver. You can use a makeshift guard with shirt cardboards, provided you change them frequently. Be sure to wipe the metal strip clean each time you move it. Or, you can use special rollers which are constructed not to deposit paint on any surface at right angles to that being painted.

When using alkyd paints, protect the walls as outlined above, and paint the ceiling in two-foot strips to prevent lap marks. Do not paint the perimeter.

PAINTING A WOOD FLOOR

❰ How can you tell if you should refinish a wood floor?

First of all, try a new coat of wax. If that does not snap up the surface, you may as well prepare to refinish the wood.

❰ How do you prepare a wooden floor for refinishing?

Remove the old wax with mineral spirits. Before the solvent dries, wipe up the dissolved wax. Use steel wool on thick spots. Sand the wood smooth. You can usually simplify the job of sanding by renting an electric sander. This will give you a virtually new floor surface.

❰ What are the main steps in finishing a floor?

(1) Staining. (2) Applying a filler. (3) Applying a sealer. (4) Buffing. (5) Applying a finishing coat.

❰ What is the first step in staining a floor?

Stain is not a finishing material, but is used to prepare the floor. Test the stain on a scrap of flooring to determine the color. Then apply it to the floor with a 3- to 4-inch varnish brush, or a rag. Work with the grain. Brush in 30-inch widths starting at one corner. Apply evenly, and remove the excess with a clean soft cloth before the stain can set. Wipe up any surplus dark stain after five minutes. Do not wipe light-colored stains. Let all stains dry overnight.

❰ When do you need a filler?

Many home floors are made of oak. Oak has pores, which must be filled in order to achieve a smooth surface. Oak floors need fillers. Fillers come as liquids, or pastes which can be reduced to liquids. Follow the label instructions carefully.

❰ How do you apply a floor sealer?

Apply floor sealer liberally, using a long-handled lamb's wool or nylon applicator. Apply across the grain first, then with the grain. Wipe up the surplus with rags, if the label instructions say to. Rags soaked in sealer may ignite spontaneously. They should be burned, or stored in containers under water.

❰ What is the procedure for buffing?

After the sealer has dried, buff the floor with steel wool, and remove all particles with a vacuum cleaner.

How many coats of sealer should be put on?

Usually two will do. Apply the second coat with the grain after the first has been cleaned, buffed, and dried.

What is the best kind of floor finish?

Varnish is the most popular and familiar floor finish. It is a durable, hard-wearing finish for heavy-duty and residential flooring. Varnish forms a surface coating which is resistant to spots and stains. Get quality floor varnish formulated to withstand abrasion. If you have not used a sealer on the floor, you will need at least two coats of varnish for a uniform gloss. If you have used sealer, you need use only one coat of varnish.

How do you apply varnish?

Do not stir or shake varnish. Flow it on liberally from a well-loaded varnish brush, working with the grain; and do not brush it as you do when you paint, or you'll get bubbles. If you get bubbles anyway, remove them by brushing back into the area with light feathering strokes before the varnish sets. Allow it to dry for eight hours, and apply a second coat. If you have not used a filler, apply a third coat. Maintain a 70-degree temperature and provide ventilation during drying.

Is it possible to varnish over an old finish without sanding it off?

Yes. Use a ground coat which hides the old surface and gives it the color of bare wood without grain. Finish with two coats of clear varnish, two coats of varnish stain, or a coat of varnish stain and a coat of clear varnish. You can get a grained effect by using graining colors over the ground coat. Use special graining tools to create the effect. After you apply the graining coat and let it dry, apply two coats of clear varnish or varnish stain.

Is it possible to use floor enamel over an old surface?

Yes. Floor enamel, which comes in a variety of colors and hides old surfaces completely, is a good finish. Simply remove all wax, oil, or grease from the surface, and apply.

Can you use shellac on a floor?

Yes, if it does not receive too much wear. It scratches easily.

How do you apply shellac?

Apply in long, even strokes with a wide brush. Allow it to dry for fifteen to twenty minutes, and then rub lightly with steel wool or fine sandpaper. Sweep it clean. Apply a second coat, and allow it to dry for two or three hours. Rub and sweep again. If necessary, apply a third coat. Allow it to dry, then rub and sweep. Do not use the floor for 24 hours.

❡ *Can you use lacquer on floors?*

Yes. Lacquer can be easily retouched with good results. Old lacquer dissolves under new, and a patch will not show. Apply with a wide brush, and follow the directions on the can.

PAINTING A KITCHEN

❡ *What is the best kind of paint to use in a kitchen?*

A coat of quality enamel protects the walls. Cooking, washing dishes, laundering, and ironing cause moisture, and moisture can cause trouble unless the walls are adequately protected. Enamel is durable and scrubbable.

❡ *What colors go well in a kitchen?*

Use cool blues, blue-greens, and blue-grays to offset the heat of the ovens and irons. Brighten them with accent splashes of yellows, pinks and corals. White is a perfect accent color; you can even use it for the walls, highlighted with splashes of both warm and cool accents.

❡ *With what do you paint cabinets and drawers?*

Use enamel for cannister, breadbox, and refuse pail.

❡ *What color should a kitchen ceiling be?*

It can be painted a lighter or darker version of the walls. A low ceiling will look better painted a light color; a high ceiling will look good painted a deeper shade.

❡ *How do you prepare kitchen walls for painting?*

Scrub with soap and water to be sure to remove any traces of grease or dirt.

❡ *How do you apply enamel?*

Using an enamel brush, flow the enamel onto the surface. Fill your brush generously, and use long, smooth strokes. Do not refill your brush, but cross-stroke over the covered area. Then, with your almost-dry brush, stroke long and smooth again. This method will spread the enamel evenly and prevent runs or sags.

Painting

❮ Is there any way to snap up dead-looking linoleum with paint?

Use a quick-drying latex floor enamel to make linoleum shine. You can also refinish linoleum with varnish or lacquer. Use lacquer only on linoleum that has been previously lacquer-coated. You can use varnish on all linoleum, except inlaid. Simply remove wax with turpentine before applying your first coat.

PAINTING A BATHROOM

❮ What is the best kind of paint to use in a bathroom?

Quality enamel is moisture-resistant and can withstand frequent cleaning with soap and water.

❮ How do you prepare the surface of a bathroom for enameling?

Wash away any dirt or grease smudges with soap and water. Next, fill any holes or cracks with a commercial filler, and let the filler dry thoroughly. Sand any too-smooth or very glossy areas to provide better adhesion for the enamel.

❮ How do you apply enamel?

(See instructions on enameling a kitchen.)

❮ How do you enamel woodwork and trim?

Keep woodwork and trim the same color as the walls. A solid color will make the room look larger.

❮ What color should a ceiling be?

Use a contrasting color on a bathroom ceiling. If the walls are cool blue, paint the ceiling warm pink.

PAINTING A BASEMENT

❮ What kind of paint can you use on a basement wall?

You can use a latex or water-thinned masonry paint, Portland cement paint, reinforced masonry paint, or swimming pool paint.

❮ How do you prepare a basement wall for painting?

Remove all dirt, dust, and any crumbly material by vigorous brushing. Scrub with water and a detergent. Use an odorless paint thinner to remove grease or oil. (Be sure you have sufficient ventilation, and do not smoke.) Fill cracks and holes with patching compound.

❲ How do you apply latex paints?

Latex paints act as their own primer. The walls need not be completely dry. Prime any metal in the wall with an anti-corrosive primer. Simply brush or roll on the latex paint.

❲ Do glossy or flat paints suit a basement better?

You can clean glossy paint more easily than flat, and glossy paints are more resistant to mildew. However, flat paints have better hiding power, and diffuse light better. Take your pick.

PAINTING METAL

❲ Should metal be painted?

Yes, as soon as it is installed. The exception is galvanized iron, which should be allowed to weather six months. Repaint old metal as soon as the undercoat shows through. Do not allow it to rust.

❲ How do you paint galvanized iron?

Scrape off dirt. Wash off grease with a paint thinner. Remove rust with a wire brush and emery cloth. Put rust-preventive primer on spots that will not go away. Fill all openings around window casings and door frames with caulking compound. Mix zinc dust-zinc oxide or other galvanized steel primer thoroughly. Apply metal primer over the entire surface. Then, put on three coats of quality finish exterior paint or enamel, allowing each to dry thoroughly. House paint or trim enamel is most frequently used for finish coats. Aluminum paint is fine, but should not be used as a priming coat on iron or steel.

❲ How do you paint galvanized iron gutters?

Paint the same as you would any galvanized iron surface. On the inside, however, you should use asbestos roof coating or cut back asphalt coating.

❲ How do you paint metal screening?

Lay the screen on sawhorses or on planks. Using an ordinary brush, scrub or brush spar varnish on the screening in all directions. You can use a zinc dust-zinc oxide primer, tinted with oil color. Turn the screen over and repeat. By dry-brushing from the back, you will open up any covered holes.

How do you paint bronze and copper?

Clean with a paint thinner. Remove loose corrosion with sandpaper. Apply a priming coat of zinc dust-zinc oxide primer. Finish with one or two coats of house paint or enamel. For a transparent finish, polish the surface to a high gloss and then wipe with paint thinner. Apply either a coat of clear lacquer, or one or two coats of spar varnish.

How do you paint aluminum?

First you must wash aluminum with a phosphoric acid compound to remove oil or grease. When the metal is dry, prime it with an exterior metal or wood primer. Zinc chromate is the most common recommendation, particularly where corrosive conditions exist. When the prime coat has dried hard, apply one or two coats of finish paint.

What kinds of finish paint can be used on aluminum?

Nearly all quality paints and enamels suitable for wood or metal will give satisfactory results. If you want to keep the appearance of the original metal, use a clear acrylic or cellulose butyrate lacquer. In that case, use no primer. Remember that a clear finish never lasts as long as a paint or enamel finish.

PAINT BRUSHES

What are the parts of a paint brush?

The bristles; the metal band called a ferrule; settings which hold the bristles in place; filler strips which greatly increase its paint-carrying capacity; and the handle which is usually of hard maple, beech, birch, or plastic.

Of what are the best brushes made?

The best brushes are bristle brushes. Horsehair and vegetable fiber brushes are inferior.

How wide should a brush be which is used for siding or walls?

A brush between 3½ to 4 inches is the best. A 3½ inch brush is easier for an amateur to handle.

What size brush should you use for trim?

A flat brush, 2 inches wide with bristles 3 inches long, is the best. For smaller trims, use a flat or oval sash brush, 1½ inches wide with 2-inch bristles.

WHICH BRUSH TO USE

PAINT AREAS   **TYPE AND SIZE OF BRUSH**

Large Exterior or Interior Surfaces of Homes, Garages, Barns, Sheds, Silos, etc.

Asbestos Walls	Floors	Wall Brush
Boats	Roof	7/8" or 1" thick
Ceilings	Shingles	3½" to 6" in width
Cinder or Cement Block	Siding	4" width—most popular
Chimneys	Stone	In some areas a Stucco
Clapboard	Stucco	or semi-Dutch Calcimine
Concrete Walls	Swimming Pools	(Block Style) is preferred.
Decks	Tile	
	Walls	

Medium Size Areas

Baseboards	Mechanical Equip.	Flat Varnish (Including Enamel Style) or
Cabinets	Moldings	Flat Sash
Cupboards	Picket Fences	2", 2½" or 3" widths.
Doors	Rain Spouts	Small Oval Varnish or
Eaves	Small Boats	#8, #10 or #12 Oval Sash.
Gutters	Steps	2" Angular Trim
Large Pipes	Table Tops	(for window sash only)
Large Windows	Shutters	

Small, Narrow or Corner Areas

Chairs	Radiators	Small Flat Varnish or
Children's Toys	Screens	1" or 1½" Sash or
Garden Tools	Scrollwork	#2, #4, or #6 Oval Sash
Ladders	Small Pipes	1" or 1½" Angular Trim
Metal Furniture	Trellises	(for window sash only)
	Windows	

Automobile (repainting) ▷ 2½" or 3" soft hair flowing style.

Furniture Refinishing (stain) ▷ 1½", 2" or 2½" soft hair flowing style.

Stenciling Designs ▷ #4 or #6 Round Stencil

❬ *What is an oval brush used for?*

You use an oval brush for painting moldings which are round, and for pipes, railings, and all other rounded surfaces.

❬ *What are the other kinds of special brushes?*

There are calcimine brushes, wall-stippling brushes, roof-painting brushes, white-washing brushes, and soft brushes for fine varnish and enamel work.

❬ *What kind of brush is best for painting a rough surface?*

Use an old, stubby brush.

Painting

❊ Are you supposed to stir paint with a brush?

Never. Use a paint paddle.

❊ What is the best way to clean a brush?

Use turpentine or mineral spirits to clean oil-base paints, enamel, and varnish. Use alcohol to remove shellac. Use mild soap and water to remove water-mixed casein, latex, and calcimine.

❊ How long do you soak the brush in the solvent?

Soak it for several minutes. Then work the bristle against the side of the container to loosen the paint. If paint is caked on the outside of the brush, use a putty knife to remove it. Squeeze the bristle material with the fingers to work the paint from the heel of the brush.

❊ How can you protect your hands when cleaning a paint brush?

Pour solvent or cleaning fluid into a plastic bag. Shove the brush into the solvent, and work the paint out, manipulating the bristles through the plastic. You can watch progress of your work through the transparent plastic, and you need not wet your hands at all.

❊ How do you prepare a brush for storing?

After it has been cleaned of paint, wash the brush with a mild soap and warm water. Shake out the excess water. Comb the bristles to straighten them out. Allow the brush to dry, either by suspending it by the handle or allowing it to lie flat. Never stand a brush on its painting edge, wet or dry.

❊ Is it wise to let a brush soak in water?

Never soak a brush in water. The bristles will lose elasticity and become soft and floppy.

❊ Is it correct to paint with the narrow edge of a brush?

Never. This causes the brush to "finger," or become separated in sections.

❊ How do you pre-condition a paint brush before use?

Suspend a new brush in linseed oil overnight. To suspend it, drill a hole through the base of the handle, insert a wire rod through the hole, and rest the rod on the edges of a paint can. Do not pre-condition it if the brush is to be used for lacquer or shellac.

PRACTICAL HOME REPAIR FOR WOMEN

❦ How do you reclaim a brush which has become worn or dry?

You can soak it in a commercial brush cleaner. Leave it in the liquid until the bristles are soft and pliable. A mixture of equal parts alcohol, acetone, and benzol is useful. If the bristles are badly bent, soak them in machine oil, and place the brush to dry on a heated piece of metal until the oil begins to sizzle. While the brush is hot, reshape and bind the bristles with metal strips. After it has cooled, wash it in mineral spirits, and rinse with benzol or acetone. Then wrap the brush in paper, and lay it flat until ready for use again.

ROLLERS

❦ What is the size of a convenient general-purpose home maintenance roller?

A 9-inch roller is recommended for most home maintenance work. Rollers range in size from 7 to 18 inches. Smaller ones are made for special tasks, such as painting trim.

❦ Of what are rollers made?

Good mohair will give the smoothest surface finish with all types of paint. Top quality mohair must be used to get good finishes with enamels and varnishes. Synthetic wool-like fabrics are used for rough production where finish is not a factor. The wool-like synthetics have pile lengths ranging from 3/8 inch to 1½ inches.

❦ Are there any special rules for painting with a roller?

Yes. The technique for painting walls, ceilings, and edges differs somewhat from the technique used with brushes.

❦ How do you roll paint on a wall?

Start in the upper left corner of the wall, rolling on two-foot strips from the ceiling to the baseboard. Use light even strokes, up and down, then crosswise. Start the loaded roller away from an already painted surface, and work toward it.

❦ How do you roll paint on a ceiling?

Paint a ceiling in narrow strips, so you can apply a second strip before the edge of the first gets tacky and shows up as a lap mark.

❦ How do you roll paint on at edges?

Your best bet is to use a special edge-and-corner roller, or a brush, to apply paint in corners or next to woodwork. On large areas, do this cutting-in as you progress with the rolling, especially if you are using fast-drying paint or enamel.

❮ What is the best way to clean a paint roller?

Roll out all excess paint on an old newspaper. Wash the roller in solvent in the conventional way. Rinse, and roll out again on additional layers of clean newspaper. The porous newsprint will suck out the excess paint, so that a final rub with a clean rag will leave the roller soft and fluffy.

SPRAYERS

❮ Of what is a paint sprayer composed?

It has two main parts: the gun and the compressor.

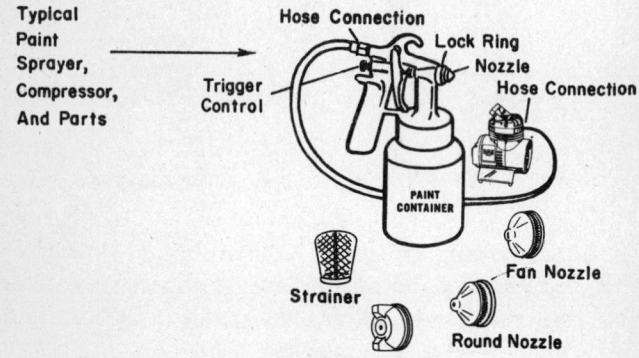

Typical Paint Sprayer, Compressor, And Parts

❮ How does a paint sprayer work?

You spray paint onto the surface by means of the nozzle in the gun. The compressor, or air storage tank, builds up compressed air which forces the paint through the gun.

❮ How is the amount of paint controlled?

Different nozzles are able to handle different amounts of paint. Capacity of a spray outfit is measured by p.s.i., or pounds per square inch of air pressure. A higher p.s.i capacity means a sprayer can handle thicker paints.

❮ How do you paint with a spray gun?

Hold the gun perpendicular to the surface being painted. Keep it 7 to 9 inches from the surface to obtain an even spray. Make the strokes with a free arm motion, keeping the gun the same

BLEEDER — Trigger controls only paint / Air

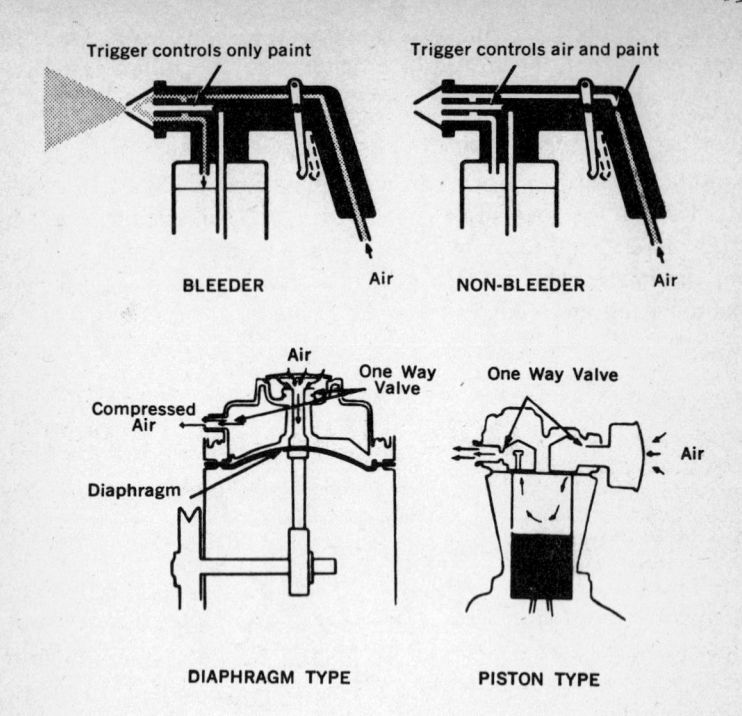

NON-BLEEDER — Trigger controls air and paint / Air

DIAPHRAGM TYPE — Compressed Air, Air, One Way Valve, Diaphragm

PISTON TYPE — One Way Valve, Air

distance from the surface at all points. Begin a stroke before pulling the trigger, and release the trigger just before ending the stroke. At corners, spray to within one or two inches of the end of each side. Hold the gun sideways, and paint both unsprayed sides of the corner with one stroke.

How do you clean a spray gun?

Remove the cup from the gun. Hold a cloth over the opening in the air cap, and pull the trigger to force air back into the container. Empty the container, and fill with the solvent specified by the manufacturer. Spray the solvent through the gun to clean out the passageways. Remove the air cap, and wash off the fluid tip with solvent. Clean the air cap in the solvent, and replace it on the gun. Never place the entire gun in solvent.

How do aerosol paint-sprayers work?

By pushing the plastic nozzle, you spray paint directly from the aerosol container.

3
Tools and Fasteners

Carpentry is actually divided into two operations which should be quite familiar to any woman: shaping and fastening. These two operations are, of course, the basic processes of dressmaking: pattern cutting and sewing.

Other facets of carpentry are supplementary to shaping and fastening. Measuring and laying out work—like the marking and cutting of cloth in dressmaking—can be considered part of shaping. All cutting operations in carpentry, such as sawing or filing, are shaping. Likewise, nailing and gluing are part of fastening—exactly like needlework in dressmaking.

In learning to perform home repairs, you must first of all familiarize yourself with the basic hand tools used in carpentry. Then you can try your luck with them.

Remember that hand tools are fashioned so that a woman as well as a man can handle them easily. You may find you have more natural aptitude and coordination than a man. It may take you more strokes of the saw to cut a board, but quite possibly the cut will be neater and cleaner when you are finished.

You can acquire carpentry techniques only by continual practice. Study the uses of hand tools in this chapter and then go to it. Once you learn what you can do with a certain tool, you will know how to adapt it to a specific repair problem.

Repair, like mending clothes, demands three things:

First, a study of the problem.

Second, an analysis of the trouble.

Third, an attack on the trouble with the proper tools and materials.

Don't fret. After awhile, you'll be able to hold a hammer and hit a nail on the head without a second thought.

Q & A

ESSENTIAL TOOLS

What are the primary tools you should have available in the home for work with wood?

A list of essential tools might vary from household to household, but the following comprises most of the tools you will need for a day-by-day home maintenance schedule:

Claw hammer, 16 ounce.
Screwdrivers, 3 and 6 inch.
Handsaw, both crosscut and rip.
Coping saw.
Compass saw.
Chisels, ¼ and ¾ inch.
Smooth plane.
Brace, 10 inch.
Bits, ¼ to 1 inch.
Screwdriver bit, 5/16 inch.
"Surform" surface-forming tool.
Level.
Marking gauge.
Square or combination square.
Glass-cutter.
Clamps.
Nail set, 2/32 inch.
Rule or tape, 8 feet.

Pliers.
Rasp or file.
Oilstone.
Vise.
Spokeshave.
Hand drill.
Miter box.
Adjustable "5" wrench.
Pipe wrench, Stillson type.
Rive-tool.

HAMMERS

(What are the main parts of a hammer?

A hammer has a head and a handle. The main parts of the head are the bell face, which is the end which hits the nail; the neck, which supports the face; the curved claw, which is on the opposite end from the bell-face; and the wedges, which are driven into the end of the handle (when made of wood) to keep the head from flying off.

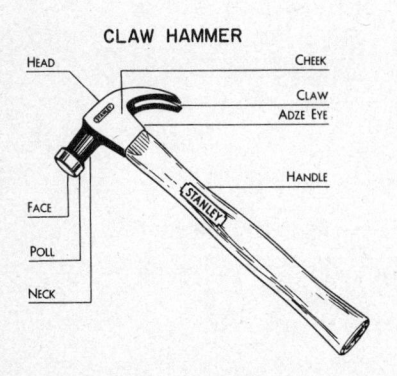

CLAW HAMMER

HEAD — CHEEK — CLAW — ADZE EYE — HANDLE — FACE — POLL — NECK

(How is a hammer held and used for best results?

Hold the hammer handle near the end. For light blows, use only a wrist action. For medium blows, use the wrist and forearm. For heavy blows, use an arm and shoulder action with slight wrist movement.

❨ In what way do you correct a nail which begins to bend as it is pounded in?

Strike the head at a slight angle in the direction opposite to that of the bend. You may have to remove the nail and start in again.

❨ What is the correct method for pulling out a nail?

Put a block of wood under the claw hammer when pulling out a nail in order not to mar the wood surface.

❨ How do you clinch nails for added holding power?

When a nail goes completely through a material, you can bend the protruding end over into the wood for extra grip.

❨ What is toe-nailing?

When nailing a piece of wood at right angles to another piece, you drive a nail in diagonally from each opposite surface of the wood into the bottom piece. The cross-strength you get adds to the success of the joint.

❨ How can you keep from splitting wood when you must nail close to the edge?

Blunt the point of the nail by turning it upside down and lightly tapping the point with a hammer. The blunted point will shear through the wood fibers, instead of spreading them apart. The sharp point is what causes wood to split.

SCREWDRIVERS

❨ What are the main kinds of screwdrivers?

There is the common screwdriver for slotted screws; the ratchet and spiral ratchet screwdriver; the Phillips screwdriver; and the cross point.

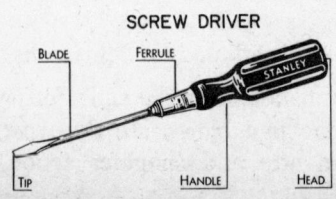

SCREW DRIVER

BLADE FERRULE

TIP HANDLE HEAD

Why do screwdrivers have different-shaped and -sized blades?

Each screwdriver is made especially for a certain kind and size of screw. Always use the right kind of screwdriver for the size screw you wish to drive.

How does a ratchet screwdriver work?

A ratchet screwdriver drives in a screw when pressure is applied on the end of the handle. The blade makes several turns with each push.

What is a Phillips screwdriver?

A Phillips screwdriver has a crossed-blade point. It is used only with a Phillips screw, which has a crossed V-slot in the head. The Phillips screwdriver cannot slip out of the slot or damage expensive finishes.

How do you use a screwdriver?

First, bore a pilot hole for the screw. For small screws, use an awl or a push drill; for large screws, use a bit or twist drill. The pilot hole should be smaller in diameter than the screw. Then apply the screw to the pilot hole, tap it in place, and screw it in with the screwdriver.

Is there any way to keep from chewing up the screwdriver slots in wood screws?

Yes. Never use a screwdriver which is the wrong size when driving a screw. The best rule-of-thumb is this: the tip of the blade should be square, so it fits into the bottom of the slot, and the sides of the blade should be almost parallel near the tip. The blade should be as close as possible to the width of the screw slot.

Can a screwdriver become dull?

Yes. To bring it back to life, square off the blade tip with a file.

SAWS

What are the main parts of a handsaw?

A handsaw is composed of a steel blade and a handle.

❦ What are the five main kinds of handsaws?

Crosscut saw, rip saw, back saw, keyhole saw, and coping saw.

❦ How does a rip saw differ from a crosscut saw?

A rip saw cuts with the grain; a crosscut saw cuts against the grain. A rip saw's teeth are filed straight across the face to a sharp square. The teeth of a crosscut saw are filed on alternate sides, producing beveled cutting edges like a series of knives. A crosscut saw makes a wider cut as it goes through the lumber.

❦ What is the proper angle at which to use a rip saw?

A rip saw should be held at an angle of 60 degrees from the board being cut.

60° angle for ripsawing

❦ What is the proper angle at which to use a crosscut saw?

A crosscut saw should be held at an angle of 45 degrees from the board being cut.

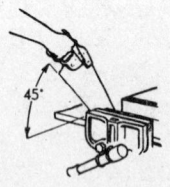

45° angle for crosscut sawing

❦ What is the proper way to hold a handsaw?

Hold the index finger extended along the handle, pointing parallel to the top of the saw blade. Grasp the wood with the other hand, the thumb placed along the line of the cut, but not in danger of being touched by the saw teeth. When you push down, the teeth cut. Use long, easy strokes.

❰ *For what purpose is a keyhole saw used?*

A keyhole saw has a thin, narrow blade which comes almost to a point. It is used for sawing curves in wood, and for work in cramped areas where a large-sized saw cannot reach.

❰ *How does a coping saw work?*

A coping saw has two separate parts: a handle or brace, and a blade. The brace is a squarish back to which the blade is mounted. Because it is thin, and because the brace is out of the way, the coping saw blade can make very irregular cuts in wood.

❰ *How do you sharpen a saw?*

There are several steps: jointing, shaping, setting, filing, and side-dressing.

(1) *To joint*: Using a mill file of the proper size, pass it gently back and forth across the tips of all the teeth until the file will touch all of them.

(2) *To shape*: File all the teeth to the correct shape, using the file at right angles to the blade.

(3) *To set*: Using a saw set, adjust the drum until it fits the size of teeth in the saw. Apply the saw set to every tooth until each tooth is in the position it was before being bent or dulled.

(4) *To file*: File each tooth sharp with a 6-inch slim-taper file. Start with the tooth nearest the handle, and continue until each adjacent tooth is pointed. In a crosscut saw, use the file at a 45-degree angle from the blade, reversing the saw as you do each tooth. In a rip saw, use the file at a 90-degree angle to the blade.

(5) *To side-dress*: Lay the saw on a flat surface, and lightly rub the sides of the teeth with an oilstone to remove any excess burr.

❰ *How do you keep a saw from binding in the wood?*

Insert a small nail in the top of the kerf, or cut. If the nail is not wide enough, try a knife blade, a wedge of shingle, or a thin slat. Keep the two sides of the kerf apart and the saw will not bind.

❰ *How can you pull a saw back into line if it strays off?*

Twist the lower edge of the handle toward the line, and guide it back with steady pressure.

◖ Should you saw directly down the middle of the marking line?

No. Keep the blade at least 1/16 inch outside a line; the saw wastes equal to the width of its blade. Margin should be left for planing, or for finishing.

◖ What kind of maintenance, other than sharpening, does a saw need?

Saw blades must be lightly oiled periodically. Wipe off the excess oil with a piece of cotton waste.

CHISELS

◖ What are the parts of a chisel?

It has a blade and a handle. A quality chisel blade is made of hard, tempered tool steel. The blade is beveled at the cutting edge.

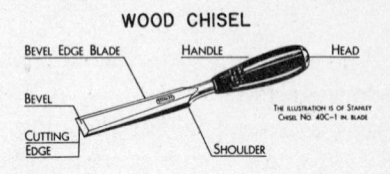

WOOD CHISEL

BEVEL EDGE BLADE — HANDLE — HEAD
BEVEL
CUTTING EDGE — SHOULDER

The illustration is of Stanley Chisel No. 40C-1 in. blade

◖ What sizes do chisels come in?

Blade widths range from 1/8 inch to 2 inches. Lengths are called "butt" (2½ to 3½ inches); "pocket" (2 to 5 inches); or "firmer" (8 to 10 inches).

◖ What are chisels used for?

Chisels are used for preparing small surface areas for the insertion of fittings, for inserting hardware, for inserting wood pieces, or in making joints.

◖ What are the two main types of chisels?

The socket chisel and the tang chisel.

◖ What is the difference between a tang chisel and a socket chisel?

The socket chisel has a handle which fits into the shank of the blade. The tang chisel has a handle which is hollowed out to receive the pointed chisel blade.

❰ In what way is a tang chisel used?

A tang chisel is used by hand. One hand holds the shank, and the other grasps the handle. The chisel blade should parallel the wood being cut. One hand guides the chisel into the cut, while the other exerts pressure on it.

❰ In what way is a socket chisel used?

A mallet drives the socket chisel. One hand guides the chisel at the handle, and the other pounds with the mallet.

❰ How do you hold a chisel to make light cuts?

Hold the bevel up and the flat side of the blade down to make light cuts.

❰ How do you hold a chisel to make deep cuts?

Turn the chisel over with the bevel down and the flat side up for deep cuts.

❰ What is the proper way to sharpen a chisel?

Hold the chisel with the bevel angle down on a whetstone or on a grindstone. Turn the grindstone away from the blade. Keeping the blade wet to prevent overheating, grind the bevel of the chisel's cutting edge uniform and flat. A chisel's angle of bevel is usually 30 to 35 degrees. When the bevel is sharpened, turn the chisel over, lay it flat on the whetstone, and remove the burrs or wire edges. The cutting edge should always be at right angles to the handle.

❰ How do you keep a chisel sharp?

Store it in such a way that the blade edge will not be banged up.

❰ What is a cold chisel?

A cold chisel is a hard-steel tool used to cut sheet metal, to

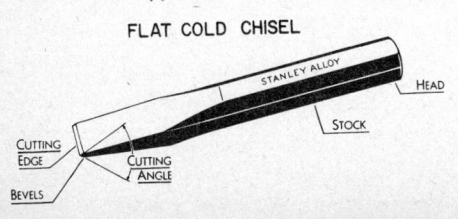

FLAT COLD CHISEL

chip metal, to cut rods and bars, and to split nuts that are frozen on bolts.

PLANES

❮ What is a plane?

A plane is a tool used to shave, smooth, reduce, or alter a wooden surface. A 30-degree beveled iron cutting blade, like a chisel's, protrudes from the bottom of a wooden or iron casing. When the plane passes over a surface, a thin shaving of wood is scooped up through a slot in the plane's bottom.

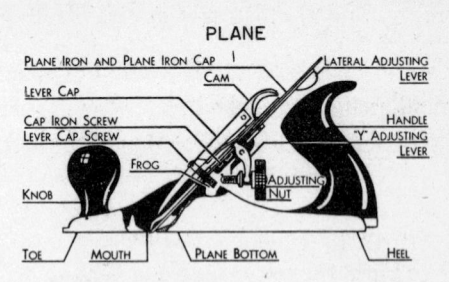

PLANE

❮ Name the main parts of a plane.

Besides the bottom, there is a cutting iron, a lateral adjusting lever to cant or slant the blade, a lever cap to hold the cutter blade tightly in position, a cam (or clamp) which secures the lever cap, and an adjusting screw which regulates the depth of the cut.

❮ How do you adjust the blade in a plane?

Lift the cam, so the lever cap can be removed. Withdraw the blade and cutter cap unit from the plane. Loosen the set screw to adjust the blade and the cutter cap. Tighten the set screw, and replace the unit. Turn the adjustment screw beneath the plane's handle to give the blade the proper protrusion. Trial-and-error will tell you when you have it right.

❮ What is the proper way to hold and operate a plane?

Grip the tool by the handle with one hand. Put the other hand on the front knob to exert downward pressure. Move the plane along the wood in a straight stroke, preferably with the grain. Use pressure at the beginning of the stroke; lift the blade off the wood carefully. A block plane can be manipulated with only one hand.

Tools and Fasteners [49

❮❮ How do you plane against the grain at the end of a board?

Plane from one end, and stop the stroke before reaching the far edge. Reverse, and start in from the other direction. Otherwise, you will split the grain at the edge.

❮❮ Is there any special precaution you should take to keep the blades from becoming dulled?

Always lay the plane on its side when storing it.

BRACES AND BITS

❮❮ What is a brace and bit?

A brace and bit are two tools used in combination to drill holes. The bit is the cutting device, formed with sharp-edged spiral blades. The brace is the handle which holds the bit and turns it.

BIT BRACE

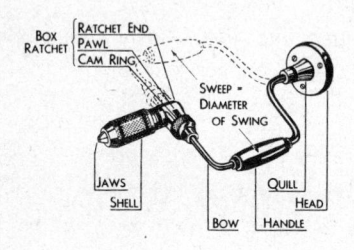

AUGUR BIT

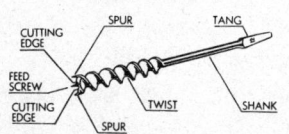

❮❮ How do a brace and bit work?

The bit is fitted into the brace by its shank, and secured by tightening the jaws in a chuck. The bit point is forced into the wood when the brace is turned, its handle describing a 6- to 14-inch sweep.

❮❮ Name the principal parts of a brace.

A brace consists of a rounded knob, a handle which slides

around the brace, a ratchet, a chuck which is a knurled metal cylinder fitting over metal jaws, and the jaws which clamp the square shank of the bit to hold it rigid.

❬ What different type of bits are there?

Bits usually come in sizes from 4/16 to 16/16 inch.

❬ Name the principal parts of a bit.

A bit has a shank, which is the tapered end that fits into the jaws of the chuck; the twist, which is the spiral cutting edge; the spur, which is the edge that circles the hole first; and the cutting lip, which is the actual cutting blade.

❬ What is a screwdriver bit?

A screwdriver bit is one which can be inserted in a regular wood brace. It can be used for driving in heavy screws too large to work in with regular hand screwdrivers.

❬ What is a hand drill?

A hand drill, shaped like an old-fashioned eggbeater, bores small holes in both wood and metal. It has a crank, a side handle, a pinion, and a chuck with jaws in which the drill fits.

❬ To what diameter will a push drill work?

A push drill is similar to a ratchet screwdriver. It will bore holes up to 11/16 inch in diameter. Pressure exerted on the end turns the drill on a ratchet. As you push again and again, the drill cuts into the wood.

❬ How do you operate a brace and bit?

Select your bit, open the chuck jaws, insert the shank into the jaws, and then lock firmly. Place the tip of the bit perpendicular to the spot to be drilled, push down, and turn the handle clockwise. To avoid splintering the bottom of the hole, remove the bit when its point comes through. Finish the hole from the underside.

❬ Is there any maintenance necessary on a brace and bit?

Keep the moving parts of the brace oiled.

❬ How can you sharpen the dull edges of a bit?

Hone the cutting edges with a light file.

Tools and Fasteners

(How is a "Surform" surface-forming tool described?

A "Surform" tool is a combination file and plane. It cuts, shapes, and smooths all at once. It is superior to a rasp, and is used to remove stock rapidly. Because it has holes behind its file-like teeth, it files without clogging, and is handy to use.

(With what materials can you use "Surform" tools?

You can shape wood, plywood, composition board, asphalt tile, hard rubber, and edges of plasterboard and plywood especially well.

(In what different forms do "Surform" tools come?

File type; plane type; combination plane and file; a round tubular file; and a pocket "Surform," 5½ inches long, perfect for the home.

LEVEL

(What is a carpenter's level, and how does it work?

A carpenter's level is necessary to find true vertical and true horizontal lines. Inside the level are tubes of glass which contain fluid and an air bubble. When placed exactly horizontal, the bubble centers in the slot. When placed vertically, the bubble centers in the end slot.

SQUARES AND MEASURES

(What is a framing square?

A framing square is an L-shaped metal ruler which will give you a right angle and which also has many other practical uses in carpentry. It is usually made with a 16-inch width and a 24-inch length.

(In what ways is a combination square used?

A combination square is used to mark and check right angles, and to give a right-angle line across a piece of lumber. It also can mark and check a 45 degree angle for mitering. The handle can be adjusted, and it slides along a 12-inch steel blade.

(How do you cut glass with a glass-cutter?

Guided by a straight edge, run the roller point of the glasscutter along the piece of glass you want to cut. Holding the glass over a piece of wood, with the edge along the line of the cut, grasp the end of the smallest portion of glass in the proper tooth grip on the glass cutter, and snap sharply. The glass will break along the marked line.

¶ When do you use a nail set?

Use a nail set at the point where you have the nail almost driven into the surface of the finish work. Apply the point of the nail set to the indented dot in the center of the head of the finish nail. Hammer on the other end of the nail set, driving the head in until it is below the surface of the wood. A self-centering nail set will prevent marring of the surface.

¶ How can you remove rust spots on the polished surface of a scissors or knife blade?

Rub ammonia on the rust spots. Allow the ammonia to soak in for a bit. Then rub the spot with a soft cloth. If you use an abrasive material, you are liable to ruin the high polish and damage the fine cutting edge.

¶ Is it possible to clamp a rod or tube or some other round shape in a vise?

Yes. You can use a web clamp. Or, if you cannot use a web clamp, you can prevent damage to the work by wrapping the round piece with thick pads of steel wool before putting it in a regular vise. This will give a firm, cushioned grip which will enable you to tighten the vise quite a bit in order to hold the piece rigid without damaging it.

PLIERS AND WRENCHES

¶ What is a pair of pliers?

A pair of pliers is actually a hand-operated gripper, with metal teeth to do the gripping.

¶ What are pliers used for?

You can grip small rods with them, hold pipes, hold wooden pegs, or studs. You can use them for bending wire, for clipping wire, or for numerous other such jobs.

Tools and Fasteners

¶ What is the most common type of pliers?

Combination pliers are the most popular, and are a must for every tool kit. A combination pliers has a "slip-joint" which allows the jaws to be opened wide at the hinge pin when you want to grip work with a large diameter.

¶ What is a wrench?

A wrench is a tool with an adjustable grip used for turning hexagonal or square nuts. The two jaws span opposite sides of the nut and grip it tightly while the operator uses the handle to apply pressure to tighten or loosen the nut.

¶ Describe the proper way to use a wrench.

Place it on the head of the nut or bolt, so that the force exerted in turning the nut will be applied to the back of the handle. Before turning, tighten the wrench jaws, so they will not slip.

How to use a wrench

¶ What is a monkey wrench?

A monkey wrench has a fixed jaw and a movable jaw, operated by an adjusting nut. The handle can be metal or wooden.

¶ For what main usage is the monkey wrench designed?

It is specifically designed for turning the hexagonal or square heads of bolts and nuts. You should never use it for turning pipe, rods, or other round objects.

¶ What is an adjustable wrench?

An adjustable wrench is also called a "crescent" wrench, because the two jaws are shaped like crescents. It is a small, handy wrench, designed for household use.

¶ What are socket wrenches?

Socket wrenches are not adjustable. A socket wrench has two

jaws, each designed to fit a specific size of nut. These wrenches usually come in sets or kits.

❮ What is a Stillson wrench?

A Stillson wrench has teeth, unlike all other wrenches described above. It is used for loosening or turning pipes or fittings, not for working nuts and bolts.

RIVETING

❮ How does a rivet work?

A rivet is simply a nail-like piece of metal with a head on one end and a knob on the other. Inserted like a bolt or nail, the knob is then struck with a hammer, flattened out, and made to stay firm.

❮ Is there a simple kind of riveting tool made especially for the homeowner?

Yes. A Rive-tool works well for all odd jobs around the house. A special hollow rivet is inserted from the top side into the material to be repaired. Then the tool itself is inserted in the rivet, clinched, and operated by handle. As you squeeze, a stem pulls up through the rivet, and the head on the bottom of the stem flares out a collar on the underside of the work. The stem breaks off at the top and leaves the rivet tightly set from both ends. You can install blind rivets in places you can't reach. If you want to rivet soft materials, such as fabric, plastic sheet, or plywood, you add a small "back-up" plate, supplied with the kit, to prevent tearing through.

LAYING OUT JOBS

❮ How does a carpenter lay out a job?

Laying out a job for shaping and fitting is the most important part of preliminary wood-working. It entails making a diagram and knowing how to read it, estimating the materials needed, measuring the materials to be shaped, and accurately marking them for cutting.

❮ How is a job measured?

Measuring is usually done with a carpenter's folding rule, or with a flexible steel rule. In measuring distances between two pieces

Tools and Fasteners [55

of framing, always keep the rule parallel to the running edge, and measure the shorter distance between two points. You do this by placing the rule's zero mark at the starting point, and extending the rule from that point. When it is impossible to lay out the rule to full length, as in measuring the inside of a closet, mark to the nearest foot, reverse the rule, place zero at the corner, and measure to the foot mark. Then, add the two measurements together to obtain the proper dimension.

(How do you measure the inside of a space with a flexible rule?

Roll out the steel tape all the way, butting the back of the rule against the other end. If the rule case is 2 inches wide, add 2 inches to the reading, and you have the full length in between.

(How can you keep flexible steel measuring tape from "creeping" when in use?

One of the easiest ways is to use a type which has a lock controlled by a grooved knob on the outside.

(Is there any set order in measuring an object's dimensions?

Mark down thickness, then width, and then length, in that order.

(What are the symbols for feet, inches, and "times" or "by"?

Feet — '; inches —"; times or by — x. A piece of framing timber two inches thick by four inches wide and five feet long would be: 2" x 4" x 5'.

(Is it necessary to draw a diagram in projecting the construction of shelves in a closet, for example?

It is always a good idea to draw a diagram. In that way, you will accustom yourself to the actual problems you will face when you have cut your material and are ready to attach it.

(How do you read draftsman's symbols?

Generally speaking, it is quite easy to figure out what the draftsman has in mind in a blueprint. Hard lines indicate what is visible; dotted lines indicate what is behind, but not visible. Extension lines indicate where an object would go if extended in size and shape. Dimension lines indicate the distance between two points.

❰ How would you read the draftsman's symbols in the picture below?

This is a side elevation of a seat on a swimming pool deck. 2" x 8" refers to the top timber and the backing for the seat. The 14" marking indicates that from the top of the deck plank to the bottom of the seat plank there are 14 inches of space. 2" x 4" indicates the size of timber used in the running brace and the seat base itself. The wide X's in the 2" x 4" shows that the plank is in cross-section; in other words, it is running at right angles to the

ARCHITECTURAL DETAIL

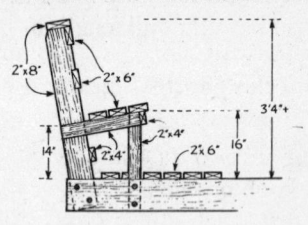

timber to which it is nailed. 2" x 6" indicates the size of the two rests inset in the back, and the three planks used as the seat. The seat tilts from 14 inches at the back to 16 inches at the front. 2" x 6"'s are used for the decking under the seat and in front of it. These planks run at right angles to the braces. The top of the back is 3 feet 4 inches above the deck planks. Note the dotted extension lines which make it easier to read the numbers placed away from the crowded part of the diagram. The small circles with squares in them indicate that the back brace and the front seat legs are bolted to the deck joists. The dotted lines extending behind the deck joists show that the legs and backs go down past the joists and are bolted on the far side. Where the 3' 4" sign adds a "plus," it simply means that the top can be higher; the measurement is approximate. The specifications not shown here indicate a ¼-inch clearance between the deck planks; this measurement is not indicated. Note how dotted lines run through sections to indicate what is on one side and what is on the other.

NAIL FASTENERS

❰ How are parts of wood and metal fastened together?
With nails, screws, glue or a combination.

Tools and Fasteners

❦ What is the simplest way to attach materials?

Nailing is the easiest and quickest way to fasten two pieces of wood together. A nail is not so strong or neat as either a screw or glue, but it is adequate for rough construction and for some cabinet work.

❦ What are the main types of nails, and for what are they used?

The main kinds of nails are common and box nails for structural carpentry; casing nails for interior trim; finishing nails for finished carpentry; and brads for light carpentry, moldings and backings. Besides these nail types, there are many other special varieties.

❦ What is the main difference between common nails and finishing nails, and for what are they used?

Common nails and box nails have flat heads and pyramid-like points. They are used for rough work with heavy boards, where nail heads are not objectionable and where they may be needed for extra strength. Common nails are used especially in framing. Finishing nails and brads have what is called a "brad head," which is a head not much larger than the diameter of the shank of the nail. The purpose of this small-headed nail is to finish work where the nail head should not show. Smaller-headed nails can be driven in flush with the surface by the use of a nail set; sometimes, they are countersunk below the surface and covered with putty. Many finish nails have a small dot indented in the center of the top to facilitate the use of a nail set.

❦ What are wire nails and box nails?

These nails have flat heads and pyramid-shaped points. Box nails are thinner than common nails, but measure the same length for the penny size. Wire nails are actually fine, miniature common nails.

❦ What are cement-coated nails?

These nails are coated with a thin layer of resin which melts when you drive the nail into wood. The resin bonds the wood fibers to the nail. Cement-coated nails are useful in flooring where the nails should never loosen.

❦ How are nails measured in length?

Nails are measured in an old-fashioned English system called the "pennyweight" system. Each nail, by its length, has a certain numerical penny designation. "Penny," incidentally, in carpentry is simply designed as "d," from the English coin system. For instance, a 2d (two-penny) nail is actually one inch in length. Common nails, finishing nails, and all kinds of nails are measured in penny length. A 3d nail is 1¼ inch in length; a 4d nail, 1½ inch in length; and so on. Each added pennyweight adds on a quarter of an inch up to 10d: From there the numbers of pennyweight vary. It goes this way: 10d, 12d, 16d, 20d, 30d, 40d, 50d, 60d. A 60d nail is 6 inches in length.

A look at the chart below will give you a comparison for various sizes and types of nails.

NAIL CHART

penny no.	length (inches)	common no./lb.	box no./lb.	casing no./lb.	finishing no./lb.
2	1	876	1010	1010	1351
3	1¼	568	635	635	807
4	1½	316	437	437	548
5	1¾	271	406	406	500
6	2	181	236	236	309
7	2¼	161	210	210	238
8	2½	106	145	145	189
9	2¾	96	132	132	172
10	3	69	94	94	121
12	3¼	64	87	87	113
16	3½	49	71	71	90
20	4	31	52	52	62
30	4½	24	46	46	
40	5	18	35	35	
50	5½	16			
60	6	11			

(How are nail heads measured?

Each nail head has a different kind of diametrical measure, depending on the type of nail.

(How is shank diameter of a nail measured?

Shank diameter, or the thickness of a nail, is measured in gauge. For instance, a 2d common nail has a shank diameter of 15. A 10d common nail has a shank diameter of 9. See the chart printed above for further information.

❧ *Is there any rule-of-thumb concerning the size of nail to use?*

Yes. Use a nail that is three times as long as the thickness of the board which is being nailed. For nailing a 1" board, use an 8d nail.

WOOD SCREW FASTENERS

❧ *What are the advantages of wood screws over nails?*

Wood screws have more holding power than nails. Materials fastened by screws can be easily separated later.

❧ *What are the disadvantages of screws over nails?*

They are harder to drive in. Drilling is sometimes necessary.

❧ *What are the main types of wood screws?*

Wood screws come with flat, oval, or round heads. They are called flat-head screws, oval-head screws, and round-head screws.

WOOD SCREW CHART

screw number	body diameter	diameter of round head	diameter of flat head
0	.060	.106	.112
1	.073	.130	.138
2	.086	.154	.164
3	.099	.178	.190
4	.112	.202	.216
5	.125	.226	.242
6	.138	.250	.268
7	.151	.275	.294
8	.164	.299	.320
9	.177	.322	.346
10	.190	.347	.372
11	.203	.370	.393
12	.216	.394	.424
14	.242	.442	.476
16	.268	.490	.528
18	.294	.539	.580
20	.320	.587	.630
24	.372	.683	.736

❧ *How are screws measured?*

Wood screws are measured by diameter, gauge, and by length The length is measured from the point of the screw to the top of the flat head, from the point to the bottom of a round head, and from the point to the middle of an oval head. The length is measured in inches. The number by which a screw is known refers to its diameter. A #0 screw is .060 inches in diameter. The largest common size is 24, which is .327 inches in diameter.

(How are wood screws ordered?

Order by gauge number for diameter, and by inch measurement for length. For instance, you order a number 6 screw in ¾, 1 inch, and 1¼ inch lengths, or whatever are available.

(How can you keep brass screws from breaking when being driven into hard woods?

Steel screws are stronger than brass screws. Find a steel screw exactly the same size as the brass screw, and use it first to cut the threads in the wood. Then remove it and insert the brass one in its place.

(What's the best way to store off-size screws, nails, and brads in the workshop?

Hang a strip of pressure-sensitive tape to the ceiling, and stick the extras onto it as they accumulate. You'll have a ready reference in front of you when you need your next odd-size screw.

(How can you remove an old rusted screw in which the slot has become useless through corrosion?

Cut the slot deeper and cleaner by clamping two or three hack saw blades together and sawing through the old groove. With the new slot, you'll be able to work the screw with your driver.

(What is a bolt?

A bolt is spiral-grooved like a wood screw, sometimes fitted with a head which can be turned with a wrench, and sometimes fitted with a slotted screwhead. It can have a nut at the other end, or it can be threaded directly into the material it is fastening. Generally, a nut and a bolt go together, and are used to fasten a piece of metal to another piece of metal or to a piece of wood.

(What is a nut?

A nut is the square fastening piece at the bottom of a bolt. It is threaded onto the bolt and secured tightly by the use of a wrench. In fastening two pieces of material with a nut and a bolt, two wrenches can be used, twisted in opposite directions.

NUT AND BOLT FASTENERS

(What are the major types of nuts and bolts?

The two major classes of nuts and bolts are carriage bolts and machine bolts.

(How are bolts measured?

Bolts are measured according to diameter, number of threads per inch, and length. Their diameters vary from ¼ to 1¼ inch. Lengths vary from ¾ to 30 inches. Holes for bolts are always drilled 3/16 inch larger than the bolt's diameter, unless a snug fit is needed. Nuts are usually square or hexagonal for use with a wrench. Actually, bolts are, in many cases, extra large screws.

(What are bolts used for?

They are used for several purposes in construction: to join heavy wooden framing members; to attach metal structural members to wood; to fasten foundation sills to walls.

(What are washers?

Washers are disks with a center hole. In plumbing, washers are made of rubber or fiber. In construction, washers are of metal. They are used to protect wood from marring when a bolt is inserted. There are flat washers, lock washers, and split lock washers. The flat washer is used against wood, either under the head of the bolt, or next to the nut, or in both spots. Lock washers, both split and otherwise, are used against metal. Lock washers are used to hold a bolt head tight against a surface when the bolt itself may be turned by vibration or usage.

(What is a toggle bolt?

A toggle bolt is a long bolt with separate wings which fit around it. Inserted in a masonry hole, the wings fold out against the hole when the bolt is screwed in.

(What is a corrugated fastener?

A corrugated fastener, also called a wiggle nail, is a rippled piece of metal, sharp on one edge. Driven into two parallel pieces of wood at the end, it will hold them together.

❊ How can you keep nuts from working loose in nut-and-bolt joints?

On the market is a new thermoplastic chemical compound with which you can keep nuts from working loose in wheeled toys, bicycles, or outboard motors. The compound works its way in between the screw head and the metal, and hardens. Only strong pressure with a wrench will loosen the nut.

❊ How do you unseat a rusted screw?

Use penetrating oil. The oil should loosen up the rust, and make it possible to extract the screw. In certain situations, it is possible to unfreeze a rusted screw by the use of a blow torch; if there is wood nearby, don't try it.

❊ How do you free nuts or bolts which become frozen in place with rusting?

Use a small propane torch. Concentrate the flame of the torch on the nut to heat it as rapidly as possible. The heat will expand the nut, and that will help loosen it. Be careful of wood nearby.

❊ What is an adhesive?

For our purposes, "adhesive" is anything which you can use to stick two different things together without the use of nails, screws, or bolts.

❊ How can you tell what kind of adhesive to use for a specific job?

After studying this guide, you should be able to pick out the proper adhesive to use for whatever you want to do.

❊ Describe the main types of "adhesives" available today.

There is a great variety of adhesives on the market today. Some of them include the following: *mucilage* or *library paste*, made from natural or vegetable resins; *animal* or *fish glue*, made from animal or fish parts; *synthetic thermosetting resin glue*, a resin powder with a catalyst and a filler; *synthetic thermoplastic resin glue*, containing a polyvinyl resin base; *casein glue*, a water-resistant protein extract; *plastic rubber cement*, a solvent-based synthetic rubber in putty form which vulcanizes chemically; *epoxy cement*, a separate resin adhesive and hardener which unites to a waterproof, shrink-proof bond; *contact cement*, an air-drying adhesive which bonds instantly; *steel paste*, a bonding and sealing product

GLUING CHART

MATERIALS	Mucilage	Animal Glue	Resin Glue	Polyvinyl Resin Glue	Casein Glue	Rubber Cement	Epoxy Cement	Contact Cement	Steel Paste	Rubber Sealant	Resorcinol Glue	Liquid Vinyl Cement	Aluminum Cement	Polystyrene Cement
Wood to Wood & Plywood		X	X	X	X						X			
Plywood Wall Panels			X		X			X						
Plastic Laminates, Wood to Wood		X	X	X	X			X			X			
Hardboard to Wood		X	X	X	X			X			X			
Wood Veneering		X	X	X	X			X						
Wood — Outdoors			X		X						X			
Wood Boats											X			
Styrene Plastic to Styrene Plastic														X
Metal to Wood							X	X						
China		X		X			X	X	X	X		X		X
Patch, Seal & Solder						X	X		X				X	
Caulk							X			X	X		X	
Model Building, Felt to Wood		X		X				X				X		X
Leather to Leather or Wood	X	X		X				X	X			X		X
Unlike Materials						X		X	X	X		X	X	
Paper to Paper or Fabrics	X	X		X								X		X
Canvas to Wood		X	X	X	X			X	X		X	X		X
Rubber to Wood or Metal						X	X	X				X		
Metal to Metal							X		X	X				
Leather to Paper	X													
Leaks in Pipes and Steel									X					

composed of steel in paste form; *silicone rubber sealant*, a flexible, weatherproof, adhesive and caulking compound; *liquid vinyl cement*, a clear-drying liquid cement; *plastic aluminum cement*, a ready-to-use metal in putty form; and *polystyrene cement*, a clear-drying liquid styrene cement for plastics. See the chart for the general uses of each.

GLUE TIPS

(How is glue best applied?

For large areas, use a paint brush. For small objects, use the glue tube itself. For medium-sized areas, use an old hacksaw blade to spread it on.

(How can you prevent dry wood grain from soaking up too much glue when you make a joint?

Give the end grain of any job a thin preliminary coat of glue to prevent it from soaking up the glue and causing a weak joint. Wait a bit before spreading the rest of the job. Give the end grain a second coat when you finish.

(What are the best step-by-step methods to use in preparing a piece of material for gluing?

If you are re-gluing a piece of broken furniture, clean off all the old glue down to the bare wood. Test out the joint before applying glue. If it is necessary, patch it with wood filler made out of glue and sawdust or wood dust. Let this harden until the joint is a tight fit. Apply glue to both surfaces to be joined. Use the right clamp or jig to hold the joint firm until dry. Let the job set undisturbed until it is dry. Use the full recommended time given by the glue manufacturer.

(What can you use to reinforce a joint while it is drying?

Nails and screws, even dowels, are useful in reinforcing the wood at a joint, either permanently or while it is drying. Always use finishing nails to reinforce a joint. To cap or hide screw heads in a furniture piece, cut a cap from a dowel, or make one with a plug cutter on a drill press. Fasten it in place with glue. Dowels or pegs can often do a good job without nails or screws, and often serve the purpose better. Reinforce with glue, of course.

(How can you keep covers on small tubes of adhesive and sealer from sticking?

Smear the threads with a thin coat of petroleum jelly before replacing the cap the first time. You can use this trick on tubes of paint, too, and on jars or cans with threaded covers.

WOOD CLAMPS

(What are wood clamps good for?

Since glue needs time to dry without being disturbed, the joint to be glued should be held firm. This is usually done by means of a wood clamp. Pull the clamp tight, and hold the joint that way, under pressure, to prevent slackening or shifting during the drying process.

(How do you keep wood from being damaged when you clamp it together for gluing?

Insert small wooden blocks between the jaws of the clamp and the wood surface.

(How do you prevent these blocks from being glued to the surface?

Insert a sheet of wax paper between the block and the finished work surface.

(When you hold two pieces of lumber together to drill matching holes, how can you keep wood clamps from slipping?

If the clamps slip too much, hold the two pieces of wood in position by driving a corrugated fastener part way into the lined-up ends of the boards so that the fastener overlaps both pieces. Pull it out when you've finished your drilling.

(What is a C clamp?

A C clamp—so-called because it is shaped like a capital C—gives an excellent clamping pressure for most glue joints. In order to keep the joint under proper pressure, cut out cushion blocks from scrap to distribute the pressure evenly. C clamps come in adjustable shapes.

4
Wood

Wood is probably the most important building material with which you will come in contact while working on home repairs. Although there are many substitutes these days—composition board, plasterboard, vinyl tile, asphalt tile, and so on—wood is easy to use because of its adaptability, simplicity of installation, and durability.

If shaping and fastening are the two operations with which carpentry is concerned, think of wood as the material to be worked —just as cloth is the material to be worked in dressmaking.

To make the dress you have in mind, you must be quite selective in the kind of cloth you buy. The same is true with the selection and purchase of wood.

In order to understand how to obtain the right wood for the job, you must know certain facts and peculiarities about lumber. The questions and answers in the following chapter have been arranged to give you an over-all picture of the wood you may buy at a building supply house, both as timber or as plywood, the two most common forms. You'll learn what certain woods are best for, and what they cannot be used for. You'll learn how to price lumber, and how to order it. And, you'll learn what to watch out for when shopping.

Q & A

WOOD TYPES

❰[*What are the main types of wood?*

Lumber is divided into two main types—hardwoods and softwoods. Hardwoods come from deciduous, broad-leaved trees, which shed their leaves in winter. Softwoods come from cone-bearing trees or evergreen trees with needlelike leaves, which do not shed in the winter.

❰[*What are hardwoods used for?*

Hardwoods are generally used for floors, for stair treads, and for furniture.

❰[*Which kinds are commonly in use?*

Maple and oak are the two most extensively used hardwoods around the home. Others are used as veneers for rare finish.

❰[*What are softwoods used for?*

Softwoods are used for framing, for rough boarding and sheathing, for shingles, and for interior trim and millwork.

❰[*What is framing?*

Framing is the structural wood which holds up a house. It is the equivalent of the skeleton of an animal. To the frame are fastened the walls, the floor, the roof, and the ceiling.

❰[*What is sheathing?*

Sheathing is wood applied to the structural framing of a house. It is the "inner skin" over which the outside surface is applied, and in new construction today is probably plywood, although it can be 1" x 8" sheathing.

❰[*What kinds of wood are used for sheathing?*

Plywood, or Southern pine, or an equivalent.

❮ What kind of wood is used for shingles?
Red or white cedar.

❮ What is interior trim?
Interior trim refers to the various strips of wood applied to corners and joints in the interior of the house. The trim applied to the junction of a wall and ceiling is called *molding*. Trim applied to the junction of the floor and wall is called *baseboard* trim. Trim applied to the outside of a doorframe or a window frame is called *door molding* and *window molding*.

❮ What is millwork?
Millwork refers to lumber used in built-in cabinets, to shelves, and to bookcases, and so on.

❮ What kind of wood is used for interior trim and millwork?
Soft pines are used for doors and molding, along with white and sugar pines.

SEASONING

❮ Is there a difference between seasoned wood and unseasoned wood?
Yes. Seasoned wood is wood which has been thoroughly dried out. When a tree is originally felled, its weight is from 25% to 70% water. Seasoning reduces its water content from 20% of the total to 6% of the total.

❮ How is wood seasoned?
It can be done by drying out in the air, by forced drying in a kiln or oven, or by a combination of the two.

❮ Is it necessary for wood to be seasoned?
Yes. If wood is not properly seasoned, it will continue to dry. As it dries, it will shrink and lose weight. When wood becomes seasoned, it increases in strength. Unseasoned wood, also called "green" wood, is unsatisfactory for building and repairing, because it will shrink after it is in place. Also, it may be too moist to take

Wood

a coat of paint. Unseasoned wood is liable to warp and twist as it dries.

❊ Does all lumber have to be completely seasoned before use?

No. For use in shelving for the workshop, the garage, or the pantry, almost any kind of lumber will be dry enough. However, for interior trim, fully seasoned material is essential.

❊ Does well-seasoned wood ever change size after it is installed?

Even moderately well-seasoned lumber can shrink 2% or more in a few days within a heated house.

❊ Can wood be used immediately after purchase?

It is best to move the wood into the heated part of the house (where it will be used) a few days beforehand. Humidity varies from room to room and from floor to floor in any house. By becoming adjusted to the humidity, the wood will become properly seasoned before it is put up.

DIFFERENT SIZES OF LUMBER

❊ Is lumber classified according to thickness and width?

Yes. The major classifications of lumber are strips, boards, framing ("dimension") and timbers.

❊ What are strips?

Strips are less than 2 inches thick and less than 8 inches wide. A 1" x 4" is a strip.

❊ What are boards?

Boards are less than 2 inches thick, and 8 inches or more wide. A 1" x 10" is a board.

❊ What is framing?

Framing timber, also called "dimension" timber, comes in anything from a 2-inch thickness to over a 4-inch thickness. The bulk of framing material is 2-inch material: 2" x 4", 2" x 6", and so on.

❊ What are timbers?

Timbers include all wood 5 inches or more in thickness.

⁌ How are woods graded differently according to quality?

Qualitative grading is based on the lack of such defects as knots, decay, stain, pitch pockets, wane, bark pockets, and skips.

⁌ What causes knots?

Knots are the cross-section of branches growing through the tree trunk. They range from pin-size (under ½-inch in diameter) to large (over 1½-inch in diameter). Tight knots are firmly embedded and are no liability. Loose knots occur on the edge of the board. They are liable to fall out.

⁌ What causes decay?

Disintegration of the wood fiber usually comes from attacks by fungus, moisture, or mold.

⁌ What causes stain?

Stain discoloration in the wood, generally blue or brown, is caused by imperfections in the tree itself.

⁌ What causes pitch pockets?

Pitch sometimes does not flow out through the bark, but becomes embedded in the wood itself. It collects in pockets.

⁌ What is wane?

Wane is bark left on the edge of a board due to imperfect cutting at the mill. Watch out: it will crumble off when the lumber is used.

⁌ What causes bark pockets?

Sometimes a tree grows eccentrically, enclosing bark inside the wood pulp, trapping it. These are called bark pockets.

⁌ What causes skips?

Undressed or rough areas of wood, called "skips," result when the milling plane which shapes the wood misses a portion of surface.

QUALITY GRADING

⁌ How are "select" or "finish" boards and strips classified?

A, B, C, and D. A and B are called B & btr. Common utility

grades are numbered from 1 to 5. Some yards sell B and C or D finish grades only; others sell select grades #1 and #2 Clear, followed by #1 and #2 Common, and so on.

❰ How is framing lumber classified?

Framing lumber and timbers are classified as 1, 2, 3, and sometimes 4.

❰ How are flooring and siding woods graded?

Softwood flooring and siding come in four grades, B & btr, C, D, and E.

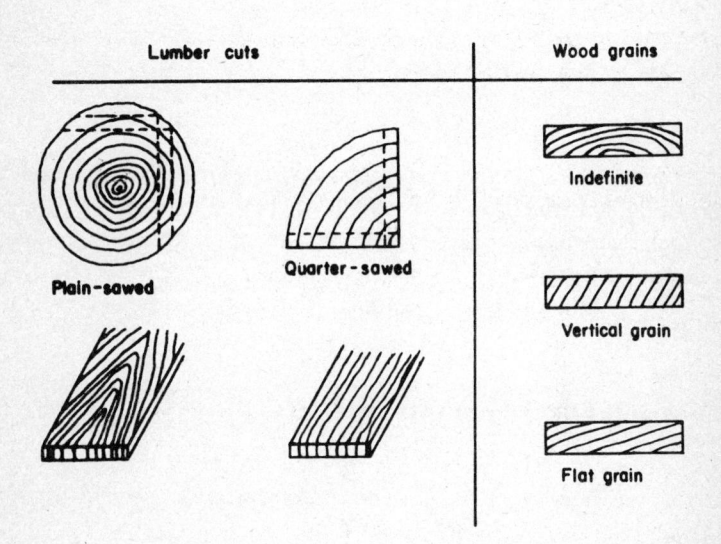

Lumber cuts

Plain-sawed

Quarter-sawed

Wood grains

Indefinite

Vertical grain

Flat grain

❰ How is oak graded?

Oak is graded differently. Quarter-sawed (sawed flat from a quarter section of the log) is clear, sap clear, or select. Plain-sawed (from a whole section of the log in from the outside) is clear, select, or No. 1 and No. 2 common.

❰ How are shingles graded?

Some shingles come as No. 1, bests, and primes. Others come in three numbered grades. Others in a single grade.

❪ What kind of wood is suitable and economical to use for interior trim?

No. 2 utility white pine.

❪ What kind of wood is suitable and economical to use for framing and structural work?

No. 2 sheathing.

❪ What kind of wood should be used on open porches or in areas subject to moisture?

B & btr vertical grain might prove better than medium grade (C select).

❪ Is a 2" x 4" actually 2 inches by 4 inches in thickness and width?

Not when you get it. All lumber is designated by the thickness and the width of the lumber according to its green, untrimmed dimensions. A 1" board is actually 25/32-inch thick. Lumber from 2 to 7 inches in width has an actual dimension of 3/8-inch less than the nominal dimension. At widths of 8 inches or more, the actual dimension is 1/2-inch less. A 2" x 4" is really 1 5/8" x 3-5/8". For tongue-and-groove lumber, the surface width is reduced another 3/8-inch.

BUYING LUMBER

❪ What is the billing unit for lumber? In other words, in what units of measurement do you purchase and pay for lumber?

You pay for wood by the board foot.

❪ What is a board foot?

It is a rough, green piece of wood 1" x 1' x 1', or of an equivalent volume. In other words a 1" x 6" strip 2' long is one board foot of lumber; likewise, so is a 1" x 4" strip 3' long. So is a 2" x 6" framing timber 1' long.

❪ How do you order lumber from a lumber yard?

You can specify the linear feet of a given material. For instance, you might order five pieces of 1" x 6" No. 2 white pine each 6 feet long. You will be billed for 5 (pieces) x 6 (total length in feet) x 6/12 (total width in feet) x 1 (total thickness in inches), or 15 board feet of common pine, at whatever price it runs per board feet. Or you may order it by the *running* foot, which means the actual number of feet a piece of lumber measures in length. 6 running feet of 2" x 4" will be a framing strip 6 feet long; it will equal 4 board feet, or course. Most yards sell various strips, boards, and framing material in running feet, too.

(In what lengths is lumber sold?

Most yards will cut it to the size you specify, but it is actually sold in standard lengths, or in multiples of 2 feet.

PLYWOOD

(What is plywood?

Plywood is building material made up of an odd number of thin sheets of wood glued together, the layers being at right angles to one another.

(What are the main advantages of plywood?

Plywood has more strength than a one-thickness board. Because of the cross-ply lamination, it has strength across the grain as well as lengthwise. It is the preferred wood product to use in covering large areas, and for jobs needing maximum strength and minimum weight.

(Is plywood made up of one kind of wood?

No. Plywood is generally composed of "inner plies" for the cross-grain wood on the inside, and "face" and "back" woods of the same species for the outside surfaces. Softwood plywood is always manufactured so there is a "balanced" panel: thus the odd number of plies—3, 5, 7. Face and back plies must be the same; inner plies are symmetrical. In a five-ply panel, plies one and five are of the same specie. Plies two and four are the same. The middle ply could be another specie altogether.

(What kind of wood is used for inner ply?

An inner ply is usually a wood of low density. Hardwoods such as bass wood, cottonwood, and poplar, are low density woods;

softwoods such as cedar, white pine, and Ponderosa pine, are also low density woods.

❪ What is a good face wood?

That depends entirely on the job to be done. A face wood can have a medium or high density. Hardwoods such as ash, beech, birch, maple, and oak, are of high density; softwoods such as Douglas fir, larch, and Southern pine, are of high density. Softwood plywood is used for so many purposes, ranging roughly from pickle vats to luxury homes, that there are special panels for special purposes. For instance, a DFPA.C-D panel would produce a very ugly cabinet—but it would produce a *better* roof deck than would a high-appearance panel such as DFPA.A-A.

❪ Does plywood warp or shrink or swell?

The tendency to shrink or swell is at a minimum in plywood. The wood is dried—or seasoned—during manufacture. It resists warping and keeps its rigid form.

❪ Will plywood split?

The impact of any blow against plywood is distributed over the whole area of the panel because of the laminated structure. Nails and screws do not cause the panel to split, even near the edges.

❪ Is plywood easy to work with?

It is the easiest kind of material for the amateur to use. It will not chip or break. It is lighter and stronger than ordinary wood, and can be moved about more easily.

❪ Is plywood good for insulation?

Low-density plywood has excellent insulating properties and good acoustical value in absorbing sound.

❪ Will plywood last as long as regular wood?

If plywood is installed correctly, it will last as long as, or longer than, any other wood around it.

❪ Can plywood be used outside the house?

There are two types of plywood: Exterior and Interior. Exterior-type plywood is bonded under heat and pressure with permanent, phenolic resin adhesives that are more durable than the wood itself. Interior type plywood is bonded with adhesives that are just as permanent under dry conditions, but which will break down under repeated wetting and drying cycles.

❪ *What causes interior plywood to break down?*

If the moisture point is allowed to rise to more than 20%, interior plywood may be attacked by mold, fungus growth, or decay. The moisture percentage in the average home is about 12%, and virtually never reaches more than 15 to 17%.

GRADES OF PLYWOOD

❪ *What determines whether a plywood is hardwood or softwood?*

The "face" wood of a piece of plywood partly determines whether it is hardwood or softwood.

❪ *What determines "type" of plywood?*

"Type" is determined by glue used to fasten the sheets together.

❪ *What determines "grade" of plywood?*

"Grade" is determined by the quality appearance of the veneer on the face and back.

❪ *What are the various grades?*

A, B, C (repaired), C, D, and N.

❪ *What is grade A?*

Quality veneer, of highest standard. No defects. Smooth and paintable. All patches and repair run parallel to the grain. Approved plastic filler in splits if they are less than 1/32-inch in width.

❪ *What is grade B?*

Similar to A, but with circular plugs, rough edges, tight knots up to 1 inch. Surface must be free from open defects.

❪ *What is Grade C (repaired)?*

This is C veneer that has had most surface defects filled. Tight knots up to 1½ inches are allowed, and so are worm and borer holes up to ½-inch. Ruptured or torn grain, solid tight pitch pockets, and sanders' skips of 5 per cent are allowed.

(What is Grade C?

The lowest quality veneer permitted in exterior type. Knots up to 1 inch, small borer holes, 3/16" splits. Plugs, patches, shims, and minor sanding defects admitted.

(What is D Grade?

D Grade is used only in interior-type plywood panels. Knots up to 2½", pitch pockets, limited splits, worm or borer holes, repair patches.

(What is N Grade?

This is special-order, "natural-finish" veneer, very select, all heartwood, free from knots, splits, pitch pockets, and other open defects. Not more than three pieces of veneer are used. May contain specific small repairs if well-matched, but no plastic filler permitted.

(What is a panel marked A-A?

It has highest standard quality on both face and back panels. A-B would indicate A quality on the face and B quality on the back.

5
Plumbing

Cold and hot running water in the home is a must to every American woman. Since all cooking is dependent on the immediate delivery of water to the kitchen, and since all matters of cleanliness are dependent on the adequate availability of water, you cannot minimize the importance of a perfectly working plumbing system.

You must repair or have repaired a leaky faucet or pipe as soon as possible; otherwise, serious damage may result. While many plumbing problems must be handled by an expert—such as burst pipes from a freeze-up—many of the ordinary plumbing repair jobs around the house are not too difficult for you to handle. Nor do they require expensive tools.

Q & A

FAUCETS

What causes a faucet to leak?

There are several reasons why a faucet leaks. The main cause is a worn washer; or, the packing around the faucet stem may become deteriorated; or, the "seat" against which the valve washer closes may become scored or pitted. And, sometimes, faucet parts become loose and need to be tightened or replaced.

❛ Can a leaky faucet be ignored until a convenient time for repair?

A leaky faucet must be repaired immediately. Seats and washers will rapidly deteriorate once a leak has started.

❛ What tools are necessary for faucet repair?

A file or hack saw, pliers, monkey wrench, and screwdriver should do the trick. There is a special tool available for the repair of pitted seats; it is called a faucet seat dresser, or "Drip-Stopper." Basically, the faucet seat dresser is a handle attached to a threaded spindle with a hard steel cutting disk at the bottom. The spindle fits into the faucet and centers the cutting disk on the middle of the faucet seat. By turning the handle, you smooth the faucet seat clean.

❛ What is the most popular kind of faucet in a home?

The most common type is usually a compression faucet.

❛ How does it work?

By turning a handle, you screw a valve stem down into a valve opening, called a "seat." This closes the valve opening, and prevents water from flowing through the fixture. At the bottom of the valve stem, a valve washer is attached with a set screw. This fits against the seat when the faucet is closed, cutting off flow. When the washer becomes old and worn, water may leak through, causing the faucet to drip. At the top of the valve stem, a packing nut, protected by washers, keeps water from traveling up the stem and spilling out the handle. The three points of trouble are: at the valve washer; at the seat, which becomes pitted through constant use; or at the packing nut.

❛ How do you replace a worn washer in a compression faucet?

See Chapter One, Page 5.

❛ How do you replace deteriorated packing?

Turn off the water supply at the shut-off valve. Unscrew the packing nut, and remove the stem from the faucet. (See Chapter One, Page 5 for instructions.) Then dig out the old packing from the packing nut. Wind new packing twine or candlewicking around the stem in the same direction the handle turns when

Plumbing

screwed into faucet. Now, screw the packing nut over the stem to hold the packing in place. Be sure you haven't got too much packing in the nut. If you have, remove it. Reassemble the faucet.

⁋ Explain how to re-dress a scored or pitted seat.

Turn off the water supply at the shut-off valve. Remove the handle, the packing nut, the faucet stem, and the washer. Using the faucet seat dresser or "Drip-Stopper" above, insert the tool into the faucet body. Turn the handle clockwise until the threads have engaged the faucet threads. Turn the handle of the dresser three or four times. Remove the tool, and look at the seat to see if it is sufficiently smooth and shiny, without grooves or scoring. If it is still pitted, use the dresser again until it is smooth. Flush out the metal particles from the seat, and reassemble the faucet.

DRAINAGE PIPES

⁋ How do you clear a stuck drainage pipe?

See Chapter One, Page 6.

⁋ How do you free a clogged trap in a toilet?

Insert the hooked end of a closet auger into the bowl. (A closet auger is a long snake-like object, the far end of which can be rotated by a handle on the near end.) Push the auger into the opening at the base of the bowl, and rotate the handle until you reach the trap. Agitate the auger until the obstruction in the trap is broken or adheres to the hook. Remove it. Empty a pail of water into the bowl. Do not flush it. If the water rushes through, the trap is free.

⁋ If the trap is free and the water still backs up, what is wrong?

Quite possibly the waste pipe in the wall may be clogged.

⁋ How do you clean a waste pipe?

Remove the trap loop under the bowl. Feed the auger downwards into the waste pipe through the connection. Twist the auger until the obstruction has broken or is hooked.

⁋ What causes hammering in water pipes?

When water is abruptly stopped in its course through a pipe, the water bangs or hammers against the sides of the pipe.

❡ *How can you correct this disturbing noise?*

Have an air cushion installed as near the water meter as possible. An air cushion is a 3-foot length of pipe capped at the top and screwed into the main pipe. The water is forced into the empty pipe length and gradually slows down as it compresses the enclosed air.

❡ *What causes rumbling in pipes?*

Rumbling may be caused by steam from the hot water system. You should have controls installed to prevent your water from overheating.

❡ *What causes thumping noises in faucets?*

The faucet parts are worn out. Replace them.

WATER HEATER

❡ *How is most water heated in a modern home?*

The most common kind of water heater in use today is a single unit which contains the supply tank and gas-, electric-, or oil-heating unit within the same insulated jacket. The water is thermostatically controlled at 130 to 140 degrees Fahrenheit.

❡ *Does the tank itself do the heating?*

No. The water is usually heated elsewhere in a furnace or stove. It is kept in the tank under 85 pounds pressure to the square inch.

❡ *What happens if the water in a tank becomes overheated and develops excess pressure?*

The tank will explode. You should have a meter, check valve, or some other device to close off the supply. A relief or safety valve will blow off any pressure above normal.

❡ *What causes dirty hot water?*

Rust and dirt carried in from the street main will give you dirty hot water. Or, you can get it from rusting of the house pipes or supply tank, or from sediment thrown by heating the water.

❨ *How can you do away with the dirty hot water?*

Let the sediment settle and draw it off. Sometimes, the installation of a water-softener unit in the incoming cold-water line will remove the main-line sediment and rust.

❨ *What size hot water tank is needed to supply a household of four people?*

About 30 gallons capacity. For each additional bedroom, or for each added person, add 5 gallons capacity. In a five-bedroom house with seven people, you should have a tank of 45 gallons capacity. Add 5 gallons for an automatic washer, and 5 gallons more for an automatic dishwasher.

❨ *What happens if water pipes become so clogged that they do not work properly?*

If water is hard, and mineral salts scale the pipes, you may have to replace the pipe. You can make the cheapest and best replacement with copper tubing; it can be pulled up through the walls alongside the old pipes, leaving them where they are.

SEWAGE DISPOSAL

❨ *What is a cesspool?*

A cesspool is a brick-lined or stone-lined underground well, where liquid sewage seeps through and is absorbed in the earth.

❨ *For how long should a cesspool last?*

Unless it overflows after filling, a cesspool should serve for many years.

❨ *What causes a cesspool to overflow?*

Generally, you'll find that overflowing is caused by a clogging-up of the openings in the masonry. Grease from the kitchen sink may be the villain. Grease floats; it is drawn into the masonry openings and closes them.

❨ *How can you clean a clogged cesspool?*

Pumping-out and emptying actually have little effect. You will need to use a chemical cleaner. Oftentimes, these don't help either.

❮ What do you do if your cesspool is permanently clogged?

The best thing to do is build another one next to the original to receive the overflow. In the new one, place a grease trap in the waste pipe from the kitchen sink. A grease trap is made of earthenware; it looks like a length of sewer pipe. When the grease enters the trap, it cannot go through the outlet pipe. You can skim off floating grease in the trap here as often as necessary. A grease trap will assure your cesspool long service.

❮ What causes the most trouble in a septic tank?

Usually, the lines of drain that carry off the discharge from the septic tank are too few; the tile size may be too small; the lines may not have enough slope; or the lines may have too much slope.

❮ When you have a septic tank, are detergents better to use than old-fashioned soap?

Absolutely not. Detergents are frequently fatal to the bacteria, which must act on the sewage in order to digest the solids and turn them into sludge that will not clog the tank.

❮ What can you do if you have to use detergents in your sink?

Use a septic tank for the house in general, and a cesspool for the drain lines from the kitchen sink, washing machine, and the tubs. Cesspools can easily take on detergents; septic tanks cannot.

❮ What about drain-cleaning compounds? Are they safe for use with a septic tank?

No. Drain cleaners will act unfavorably on bacterial action in the septic tank.

❮ What can you do if bacterial action in the septic tank stops for one reason or another?

You can start it once again by running a quantity of water into any of the plumbing fixtures. By dissolving yeast in tepid water and letting the mixture drain into the tank, you will restart the bacterial action in the septic tank.

❰ How can you keep tree roots from endangering sewer lines?

Kill them by dissolving a half pound or so of copper sulfate crystals (blue vitriol) in a plumbing fixture and letting it drain into the sewer. Repeat the treatment every four weeks.

6
Heating

Repairs in home heating systems are quite complex and call for the expert hand of the licensed professional. But there are some points of maintenance and repair which you as the lady of the house can handle yourself. The trick is to know enough general heating theory so you can decide whether or not to call in outside help.

If your house is insufficiently heated, you may have too small a heating unit for the size of the house. This situation frequently occurs in homes which have been expanded from year to year to fit the needs of a growing family. In that case, you should consult a heating engineer for an estimate on a new and bigger system.

Sometimes the heating plant itself is not the problem. Your house may be inadequately insulated. Then you should check around the windows and doors for possible drafts due to leaky framework.

Most of the simple repairs which you should know about are described below.

Q & A

HEAT

In a home heating system, where is the heat created?

Heat is generated in the combustion chamber of the heating plant. Cast-iron boilers and steel boilers are most commonly used for this purpose.

❬ How is the heat carried from its generating source to the various rooms of a house?

In a modern home, there are three general mediums by which heat is carried from its source: by steam, by hot water, and by forced air.

❬ For generating heat, what fuels are commonly used in the modern home?

Heating plants are fueled by coal, by oil, by natural gas, and by electricity. Coal, oil, and gas usually transfer the heat to steam or hot water for distribution. Electricity uses hot air as a medium.

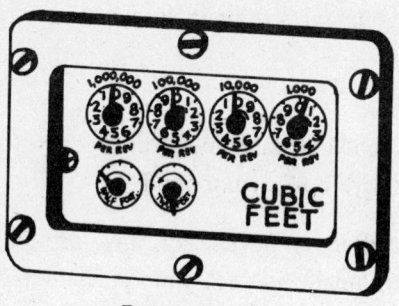

Typical gas meter

❬ What are the several ways in which heat travels through the air?

By conduction; by convection; and by radiation. Conduction is the transference of heat through matter. Convection is the transference of heat by means of air circulation. Radiation is the transference of heat by wave motion, without a medium.

❬ In what way is heat generally distributed in the room to be heated?

By radiators or convectors. Radiators throw the heat out directly from the surface of the radiator. Convectors distribute heat indirectly by means of air currents.

❬ What is radiant heating?

Radiant heating generally refers to heat which comes up through the floor of a room. In a cement-slab house, heating coils are embedded in the concrete on construction. When hot water passes through the coils, the heat is transferred through the cement and into the room by radiation.

❦ How does a forced-air system work?

Air is heated in the heating plant and is then passed through the entire structure by hot-air ducts. The heat arrives in each room through wall grills, floor grills, ceiling grills, or the like. Electric heating is strictly forced-air heat.

❦ What are some of the reasons that a hot-water system will lose efficiency?

Faulty valves or leaks; too-hard water in the boiler; low water level in the radiators; or a combination of several factors.

❦ What causes mineral sediment to form on the interior surface of a boiler?

Too-hard water.

❦ Can you cure too-hard water in a boiler?

Yes. Soften it with boiler compound.

❦ How can you tell if you have leaky valves or pipes?

You must continually inspect your pipes and radiators to make sure that none of the valves or pipes are leaking.

RADIATORS

❦ How much heat does a radiator actually supply?

The amount of heat supplied by a radiator is exactly proportional to the area of its outside surfaces. Recently, cast-iron radiators have been replaced to a great extent by finned radiators because of the added surface area supplied by the fins. The fins are placed parallel to each other, extending out from the pipe through which hot water or steam passes. As these plates warm up, they throw the heat out into the room. A contractor can tell you exactly how much warmth an individual radiator will give. It is measured in units called "square feet of radiation."

❦ Is there any way to save heat loss from radiators?

Place a sheet of aluminum or other reflecting material against the wall behind the radiator. That will retard the flow of heat out of the radiator to the wall, and will reflect it into the room.

❨ What amount of radiation heat is needed to warm a house?

A common rule-of-thumb for determining radiator heat needs is as follows: Allow 1 square foot of radiation for each 2 square feet of glass window area; 1 square foot of radiation for each 20 square feet of outside or exposed wall; 1 square foot of radiation for each 200 cubic feet of contents. The figure is for steam heat. For hot-water heat, increase the total by 60%. For a north or northeast room, increase the total by 25%. For a west room, increase the total by 15%. For an east room, increase the total by 10%. When you are all through adding and multiplying, add 50% just to be on the safe side.

❨ How are holes in leaky radiators fixed?

You can patch small holes with iron cement. Actually, you should replace the radiator.

❨ Can you repair leaky valves?

Unless the valves are faulty (in which case they should be replaced) you can repack, redress, retighten, and replace the valves which leak.

FIREPLACES AND CHIMNEYS

❨ What causes a fireplace to smoke?

The chimney may be too low at the top for the smoke to be carried away; the flue may be clogged; the throat and wind shelf may be badly constructed; the throat damper may be closed; or the opening of the fireplace may be too high for its width.

❨ Can you correct a wrongly shaped fireplace in an already-built chimney?

You can set a sheet of metal across the top of the fireplace opening to cut down the height of the fireplace. The best way to find the proper ratio of height to width is to experiment by placing boards across the top and sides.

❨ What is the best way to keep embers from flying out of a chimney top?

You should have a spark box at the top of the flue. A spark box is a heavy wire netting with meshes an inch square. Make a 5-sided box of the netting, and set it into the flue top. Let the box part extend at least a foot above the flue top.

❪ How do you clean a chimney flue?

Stuff a burlap bag with excelsior. Weight it with two or three bricks. Tie this to one end of a rope, and lower the bag down the flue. Swing the bag about in a circular motion to remove the soot.

❪ In what manner do you check the tightness of a chimney flue?

Build a fire and let it burn briskly. 'Place a square yard of tar paper on top of it, smothering it. This will give you a big smoke cloud. Cover the top of the chimney with a piece of wet carpet before the smoke all goes out. Now watch to see at what point in the chimney the smoke tries to escape.

❪ What causes a house to become stale and stagnant in winter?

The humidity has been burned out of the air.

❪ Can you correct this defect?

Yes. Open the windows for a short interval to renew the atmosphere. Humidify the rooms by placing a pan of water on the radiator, or purchase a commercial humidifier which will automatically replace humidity in the air.

ELECTRIC HEAT

❪ How does an electric heater work?

When current runs through a high-resistant wire, it heats up quickly. Air passed over a hot wire is heated by radiation and convection. This air, in turn, is circulated to other parts of the house in ducts, exactly like any other type of forced-air heat.

❪ What are the main classifications of electric heating systems?

There are 5: a wall- or ceiling-mounted radiant heating unit; a wall-mounted convector of both natural or fan-forced types; a baseboard system which falls within the radiant and natural convection classifications; a radiant heating system using embedded wire or some other method which becomes part of the building construction; and a forced-air system using a central heater or duct heaters.

Types of electric heat

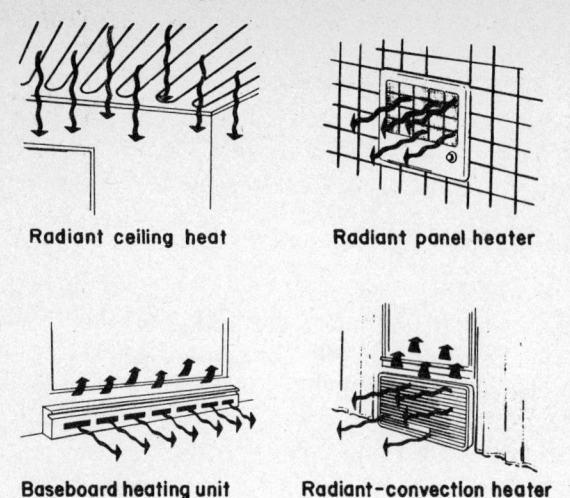

Radiant ceiling heat

Radiant panel heater

Baseboard heating unit

Radiant-convection heater

❪[*How much voltage strength do most heating systems demand?*

Most electric heating systems run off a voltage of 240. There are, however, several wall-type one-room heaters which will work on a 120-volt circuit.

7
Electricity

Generally speaking, you should know a great deal about electricity before you try to repair the wiring in your home. House current can be dangerous if improperly handled. Complicated repairs to electrical wiring should be performed only by a licensed electrician.

However, there are simple repairs which you can make. Before you begin to dabble with electricity, you should know a number of things about electrical theory and how it relates to the wiring in your home. You may find to your surprise that your present wiring is not adequate to take care of your electrical appliances. If this is the case, you should bring in an electrical engineer to plan out a modernized system to fulfill your needs.

Q & A

ELECTRICITY

❮ By what means is electric power brought to an appliance or a motor?

Two wires are needed to supply power for an electric motor. One wire carries the current to the motor, and another carries it away, or "grounds" it. In the home, both conductors are usually contained in a double-strand cord.

❮ In what manner does electric current move through a wire?

It flows through copper wire in much the same way that water

Electricity

flows through a pipe. The more electric current running through a wire, the more light and heat it will produce.

❬ In what unit is a current of electricity measured?

Electric current is measured in a unit called an ampere. All fuses, switches, and outlets are rated in amperes. The sizes of electric wires and cables are made to carry certain loads of current, measured in amperes.

❬ What happens when a wire tries to carry more electric current than it can?

The wire becomes overloaded. It will heat and burn. Overloading is the primary cause of trouble in electric wiring.

❬ How is the force behind the electric current measured?

The force of pressure of an electric current is measured by voltage. If the amperage is comparable to the amount of water flow, the voltage is comparable to the force it would generate in a drop down a waterfall. Current will not flow without voltage.

❬ How are the current (amperage) and the pressure (voltage) measured proportionally together?

Current and pressure are measured by a unit of power called a watt. The power (watts) of an appliance is the amount of pressure (volts) it takes to push a certain current (amperes) to make the appliance work. Wattage equals amperes times volts. An appliance using 2 amperes of electricity delivered at 120 volts will consume 240 watts.

❬ What is a kilowatt-hour?

For purposes of measuring the consumption of electrical current, power companies charge consumers by the kilowatt-hour. A kilowatt is 1000 watts. A kilowatt hour is simply the amount of thousand-watt units used over the period of an hour. Power consumption is measured by electric meters in kilowatt hours. Two amperes delivered at 120 volts for an hour will equal 240 watts, or a KWH consumption of .240 KWH.

❬ What is a voltage drop?

When wires of inadequate size are used in a house-wiring system, outlets put to use will not be able to supply adequate electricity to the appliance. This causes a "voltage drop."

❲ *What is an electric circuit?*

Electricity must start at its source, travel through the appliance, and then return to its source. The route of its travels is called an electrical circuit.

CURRENT

❲ *What kinds of electric current are there?*

There are two kinds of electric current: Alternating Current and Direct Current.

In direct current (D.C.), the flow of electricity goes from the power source, through the appliance motor, and back to the source, in one direction only. A battery supplies direct current, as in a flashlight.

Alternating current (A.C.) is current produced by a generator; every half-rotation changes the direction of the current. A complete rotation from plus to minus and back to plus is called a cycle. Commercial A.C. is normally 60 cycles: the current changes direction 120 times a second.

❲ *What is the most common voltage and current in use today?*

Most appliances and lights are made to use a 60-cycle, 120-volt A.C. current; residential areas are supplied with it. Big appliances like electric stoves and electric heating units use a 220 volt A.C. current. Be sure you know what current and voltage your power supply gives.

❲ *How do you read an electric meter?*

Electricity consumption is measured by meter in kilowatt hours. The newest electric meters are direct-reading, and require no explanation. However, old-fashioned meters have four dials, each numbered from 1 to 10. The pointers on the first and third dials turn counterclockwise, while the second and fourth pointers turn clockwise. The first dial measures thousands of kilowatt hours, the second measures hundreds, and so on.

❲ *What are the various kinds of electric outlets?*

There are four types of outlets in the home: fixed light outlets; convenience outlets; special purpose outlets; and control outlets for switches.

What are fixed light outlets?

These are built-in light sockets.

What are convenience outlets?

Convenience outlets are plates built into the walls into which appliance cords may be plugged.

What are the various kinds of sockets?

There are switchless, pull-chain, push-button, and weatherproof sockets.

How is a light socket constructed?

Beginning at the point where the wire enters, it is composed of a bushing; a metal cap; the socket body in which the electric terminals are located and where the wires are secured; the brass screw unit in which the light fits; an insulating paper shell; and a brass shell which fits over all.

WIRE

What is electric wire made of?

Insulated copper wire is the standard type of wire used for conducting current in the home.

How much current does the average wire carry?

Each size of wire has a specific capacity. For instance, wire size 14 (the most commonly used in the home) carries a maximum of 15 amperes; size 12 carries 20; size 10 carries 30; size 8 carries 40; size 6 carries 55; and size 4 carries 70.

What do different colored wires signify?

Whenever you see a black wire, it is a "hot" wire. That means that the current travels through that wire to the appliance. When the wire is white, it is usually a neutral wire, a ground, meaning that the current travels back through that wire to the source of power after leaving the appliance. Other colors generally indicate a neutral or ground wire. Fuses and switches must always be placed on the "hot" side of the line in order to control the current coming from the power source.

❮ What are the varieties of outer insulation coverings found in home wiring?

Extension cords are usually of three different types: fabric-covered or all-rubber lamp cords are used for portable lamps, radios, and other low-power equipment; heavy-duty cords, which have a rubber covering, are larger and better insulated than lamp cords and are used for refrigerators, vacuum cleaners, and sewing machines; heater-cords, used with heat-producing appliances, are thickly insulated with asbestos to keep the heat from scarring and burning the outer fabric.

❮ What is armored cable?

Generally called BX cable, this construction wire is covered with a thin, flexible metal outside, and is used for heavy-duty wiring installations. You must use steel boxes with BX cable installations.

FUSES

❮ What are fuses?

Fuses are specially built to prevent overloading wires. A fuse is simply a strip of metal with a lower melting point than the wire conductor in the circuit. When too much current passes through the fuse, the metal melts, and the current stops flowing.

❮ Where are fuses kept?

Your fuse box is probably in your garage, your cellar, or your utility room. Fuse boxes come in many different designs and combinations. The most important part of each fuse box to you is the socket assembly for each fuse. When a fuse has blown out, you can see the broken strip across the center under the transparent cover. In such a case, remove the fuse. Replace it with a new one of the same capacity, never larger.

❮ What are circuit breakers?

A circuit breaker is a fuse which does not "burn out." When an overload occurs, the circuit breaker cuts out and breaks the circuit. You need only reset the circuit breaker by moving a lever.

❮ Is there a simple rule-of-thumb for determining the exact wattage a circuit is carrying?

Yes. Add the wattage of every appliance attached to a circuit and divide by 120, following the formula: amperes equal watts divided by volts. A 60 watt light, a 140 watt lamp, and a 1000 watt heater add up to 1200 watts. Divided by 120, the voltage in the average house circuit, you get 10 amperes. The answer of 10 amperes gives you the total current drawn by the circuit when all the appliances are working.

(Will No. 14 wire, rated to carry 15 amperes, perform efficiently at 15 amperes?

No. No. 14 wire operates inefficiently above 8 amperes. Most wires operate efficiently only slightly above half the maximum.

(Should you place a penny in a fuse box when the fuse blows out?

Never place a copper slug in a fuse box. You may burn up your house by overloading the circuits!

CIRCUITS

(What kind of circuits are there in the average home?

General-purpose circuits; small appliance circuits; and individual circuits.

(What does the average household general-purpose circuit serve?

It serves power for the lights all over the house, and the convenience outlets everywhere, except in the kitchen, laundry, and dining areas.

(What is the capacity of the average general-purpose circuit?

If a 15-ampere fuse or circuit breaker is used with No. 14 wire, you can connect a total of 1800 watts to one general-purpose circuit. If a 20-ampere fuse or circuit breaker is used with No. 12 wire, you can connect a total of 2400 watts to one general-purpose circuit.

(How many general-purpose circuits should a household have?

You should have one 1800 watt circuit for every 375 square feet of floor; or you should have one 2400 watt circuit for every 500 square feet of area.

PRACTICAL HOME REPAIR FOR WOMEN

Check your fuse box for adequate power supply

30 amperes may be only 120 Volt	60 amperes 120 and 240 Volt	100 amperes 120 and 240 Volt
Obsolete	Obsolescent	Adequate
Typical 30 Amp. fuse type main switch	Typical 60 Amp. fuse type combination main switch and branch circuit panel	Combination main breaker and branch circuit panels
Typical 30 Amp. combination main breaker and branch circuit panel	Typical 60 Amp. combination main breaker and branch circuit panel	150- and 200-ampere panels are larger but similar in appearance to 100-ampere panels. *Panels of these capacities vary widely in appearance. The exact rating is shown on the label.
Total supply: 3,600 Watts	14,500 Watts	24,000 Watts

❪ *What does the average household small appliance circuit serve?*

It serves power for the convenience outlets, excluding the lights in the kitchen, laundry, and recreation areas, where portable appliances are most often used.

❪ *What is the capacity of the average small appliance circuit?*

If a 20-ampere fuse or circuit breaker is used with No. 12 wire, you can connect a total of 2400 watts to a two-wire circuit. If two 20-ampere fuses or a double-handled circuit breaker are used for a 3-wire circuit, you can connect a total of 4800 watts to it.

❪ *How many small appliance circuits should a home have?*

At least two 2-wire circuits, or one 3-wire circuit. Large homes need more.

❕ What does the average individual circuit in a home serve?

You need a separate circuit for every large electric appliance such as an automatic heating plant; electric range; dishwasher-waste disposer; electric water heater; home freezer; room air-conditioner; and so on.

❕ What is the capacity of the average individual circuit?

Individual circuits vary, depending on the rating of the specific appliance attached to it.

❕ How many individual circuits should you have?

You should have at least one for every piece of large equipment which draws anywhere near a thousand watts or more.

❕ How many amperes of power is the average modern household electric circuit equipped to supply?

Most homes built within the past twenty years will supply about 60 amperes at 120 to 140 volts. Many built before that will only supply 30 amperes at 120 volts. It is a very good idea to look over your service entrance equipment right now to see if you are loading your wiring too heavily with modern electric appliances.

❕ How many watts does a one-horsepower appliance draw?

You can figure that one-horsepower is equal to about 1,000 watts. An appliance or motor which is stamped "¼ horsepower," will draw about 250 watts while in operation.

❕ What conditions can cause a voltage drop?

Branch circuit wires may be too small. Branch circuits may be too long. Too many lamps and appliances may be drawing electricity from one branch circuit.

❕ In what voltage rate is most electricity delivered to the average household?

Household electricity is generally delivered at pressures of approximately 120 and 240 volts. Most plug-in appliances and all lamps use electricity at 120 volts. Many major electrical appliances require 240 volts. Most homes built before 1949 have only 120 volt service available.

❨ Why are many appliances marked at 115 volts or 110 volts?

In figuring voltage, it is best to assume that the appliance and the voltage of the house itself is actually 120, even though a particular appliance may be rated or may draw a bit less. In many instances, rating is approximate.

WATTAGES OF APPLIANCES

❨ What are average wattages of some typical home appliances?

Below is a typical list of appliances usually connected to General Purpose and Appliance Circuits. The wattages are average.

Automatic Toaster	1100 watts
Broiler-Rotisserie	1320-1650 watts
Coffee Maker	Up to 1100 watts
Deep-Fat Fryer	1350 watts
Waffle Iron or Sandwich Grill	Up to 1100 watts
Electric Sauce Pan or Skillet	1100 watts
Mixer	100 watts
Radio	100 watts
Television	300 watts
Built-in Ventilating Fan	100 watts
Electric Roaster	1650 watts
Refrigerator	150 watts

(Each time your refrigerator starts, it takes several times this wattage just for an instant. That is why you sometimes notice the lights dim down when the refrigerator starts to operate.)

Automatic hand iron	1000 watts
Ironer	1650 watts
Floor Lamps (each)	150-300 watts
Table Lamps (each)	50-150 watts
Vacuum Cleaner	125 watts
Fluorescent Lights (each tube)	15-40 watts
Portable Heater	1000 watts
Portable Electric Fan	100 watts
Electric Bed Cover	200 watts

❨ What are the average wattages of some typical individual circuit appliances?

Below is a typical list of appliances which should be connected to individual circuits. The wattages are average.

Electric Range .... 8000-16000 watts
Built-in Cook Top .... 4000 watts
Built-in Oven .... 4000 watts
Electric Water Heater .... 2000-4500 watts
Mechanism for fuel-fired Heating Plant .... 800 watts
Dishwasher-Waste-Disposer .... 1500 watts
Waste-Disposer alone .... 500 watts
Automatic Washer .... 700 watts
240 volt Electric Clothes Dryer.................................. 4500-9000 watts
Home Freezer .... 350 watts
Water Pump .... 700 watts
Built-in Bathroom Heater (each) .... 1000-1500 watts
Room Air-Conditioner (¾ ton) .... 1200 watts
Central Air Conditioning and/or complete Electric House
   Heating .... Total wattage varies with each installation

❬ *Should you personally install a new wiring system in your house if you feel the present one is inadequate?*

No. You should have an electrical engineer inspect your house and draw up a new wiring plan. The new circuit should be installed by a licensed electrician.

PLUGS AND OUTLETS

❬ *What causes an overload of current in a circuit?*

A short-circuit can cause an overload by letting too much current flow through the circuit. Too many appliances hooked into one circuit can cause an overload if they draw current above the capacity of the circuit wire. Electrical devices use more current when they start up; an overload may result from too much pull at one time.

❬ *Is it possible to accidentally plug a 240-volt plug into a 120-volt outlet?*

No. The prongs in a 240-volt plug are horizontal; the prongs in a 120-volt plug are vertical.

❨ What is a 3-prong outlet designed to take?

A 3-prong outlet serves portable power tools and various appliances which need special grounding. The third hole is a special extra ground to take away electric potential which may be generated in the casing of the hand tool.

❨ How can you use a 3-prong 120-volt plug if you have only 2-hole 120-volt convenience outlets?

Use a converter which fits over the three-prong plug. The third ground plug is then attached to the screw which holds the plate to the receptacle outlet.

❨ How many regular convenience outlets should the average room have?

Most appliances and lamps are constructed with 6-foot cords. Therefore, it is desirable to have outlets placed so that any point along the floor line of an unbroken wall is within 6 feet of an outlet. Additional outlets should be provided in any smaller but usable wall space 2 feet or more in length.

❨ When a fuse blows out, or a circuit breaker goes out, what should you do?

See Chapter One, Page 4.

FLUORESCENT LAMPS

❨ Do fluorescent lamps have any special advantages?

They give more light for each watt of electricity used.

❨ What are their disadvantages?

The initial cost of the fixture and the tube runs high. And, if your current does not run to 60 cycles a second, you are apt to get a flickering light.

❨ For what reason does a fluorescent tube turn brown or black near the ends?

It is getting old. You should replace it.

❬ Is the blinking of a fluorescent lamp, when first turned on, a usual thing?

No. The starter may be out, or the lamp may be dying. Have it checked.

❬ The normal life of a fluorescent tube is approximately how many hours?

About 2,500 hours.

❬ Will a fluorescent lamp always blink?

It should not. It may have loose fixture contacts. See if there is any vibration when the lamp is in position. If the blinking persists after the switch is thrown, and then burns normally, you quite possibly have a defective starter.

❬ Can cold temperatures affect fluorescent lamps?

A fluorescent tube is not efficient under 50 degrees Fahrenheit. Special low-temperature tubes are available for such conditions.

❬ If the ends of a fluorescent tube remain lighted or reddish, is something wrong?

Yes. You probably have a defective starter.

❬ Is the humming of a fluorescent lamp curable?

The ballast coil may be loose in its mount. Simply mount the ballast on rubber pads or washers.

❬ Can you make it easier to find light switches in dark places like cellars and attics?

Yes. Paint the wall switch plate with luminous paint. Or, you can replace the switch with a new one made of a tiny dim bulb which glows all the time when the light is off.

HEATING APPLIANCES

❬ What difference is there between a heating appliance and a motorized appliance?

In a heating appliance, like a toaster, a coil of high-resistant metal becomes heated as electric current passes through it. In a motorized appliance, like a vacuum cleaner, an electric motor is activated by an electric current; this motor pumps up dirt and dust, or provides freezing for a refrigerator.

❰ Which heating appliances can be fixed at home, and which can't?

Generally speaking, there are two types of heating appliances: those with exposed elements, and those with enclosed elements. Those with exposed elements are easier to check and repair than those with enclosed elements. Irons, percolators, or heating pads which have enclosed elements should go to a service man for repair.

❰ How do you take care of an electric iron?

Polish your electric iron occasionally with waxed paper. To do so, heat your iron and slide it over the paper once or twice. The wax will make it glide more easily over clothes.

❰ If a heating element in an appliance needs replacement, where can you get one?

You can buy heating elements from an electrical supply dealer. First, examine the appliance in question to see the type and size of element you want.

❰ What kinds of toasters can you repair yourself?

Of the three types of toasters—manually operated, semi-automatic, and automatic—only the first should be repaired at home. Its heating elements can be easily replaced. If the working mechanism of a semi-automatic or automatic toaster is out of order, you had better have a serviceman fix it.

❰ How do you repair a broken heating element?

If the break is within an inch of the terminal to which it was attached, clean the end of the wire and reattach it. Make sure the wire loop is fastened to the screw in the same direction the screw turns to tighten. If the break is further than an inch from the terminal, clean the ends of the wire, insert them both in a small nut and bolt, and tighten the nut so that the two ends of the element are attached. Or, you can remove the old element, loop the two broken ends of wire together, and touch them with nichrocite paste which fuses with nickel and chrome. When the current goes on, the heat will melt the paste and solder the joint to the nickel and chrome wire.

Electricity [103

¶ What kind of special care should you give a toaster?

Never put a toaster in water. Do not use a wet cloth to clean the inside. Use a damp cloth or a soft-bristled brush to take out the crumbs.

¶ Can you repair the coil on a "radiant-type" electric heater?

Yes. In these, the coiled heating elements are wound around a cone-shaped insulator. Fasten the broken ends of the coil with a small nut and bolt, as described. If the break looks too complicated, call in a service man.

¶ Is it possible to repair a hot plate which has a broken element?

Study it to see where the break is located. Either attach the end to the terminal, or bolt the break together with a small nut and bolt.

¶ What can you do if you spill excessive liquid onto the hot-plate base?

Pour it out, wipe the hot plate with a dry cloth, and turn on the power to burn off the remaining spill.

¶ How do you fix an automatic steam iron?

Generally speaking, all automatic electric irons should be repaired by the manufacturer, especially when parts need replacement.

¶ Can an iron which heats too slowly be fixed?

There may be nothing wrong with it. Check to see if you haven't plugged it into an extension or light socket instead of a direct convenience outlet.

¶ How do you control an iron which overheats?

Check to see if the thermostat is broken. If so, have the manufacturer replace it.

¶ What is wrong with an iron which does not heat at all?

Check the cord and the plug. If these are all right, you can correctly assume that the heating element is burned out.

❨ How do you repair the heating element of an electric iron?

Unscrew the bottom plate or sole. You'll find that the element is either exposed or enclosed in a metal case. If the element is exposed, find the break, clean the wire ends, and splice them together. Press the splice flat. Do not solder or tape it. If the element is enclosed, replace the whole unit, and take it to a serviceman.

❨ Why won't an electric percolator work?

Three possibilities exist: the fuse has blown; the valve is clogged or incorrectly set in the heating socket; or the heating element has burned out.

❨ How can you tell the condition of the heating element?

Check the fuse box of the percolator. If the fuse is out, the element has burned out. A burned-out element must be replaced by an electrical repair man.

❨ How do you repair a percolator which has a clogged valve?

Force water through the valve, or use a small round brush to clean it out. If the unit still does not work, clean the heating socket and the valve, and make sure that the valve sits firmly in the socket.

❨ How should appliances which have enclosed elements be repaired?

Electric blankets, heating pads, curling irons, waffle irons, electric roasters and the like all contain enclosed heating elements. You should have a repair man fix them.

APPLIANCE MOTORS

❨ What kind of electric motors are usually found in home appliances?

The usual appliance motor is a Universal-type motor. One type runs on A.C., and a different type runs on D.C.

❨ In appliance motors, what are the three main troubles?

The motor will not start; the motor runs hot; or the motor runs too slowly.

Electricity

❰ Are there any usual causes for such mechanical defects?

Any of the foregoing troubles may be caused by: an inadequate or defective power supply; unoiled or dirty parts; defects in the wiring of the motor; or a defective belt connection.

❰ Is there some kind of special check list available to help search out the trouble in a motorized appliance?

Yes. (1) Check the power supply. Be sure the cord and the socket are in working order. See if the cord is large enough to carry the power needed for the motor. (2) Check to see if the motor is oiled properly. Proper oiling may cure a motor which tends to run hot or slow. The oiling instructions usually accompany those motors which have to be oiled once a year. Never tamper with motors sealed in metal housings. These are "self-lubricating." Never oil a part unless it is clearly marked "oil," or unless a lubrication chart accompanies the appliance. There you'll usually find the grade and the type of oil carefully named. If it is not, use light machine oil or an oil specifically made for electric motors. (3) Check the motor to see if it needs cleaning. If it does, clean all the dirt and grease out of the open windings with a dry clean cloth or a soft-bristled brush. (4) Check any belt adjustment. Keep all oil or grease off the belt and the pulley. Be sure the belt is tightly installed. Most belts are controlled by wing screws or slot bolts. Turn the screw or adjust the bolts until the belt is tight.

VACUUM CLEANERS

❰ What are the two kinds of vacuum cleaner?

There are cylindrical horizontal cleaners, and upright cleaners.

❰ How can you get the best performance from an upright cleaner?

If it is not picking up enough dirt, check the position of the nozzle: it may be too close or too far from the surface being cleaned. Turn the screw until a twenty-five-cent piece will slide easily between the nozzle and the floor. For cleaners with revolving brushes, slide a half dollar in between the nozzle and the floor surface.

❬ *In a vacuum cleaner how do you fix a non-functioning belt?*

First inspect the belt to see that it is firmly set around both the brush and the motor shaft. Next clean all string, hair, and other dirt away from the belt. If it does not work then, replace the belt.

❬ *With what frequency should you lubricate the average vacuum cleaner?*

Do not touch it with oil unless there are specific instructions accompanying the appliance. If there are instructions, follow them carefully.

FANS

❬ *What sometimes causes noise and vibration in an electric fan?*

Usually, bent fan guards are the cause. Revolve the fan blades by hand, and check them carefully to see if any touch the guard. Bend the bent fan guards away.

❬ *How do you repair a fan motor which overheats?*

Oil it to see if that is the trouble. Check for any broken parts. Find out if the motor is clean. If dirty, clean it, carefully examining the parts as you do so. If there are any bad parts, let a repair man overhaul it and replace them.

❬ *Where do you lubricate a fan?*

Oil holes appear at each end of the motor shaft. Place oil in these holes at the beginning and end of each season of use. There are three types of oil holes in fans: a hole; a cup; or a wick. Oil holes should be lubricated every day the fan is in use; oil cups should be lubricated once a week; oil wicks need attention only once a year. In all cases, follow the instructions which came with the fan.

REFRIGERATORS

❬ *What causes an electric refrigerator to run hot and emit a bad odor?*

The motor is defective. Don't fool around with it. Have a repairman in to fix it.

Electricity

(How do you fix an electric refrigerator which runs too much?

An electric refrigerator which runs too much may have a dirty condenser; the door may leak air; or you may have your refrigerator too near a stove or other hot surface, such as a wall. A refrigerator with a condenser at the back should be at least 4 inches from a wall and 12 inches from a ceiling.

(Is it necessary to clean refrigerator condensers?

It is recommended that refrigerator condensers be cleaned at least once a year. You'll find the condenser at the back or the bottom of the box. Before you clean it, always disconnect the power. Clean the cogs with a vacuum cleaner brush attachment, or with a long-handled brush.

(Is it easy to tell if your refrigerator door leaks?

A simple test will suffice. Place a thin piece of paper between the door and the frame. Close the door tight. If you can pull the paper out without feeling a tug, the door gasket is loose and does not fit correctly. (The gasket is the rubber insulating lining around the door.) Unscrew the old gasket, and replace it. If your door handle seems loose, adjust the latch.

(Is a refrigerator which needs too much defrosting out of order?

Check for a leaky door, as described above. If that is not the trouble, you may be keeping the temperature in the refrigerator too low. The temperature should never be lower than 35 degrees, and it should be kept at 40 to 45. Below 35 causes frost to form too rapidly: this in turn causes faster defrosting demands.

(How do you fix a refrigerator freezing compartment which does not freeze ice?

Check the float valve to see if it is covered with ice. If so, turn off the refrigerator, fill the ice traps with hot water, and put them in the freezing compartment. By the time they cool off, the float valve should be thawed and loosened.

8
Floors

The floors in your home may be one of a number of different kinds. It may be a hardwood floor, a wall-to-wall carpeted floor, an asphalt tile floor, a ceramic tile floor, a parquet floor, a terrazzo floor, or even a cement-slab floor.

Since floors are in constant use whenever you walk from one end of the room to the other, they are always in the process of being worn down.

If you need to correct squeaking boards, air leaks, warping, sagging, or other defects, it is essential for you to know what is underneath the surface of a floor.

The following questions and answers should not only clarify the theoretical causes of flooring troubles, but afford step-by-step methods of clearing them up.

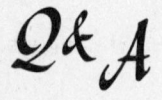

Q & A

SUBFLOORING

❨ What actually holds up a floor?

The average wooden floor in a house is held up by framing members called joists which run from foundation to foundation. It is to these joists, usually 2" x 10", 2" x 8", or 2" x 12", that the average floor is attached.

❪ What supports these joists?

The joists are attached to the foundation of the house by running strips of framing lumber, called plates. These plates are firmly bolted to the foundation.

❪ How wide apart are the joists laid?

Floor joists are usually separated by 16-inch intervals, depending on the type of subflooring above. For instance, with 2.4.1 plywood (1½" thick), the supports can be on 48" centers.

❪ What is attached to the top of the joists?

The subflooring is attached to the joists.

❪ What part of the floor lies directly above the subflooring?

In some floors, the finish floor is applied directly to the subflooring. In others, a thickness of wood usually ⅜-inch, called underlayment, is laid to take such finish floors as tile, carpet, or linoleum. These finish floors are attached directly to the underlayment.

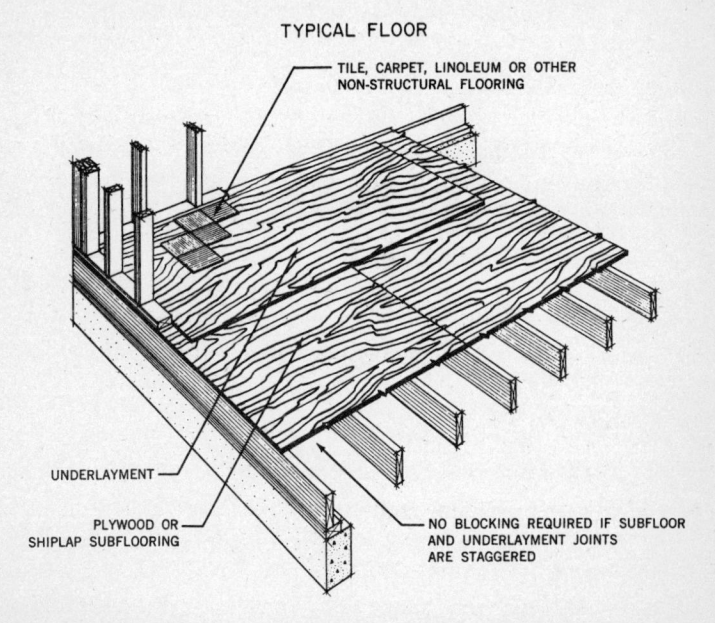

TYPICAL FLOOR

- TILE, CARPET, LINOLEUM OR OTHER NON-STRUCTURAL FLOORING
- UNDERLAYMENT
- PLYWOOD OR SHIPLAP SUBFLOORING
- NO BLOCKING REQUIRED IF SUBFLOOR AND UNDERLAYMENT JOINTS ARE STAGGERED

❪ Can the finish floor be attached directly to the joists?

It is possible to put in a single-floor surface.

❮ To separate the subfloor and the finish floor, what kind of material is used?

A layer of building paper separates the subfloor from the finish floor.

❮ Of woods, what is the most common kind of finish floor in the average house?

Tongue-and-groove hardwood, laid parallel to one of the walls of the room, is the most common. It is secured to the subfloor with flooring nails.

❮ Are there other kinds of finish floors?

Yes. They are attached to the subflooring, unless an underlayment is used to provide a stronger, smoother surface. Asphalt tiles, called "resilient tiling," linoleum of all kinds, parquet floors, and vinyl types of flooring can all be attached either to subflooring or to underlayment.

❮ What is the difference between a cement slab floor and a wooden floor?

A cement slab floor is solid concrete, poured in a form and allowed to harden. Asphalt tile or any other finish floor can be applied directly to the cement slab, usually with mastic adhesive. See illustration on page 109 for typical wooden floor.

FLOOR REPAIR

❮ What causes a sagging floor?

The main cause of a sagging floor is a serious warping of the floor joists. It can also be caused by an actual sinking of the house foundations.

❮ How can a homeowner repair a sagging floor?

If you have a basement underneath the sagging floor, it is possible to use a screw jack and a piece of timber to lift the floor from underneath.

❮ How do you operate a screw jack?

Lay a 4" x 4" timber along the basement floor directly below the sagging spot. Set the screw jack on this timber. Cut a piece of

Floors [111

4" x 4" timber exactly long enough to reach from the bottom of the sagging floor above to the top of the screw jack less 4 inches. Now cut a piece of 4" x 4" timber long enough to stretch from one end of the bulge to the other. Lift this last timber to the ceiling, and hold it in place with the vertical timber cut to fit. Operate the screw jack slightly, so that it lifts the ceiling timber. Do not do any more at once. Wait a day, and raise the jack slightly. Never raise the sagging floor more than a fraction of an inch a day. Keep checking the position of the floor until you have it level. When it is level, measure the distance between the 4" x 4" nailed to the floor above and the 4" x 4" on the floor of the basement. Cut this 4" x 4" to length, and stand it vertically on the floor under the top 4" x 4", so that it props it up. Remove the screw jack and its supporting beam.

USING A SCREW JACK

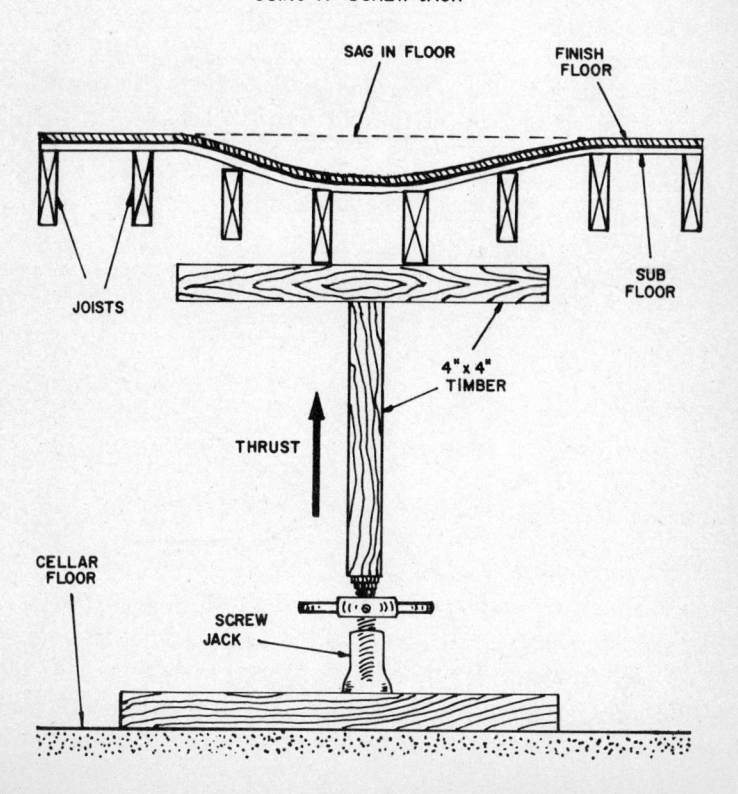

(How can you fix a sagging floor which has no basement underneath?

It is best to remove the finish flooring, and cut strips of wood called "filler strips" to level up the sagging spot; then put filler compound in around the strips with a putty knife. Filler compound is a semi-plastic material. After checking with a level, nail back the finish flooring.

(What is the best way to remove damaged and worn floorboards?

It is advisable to re-lay a section of the floor. With a brace and bit, bore a hole in one of the boards as near to the joist as possible. With a keyhole saw, cut across the first board. Then remove the first board, and any more that are necessary. Measure and cut new boards to the sizes required by the opening in the floor. Square the ends with a chisel or plane. Nail a cleat of 2" x 4" timber against each joist to support the edge of the new board wherever needed. Beginning with the groove end, fit the boards back in, nail them to the cleats, and sand down the joints. Shave off the tongue on the end of the last board which must be fitted in, and nail it in.

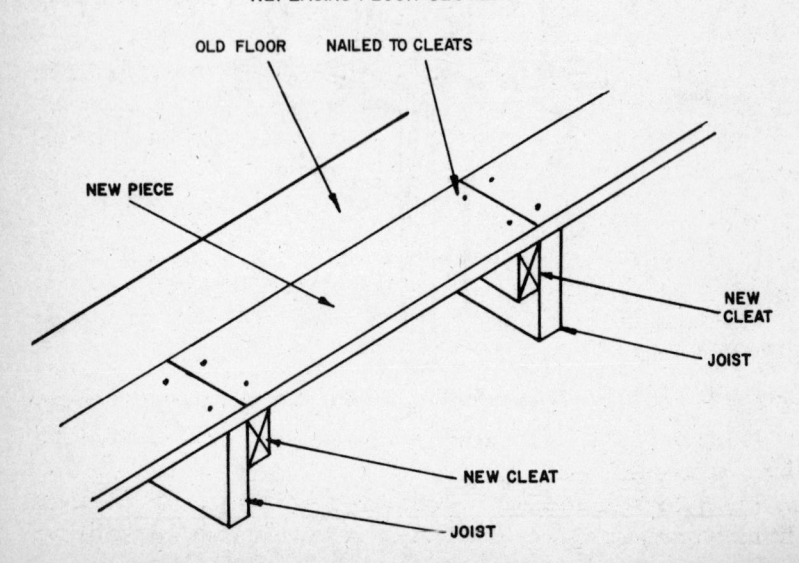

REPLACING FLOOR SEGMENT

Floors

❪ What kind of nail should you use to silence a squeaking floor?

You can toe-nail two nails, pounding them in at cross angles. Or, you can use a cement-coated finishing nail; a resinous material on the outside of the nail melts from the friction of being driven in, and the resin bonds the nail to the wood fibers.

❪ When a squeak in a floor is caused by two finishing boards rubbing against each other, how can you stop it?

Sift powdered graphite down between the boards.

FLOOR SURFACES

❪ What are the different kinds of floors?

A resilient tile floor; a non-resilient tile floor; or a wood or cork floor.

❪ Name and describe the types of resilient tile floors.

(1) *Asphalt Tile* is a mixture of asbestos fibers, lime rock, inert fillers, and colored pigments with an asphalt or resin binder. It is brittle, and is bonded to the floor with mastic, either directly or over a layer of felt.

(2) *Rubber Tile* is composed of rubber which is colored by mineral pigments, and sometimes contains asbestos fibers.

(3) *Vinyl and Vinyl Asbestos Tile* is similar to asphalt tile, except that vinyl-type resins are used as a binder, instead of asphalt.

(4) *Linoleum* is a mixture of linseed oil, resin, and ground cork pressed upon a burlap backing.

❪ Name and describe the types of non-resilient tile floors.

(1) *Terrazzo* is made up of marble chips or rock chips which are set in a mixture of Portland cement and then buffed flat.

(2) *Ceramic Tile* is composed of clay mixed with water and fired in a kiln.

❪ Name and describe the various kinds of wood and cork floors.

(1) *Hardwoods* are usually oak and maple, with beech and birch occasionally used.

(2) *Softwoods* are usually Southern pine, Douglas fir, Western hemlock, and various types of other softwoods such as ponderosa pine, redwood, and eastern white pine.

(3) *Cork Floors* are made of cork curling and granulated cork compressed in molds.

❮[How do you lay a resilient tile floor?

A resilient tile floor can be laid on any truly flat surface, or it can be laid directly on an underlayment of plywood. The tile is attached to the surface by mastic supplied by the tile manufacturer.

❮[Upon what kind of a surface must it be laid?

The surface for a resilient tile floor must be smooth and flat. If you plan to lay resilient tile on concrete, wash the concrete first to remove all grease or oil stains. If you plan to lay it on a wood subfloor, be sure the surface is smooth and flat. If there are irregularities, plane them down and sand away any differences. If the floor is not in good shape, lay a plywood underlayment which will take the finish tiles directly. Be sure the plywood is Underlayment Grade.

❮[Explain the steps in laying a resilient tile floor.

Remove all baseboards. In the center of the room, lay a cross, with a single line of tile going toward each of the four walls. Draw a straight chalk line on the floor parallel to each of the arms of the cross. Lay one quarter section of the floor. Starting from the center tile, lay the tiles in toward the corner. When you come to the wall, cut your tiles and fit them in carefully. When the floor is all laid, replace the baseboard.

❮[Is there any easy way to fit a border tile against the wall on the last row?

Take two loose tiles. Mark one A and the other B. Lay tile A exactly on top of the last cemented tile nearest the border space. Place tile B flush to the wall, on top of A, and mark tile A with a pencil along the edge of B. With household shears, cut A along the pencil mark. Insert tile A into the border space, with the rough edge against the wall.

❮[What is the best day-to-day plan for maintaining a resilient tile floor?

Dry-sweep it with a treated dust cloth or mop. Occasionally damp-mop or wet-mop it with a synthetic liquid detergent.

❮ Is there some special finishing which is recommended for resilient tile floors?

Yes. After cleaning as above, let the floor dry, and apply two coats of water emulsion resin floor finish. Let it dry out thoroughly.

LINOLEUM

❮ What kind of cleaning is recommended for linoleum?

Only pure soap suds should be used, with a mop or cloth. Do not use harsh caustic soaps or scouring powders, or you will destroy the gum which is the principle part of the material. Be careful not to flood linoleum with water when you wash it, or it will work through the joints and soften and loosen the cement.

❮ How often should linoleum be waxed?

You should wax linoleum once a month.

❮ If the pattern wears off, is it possible to paint linoleum?

Yes. Either lacquer or paint can be applied to linoleum. All wax must be removed first by benzene, naphtha, or clear gasoline.

❮ How do you eliminate a bulge in linoleum?

If the bulge is near a seam, lift the edge, and apply linoleum cement to the floor directly beneath. Lay weights on the area to hold the linoleum firm. If the bulge is in the center of a strip, slit it with a razor blade along the pattern. Press cement into the opening, spread it with a thin stick, and press the bulge down and apply weights.

❮ Is it possible to patch damaged linoleum?

Cut a new piece of linoleum, and lay it directly on top of the old damaged spot. With a sharp knife, razor, or linoleum knife, cut through the new piece and the old linoleum, so that both pieces are exactly the same size. Remove the damaged linoleum, and apply the new to the hole with linoleum cement.

❮ Can you fill small holes in linoleum?

Smooth the edges with fine steel wool. Pound a small piece of linoleum into fine powder with a hammer. Mix the pulverized linoleum with spar varnish to form a fairly thick paste. Force this paste into the hole to fill it. Allow the paste to dry. Smooth it with No. ooo sandpaper and then wax.

❮ *Explain the steps in laying a new linoleum floor.*

After removing the old linoleum, plane any rough floor boards smooth, and replace defective boards. Wash the entire floor, and let it dry. If the floor is in bad shape, cover the surface with a layer of plywood for a firm smooth base. Remove the quarter-rounds at the foot of the baseboards. If the linoleum is not felt-backed, fit a felt base, and cement it to the smooth floor with the special cement provided. Be sure there is no overlapping, and no air bubbles. Unroll the linoleum you plan to lay, and let it lie in the room overnight with the temperature at about 65 degrees. With a linoleum knife, cut the linoleum to fit the walls, the door jambs, and any other obstacles. With a cement spreader or putty knife, apply cement evenly on either the floor or the previously laid felt base. Do not spread it over more than several square feet at a time. Press the linoleum firmly onto the cemented surface. Correct for air bubbles. When all the linoleum is laid, roll it on with a heavy roller, such as a garden roller. Place bricks or other weights on all the seams. Replace the quarter-rounds to the baseboards. Attach them to the baseboard, and not to the floor: linoleum contracts and expands with heat, and it should have breathing room.

NON-RESILIENT TILE FLOORS

❮ *What causes deposits of mineral salts on the surface of a terrazzo floor?*

This formation appears only on new floors, and will clear up by routine maintenance.

❮ *Can you seal a terrazzo floor?*

Sealing is recommended. Use a special terrazzo sealing compound. Allow it to dry, and then buff.

❮ *Is there any standard maintenance for a non-resilient floor, such as terrazzo or ceramic tile?*

Dry-sweep with treated dusting cloth or mop. Use a synthetic liquid detergent.

❮ How do you re-seal a terrazzo floor?

Periodically, buff terrazzo sealing compound in with polishing brush, steel wool, or a synthetic polishing pad.

❮ May acid solutions ever be used on non-resilient floors?

Absolutely not. Acid solutions cause permanent damage to all surfaces.

WOOD FLOORS

❮ For outdoor construction what are the best floor woods to use?

Redwood, Western red cedar, and Southern cypress are best for porches, summerhouses, decks, and so on.

❮ The principal hardwood floorings are what?

Oak and maple are the most common, with beech and birch next in popularity.

❮ Is most hardwood flooring tongue-and-grooved?

Yes. It is side- and end-matched for tight construction.

❮ How wide does hardwood flooring come?

It can be obtained in face widths of 1½ to 3¼ inches. The thickness of oak runs from 11/32 to 25/32 inch; the thickness of beech, birch, and maple generally runs 25/32 inch.

❮ Does softwood flooring come wider than hardwood flooring?

Southern pine comes in widths of 2⅜ to 3¼ inches.

❮ For what is softwood flooring like Douglas fir and Western hemlock used?

Bedroom floors and guest rooms can be made of softwood flooring since there is not quite so much traffic. Softwoods tend to go to pieces under heavy wear.

❮ Where are Western red cedar, redwood, and Southern cypress flooring used?

You can use them satisfactorily in store rooms.

FLOOR WAX

❮ *On a shellac surface, what kind of wax is best to use?*

Use paste wax on shellac, not a water-emulsion, self-polishing type. The water in this may turn the shellac white.

❮ *When should wax be applied to a freshly painted floor?*

Do not apply wax until 8 hours or more have elapsed after the final coat of a floor was applied.

❮ *On floors which have been coated with varnish, shellac, enamel, or floor sealer, what is the most economical and efficient kind of maintenance material to use?*

Use wax.

❮ *What is the best way to apply wax?*

Build up a good foundation with at least two coats of a good paste wax. Use an applicator or cloth, and permit the wax to stand until the volatile thinner evaporates: say 15 to 30 minutes. Then, polish the floor with an electric floor-polishing machine. Apply a second coat of wax, and repeat the process. The floor can be maintained with paste wax, liquid wax, or water wax.

❮ *Should wax be applied to wood surfaces in thick applications or in thin?*

Wax should always be applied in a thin layer. If applied too thickly, it tends to build up a soft film. The film will hold dirt, become slippery, and smudge and smear. Also, the heavy film will resist your attempts to buff for a good gloss. The best way to apply wax is to put it on in a thin film, allow it to dry for about twenty minutes, and then buff it vigorously with a clean soft cloth.

POWER SANDING

❮ *Is it possible to renovate discolored and worn floors?*

Yes. Generally speaking, the best way to renovate a dingy floor is to power-sand it.

❲ How do you refinish a floor which was originally treated with oil?

An old oil finish becomes embedded in the wood of a floor. Power-sand the surface down. Or, you may be able to clean the floor sufficiently by buffing it with No. 3 steel wool. Or, you can use mild alkalies, to change the embedded oil to soap by chemical process. In this case, use lye, washing soda, a water solution of tri-sodium phosphate, or a commercial cleanser manufactured for the purpose. However, if the oil in the floor was mineral oil, chemicals won't work. You'll have to sand.

❲ To remove oil, how do you apply the alkali solution?

Use a mop. Flood one small area of the floor at a time. Allow the solution to stand for a few minutes. With a stiff brush or a wad of No. 1 steel wool, scrub the area vigorously. Flush it with clean water, and continue scrubbing to remove the soap which has been formed. Rinse, and let the floor dry thoroughly.

❲ How do you bleach a gray floor?

Use a saturated solution of oxalic acid in water. Wear rubber gloves; the acid is poisonous. Rinse off the oxalic acid with clean water. Mop the floor, and let it dry out thoroughly. Smooth off any raised grain with sandpaper or steel wool. Apply new finish.

❲ How do you refinish old floors originally coated with varnish, enamel, or similar materials?

Power-sand them, or clean with liquid paint or varnish removers.

❲ In renting a sander, are there any precautions which the average person should use?

(1) Never rent the sander until the day you intend to use it. Be sure you have nailed down all loose boards, have moved all furniture out of the room, and have cleaned everything completely. (2) Always rent an edger when you rent a sander. The edger lets you sand close to the walls, stairs, and other places where the larger machine won't reach. (3) Be sure to tell your dealer what kind of floor and finish you have. He will be able to tell you which kinds of abrasive to use, and whether two, three, or more sandings are needed. (4) At the end of each cut, raise the sander from

the floor before the machine comes to a standstill. Never let the drum touch the floor when the sander is not in use. (5) The sander cuts equally well backward or forward. (6) Hold the dust emptied from the sander's dust bag in a closed metal container. (7) Don't rush the job. Take short steps when guiding the machine. (8) Vacuum the floors after sanding and before applying the finish.

❘❘ What are good general maintenance procedures for floors?

Sweep or dry-mop floors which have been carefully finished. Never touch them with water if you can possibly avoid it. Keep a cotton floor mop barely dampened with a mixture of 3 parts of kerosene and 1 part paraffin oil: this is the best solution you can use for dry-mopping. When the mop becomes dirty, wash it in hot, soapy water, dry it, and dampen it again with kerosene and paraffin.

❘❘ What do you do with patches you can't remove with kerosene and paraffin?

Rub lightly with fine steel wool moistened with turpentine.

❘❘ How can you polish with steel wool and not irritate or stab your fingers?

Grip the steel wool in a large-size paper clamp of the type sold at a stationery store. It has a handle at the top. With the wool pressed between the spring jaws, enough of the material projects from the open end to do the job.

❘❘ What kind of floor finish will best withstand water and stains?

If it is waxed and kept in good condition, a varnish-finished floor is a fine protection against water stains.

❘❘ In a bathroom, what are the best kinds of floors to install?

You can install any kind of resilient tile flooring in a bathroom. Rubber tiles are excellent. Asphalt, vinyl, and vinyl asbestos work well. Ceramic tiles are good. Caulking material may be used to waterproof the joints between the tub and the floor. Be sure to caulk all joints which could be subject to moisture and water. Besides caulking material, you can buy rubber strips of sealing, which can be placed in strategic spots.

Floors

(For use under a stove or a cooking appliance which heats up, what is the best kind of flooring?

Ceramic tile is desirable. Steel tile can be purchased, too, with adhesive on the back, covered by wax paper. Just pull off the wax paper, and affix the tile to the floor.

FLOODED BASEMENTS

(What is the greatest serious disadvantage a basement can give you as a homeowner?

It can flood in the rain.

(What is the main reason for flooding?

Water always seeps into the ground when it rains. How far down it goes depends on the geological structure of the soil. If you dig far enough, anywhere, you can usually reach water. The exact spot at which water begins is called the water table. The depth varies in summer and winter, but not by too much. If your basement happens to be located either touching or within 6 to 8 feet of the water table—watch out! The first heavy rain can bring a flood into your basement.

(From what direction does the water come?

The main pressure comes from directly below. The water will usually enter through your floor, not your walls, exerting tremendous pressure. If the floor is not strong, the water may break the surface.

EPOXY RESIN WATERPROOFING

(Can you waterproof an already-built basement?

Epoxy resin materials have been found to do the job of waterproofing effectively. Epoxy is an almost impervious plastic material which forms a film resistant to alkalies, acids, and moisture. You can obtain epoxy resins in clear waterproofing compounds, opaque-colored compounds, and opaque and colored with sand added. The sand, incidentally, adds the extra bulk needed for patching foundations or floor cracks, or for laying a new floor surface over an irregular or broken flooring.

❪ *How is epoxy resin sold?*

You buy two containers, one with the resin and the other with the hardener. Mix these two, and the hardening begins. The epoxy bonds with the concrete and will resist even the pressure of a high water table.

❪ *Can epoxy be applied directly to concrete?*

Only if the concrete is clean and has no paint or dirt on it.

❪ *How can you remove paint from concrete?*

Use caustic soda or a strong solution of tri-sodium phosphate in warm water, if the paint is rubber- or oil-based. Cold-water paint and calcimine may be removed with muriatic (hydrochloride) acid and water. Wear old clothes, heavy gloves, and goggles to protect your eyes: these acids are corrosive. Mix in a non-metal container, using a wooden paddle for stirring. Flush the walls afterward with clear water, and dry thoroughly. Epoxy resins will bond only to a clean dry surface. If you have applied cement paint, you need not remove it before applying epoxy.

❪ *How do you apply epoxy resin?*

Use a brush or trowel, depending on the consistency of the material being used. Trowel it on the floors, and brush it on the walls.

❪ *How can you keep your basement air dry?*

(1) Plenty of ventilation is the only answer. Generally, your basement windows are above the level of the ground, so there will be little or no air circulating along the floor. Use an electric fan directed along the floor and toward an open window at the opposite end of the basement. (2) You can also use a small dehumidifier. This is a refrigeration unit similar to an air-conditioner. Cooling coils pull moisture out and let it drip down into a drain. You may get as much as a gallon a day out of a basement with a dehumidifier.

9

Outside Walls

Nothing is quite so important to a house as its outside appearance. Doors, windows, trim, and exterior surfaces give a house whatever beauty, character, or style it has.

However, the outside walls are even more important to the comfort of those who live inside the house than to the esthetic sensibilities of the viewer.

A leaking wall can cause as much trouble as a leaking roof. Wind can whip *in* as much cold air through a faulty wall as it can whip *out* warm air from inside.

In order to make simple but effective repairs to the walls of your home, you should know a little bit about the basic laws of structure.

The following chapter contains a theoretical discussion of the structure of the outside walls of a typical house, and then answers questions on how to repair faults in them.

Q & A

WALL PARTITIONS

❨ *What holds up the wall of a house?*

The average wooden wall of a house is held up by 2" x 4" framing lumber, called studs, which run vertically from the floor to the ceiling. The outside wall and the inside wall of the house are attached to these framing timbers.

❨ *In turn, what holds up the studs?*

At the bottom, the vertical studs are nailed to a long horizontal 2" x 4" running along the foundation and attached to the top of the sub-flooring. This timber is called the sole plate.

❨ *To what are the studs attached at the top?*

The studs are fastened to a horizontal 2" x 4" running along the top of the wall. This timber is called the top plate.

❨ *How wide apart are wall studs placed?*

In most outside walls, the studs are placed 16 inches apart (written 16" o.c. on plans). Sometimes, the studs are 20 inches and 24 inches apart. Generally, however, most studs in modern houses are 16 inches apart.

❨ *How are doors built into this wall framework?*

At each side of the door, to make the frame, double studs are nailed together, extending to the top of the frame. At the top of the door frame, two horizontal 2" x 4" "headers" run across to the double studs on both sides.

❨ *How are windows built into wall partitions?*

On the bottom of the window and at the top, two horizontal 2" x 4"s run across connecting the two studs which frame the

TYPICAL WALL STRUCTURE

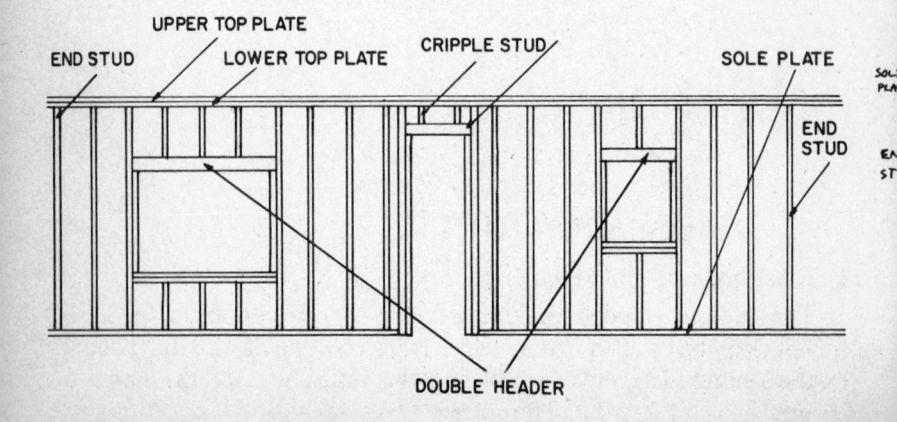

Outside Walls

window. These are called "double headers." The vertical studs run double for the length of the window frame. Extending up from the top of the frame to the top plate and down from the bottom to the floor plate are cripple studs.

(What is attached to the outside of the wall studs?

To the outside of the partition, wood sheathing is attached directly. The sheathing does not occur over the window frames and door frames.

(What is placed on the outside of the sheathing?

A layer of building paper helps insulate the sheathing from the outside. However, if you are using a plywood siding, you can nail the paneling directly to the studs without any need for building paper. These panels are tongue-and-grooved, and because they keep out water and moisture completely, there is no reason for using building paper.

SIDING

(What is attached to the outside of the building paper?

The siding is fastened to the sheathing and studs. Sometimes, as in the case of shingles, a layer of insulation board is placed between

TYPICAL EXTERIOR WALL

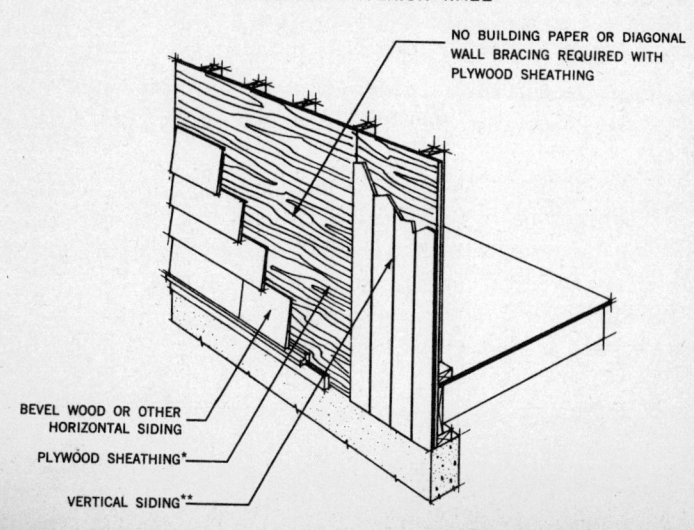

NO BUILDING PAPER OR DIAGONAL WALL BRACING REQUIRED WITH PLYWOOD SHEATHING

BEVEL WOOD OR OTHER HORIZONTAL SIDING
PLYWOOD SHEATHING*
VERTICAL SIDING*

the building paper and the shingles. In a brick house, a sheet of air space occurs between the building paper and the veneer of

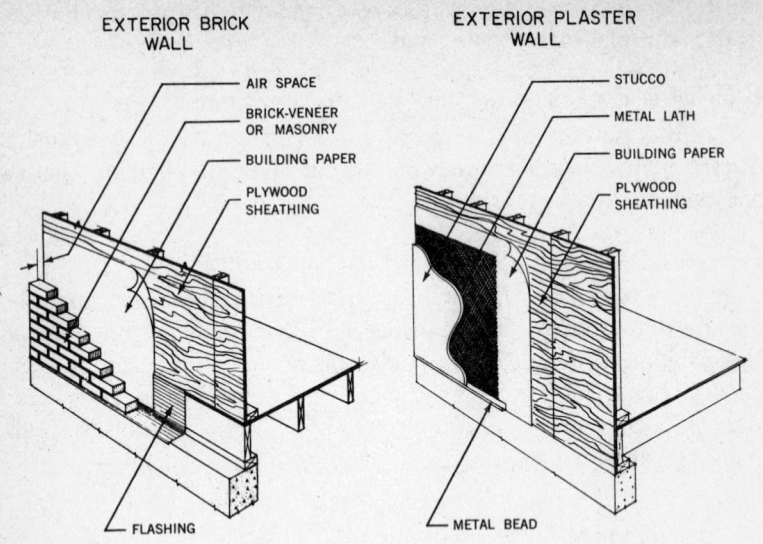

EXTERIOR BRICK WALL
- AIR SPACE
- BRICK-VENEER OR MASONRY
- BUILDING PAPER
- PLYWOOD SHEATHING
- FLASHING

EXTERIOR PLASTER WALL
- STUCCO
- METAL LATH
- BUILDING PAPER
- PLYWOOD SHEATHING
- METAL BEAD

brick or whatever kind of masonry is used as the siding. In a stucco house, metal lath is attached outside the building paper to the sheathing, and the stucco is plastered onto the metal lath.

❡ *Describe the different cuts of wood siding.*

(1) *Bevel Siding* is the most widely used. It consists of boards sawed in half so that one edge is thicker than the other.

(2) *Drop Siding* is also used, especially on a house which may not use sheathing. Boards are patterned along the upper edge, and grooved or lapped on the lower. These two sidings are applied horizontally.

(3) *Vertical Siding* is becoming increasingly popular on one-story houses. It consists of square-edged or tongue-and-grooved boards applied vertically, usually with narrow strips called battens nailed over the joints. Vertical siding makes a squat house look taller.

(4) *Plywood Siding* comes in beveled form as well as in a number of vertical and board and batten designs.

STUCCO AND BRICK

❡ *How is stucco applied to an outside wall?*

A stucco finish usually consists of a scratch coat over metal lath, a second coat of stucco ⅜ inch thick, and a finish coat ⅜ inch thick. Stucco plaster is made of 1 part Portland cement and 3 parts sand with some lime added.

❡ How do you repair a crack in stucco?

Cut out the crack completely. With a wire brush, remove all loose particles. Roughen the surface with a chisel or pointed hammer. Soak the old concrete with water. Mix cement in water until it is as thick as paint, and brush the old concrete around the hole. Mix stucco compound, 1 part Portland cement to 3 parts sand. Apply this mix to the hole. Before this dries completely, apply a second coat; then apply a third.

❡ How should you repair old stucco which is cracked all over?

When the plaster clings firmly to the lath, try putting on an entirely new surface. Clean first. Roughen it so the new stucco will bond. Then apply the stucco.

❡ Is it possible to waterproof stucco?

Yes. Buy waterproof for stucco at a paint or hardware store. Apply the waterproofing over the outside of the stucco surface. Follow the directions of the manufacturer.

❡ Can stucco be painted?

Yes. Use specially manufactured stucco paint, and simply follow directions. Or, use house paint, the first coat being a mixture of one-third paint, one-third spar varnish, and one-third turpentine. For the second coat, use 1 pint of turpentine to 1 gallon of paint. For the third coat, use house paint as it comes in the can.

❡ Do brick walls ever leak?

Yes. Frequently hairline cracks will form in the mortar, allowing moisture to saturate the mortar and come through.

❡ Is it possible to waterproof a brick wall?

Mix a sealer with equal parts of spar varnish, red-lead paint, and turpentine. Caulk up all crumbling mortar joints in the wall. Apply the sealing compound to the dry brick surface, and let it soak in. Then finish the coat off with any good house paint. You can also get transparent liquid waterproof.

WALL LEAKS

❲ *How do you repair wooden shingles which have broken?*

If the shingles are intact, but loose, merely nail them back with copper, aluminum, or galvanized rust-proof nails. Accompanying drawings show how two kinds of roof protect your house against exposure to weather. See page 129 opposite.

❲ *Is there any way to weather-proof shingles on the exposed side of the house?*

Yes. When you put a loose piece of damaged shingle back on, place roofing paper underneath it before nailing.

❲ *How do you repair a shingle which has split into many pieces?*

Remove all the pieces, and insert a new shingle of the same size and thickness in its place. Nail only with rust-proof nails.

❲ *How can you fill up cracks and splits in an outside wall?*

Force in caulking compound with a caulking gun.

❲ *How do you care for peeled or blistered paint?*

Peeled or blistered paint is caused by application on green, undried wood. You must remove the paint, clean the surface thoroughly, and repaint.

❲ *How do you correct a warped clapboard?*

Nail it firmly with aluminum or galvanized rust-proof nails.

❲ *If nailing down the clapboard will not improve a warped section, what should you do?*

You must remove the clapboard and replace it. If the nails have already pulled through the board, simply pull off the wood. If it is still tightly nailed, slip a hacksaw blade up through the bottom of the board and saw through the nails. Or, pound the clapboard in, and jockey the nail head out to where you can pull it loose with a claw hammer or a nail claw. Make a vertical cut at each end of the damaged section. Remove the bad section. Pull out the split-off part overlapped by the next course up. Paint a segment cut to fit this old section. Paint it on both sides to protect it from

Outside Walls [129

moisture penetration. On the side of the house, fill both the cracks in the siding with caulking compound; do not use putty. Attach the new, painted piece of siding where the old one was.

TYPICAL FLAT ROOF

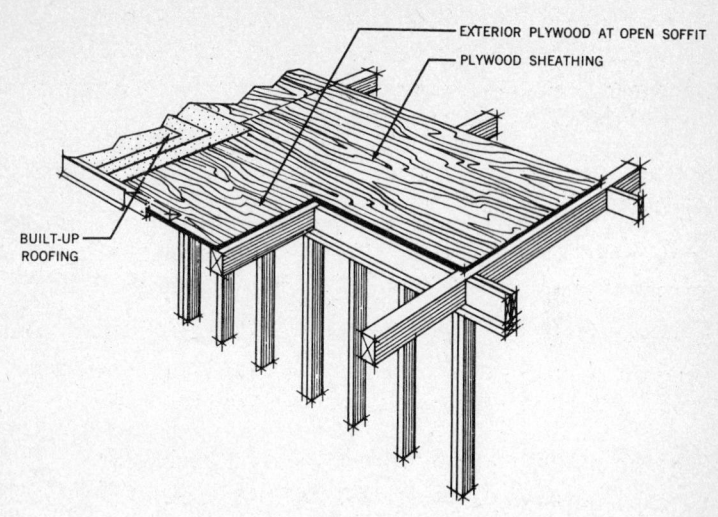

- EXTERIOR PLYWOOD AT OPEN SOFFIT
- PLYWOOD SHEATHING
- BUILT-UP ROOFING

TYPICAL PITCHED ROOF

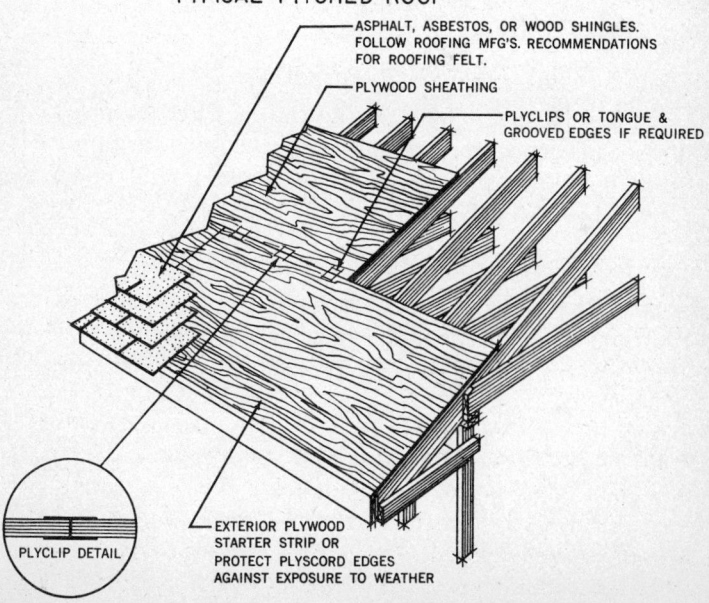

- ASPHALT, ASBESTOS, OR WOOD SHINGLES. FOLLOW ROOFING MFG'S. RECOMMENDATIONS FOR ROOFING FELT.
- PLYWOOD SHEATHING
- PLYCLIPS OR TONGUE & GROOVED EDGES IF REQUIRED
- PLYCLIP DETAIL
- EXTERIOR PLYWOOD STARTER STRIP OR PROTECT PLYSCORD EDGES AGAINST EXPOSURE TO WEATHER

❰ *How are window frames constructed to keep out moisture and cold?*

Windows are fitted into the frames after the sheathing is applied. Moisture-proof building paper is placed in such a way that no water can come in through the joint of the rough frame and the window frame. Thus, all water is shed and cannot enter through the window joints.

❰ *How can you fix a leaky joint around a window?*

The best way is to caulk it. If pieces of shingle or siding have come loose, check the building paper beneath. If it has torn away, remove the siding or shingle, attach the building paper with waterproof adhesive, and apply the siding or shingle again. Then caulk if the leakage continues.

CAULKING

❰ *What is caulking compound?*

Caulking compound is a plastic-like semi-solid, composed of a uniform blend of pigments, oils, and thinners. It is used to seal gaps in construction, preventing cold air, rain, sleet, and snow from entering.

❰ *Where is caulking compound generally used?*

It is generally used where two dissimilar materials meet: around windows and doors; roof joints; joints between masonry blocks; floor-wall junctions; wood column junctions; around outlet boxes; and gaps between rough attic floors and chimneys.

❰ *How do you prepare a surface for caulking?*

Be sure the surface is free of dirt, dust, moisture, or grease. At the time of application, the temperature should not be below 40 degrees. Gaps deeper than ⅝ inch should be filled with oakum before caulking.

❰ *What are the three types of caulking compound?*
Gun grade, knife grade, and rope form.

❰ *How do you apply gun-grade caulking?*
Packaged in cans and in cartridges, gun-grade caulking is made

for use with a caulking gun. There are two kinds of caulking guns. One consists of a cylinder filled with caulking compound. The compound is kept under pressure, and is forced out when the plunger is depressed. The other type of gun is a simple hollow frame with a handle, trigger, and plunger. A tube of caulking compound is put into the hollow. Pressure on the trigger compresses the end of the tube to force out the compound. When applying gun-grade caulking, hold the gun at a 45-degree angle to the surface, in the same plane as the surface and not at right angles. The hole to be filled should be at least ⅜ inch deep.

(What is rope-form caulking?

This type of caulking comes in rope form, which is simply unrolled and pressed firmly into the crack with the fingers. Rope caulking is ideal as a temporary seal because it can easily be removed. It is excellent against drafts, moisture, and dust around windows, screens, and louvers.

(What is knife-grade caulking?

Knife-grade caulking compound can be applied with a putty knife or spatula. This type of caulking is particularly suited for medium-sized cracks and crevices.

(How can you caulk around bathtubs, sinks, and windows when the space is too small for easy access?

Try an aerosol caulk, which is built for getting into awkward spaces. When you press the plastic nozzle sideways, the compound is forced out in a smooth, continuous ribbon to fill cracks in wood or plaster, as well as around tile and plumbing fixtures.

(Is caulking ever needed to correct flashing?

Yes. Joints between the window and door frames and walls are covered by flashing, but many times the wood will shrink away and the joints will open. You must close these holes by caulking.

(Where else do cracks appear?

Cracks also appear between the siding and the foundation, at the tops of walls near the roof line, below the rafter line, and at the point where the chimney fits against the wood siding. Caulk these leaks.

❡ Can you caulk joints between wood and metal?

Yes. But it is best to give a priming coat to the area before applying the compound. A priming coat will keep the metal surface from rusting, and will keep the porous wood from extracting the oil from the caulking compound.

❡ What is tow and oakum?

Both tow and oakum are stiff ropy materials which can be inserted in large cracks.

❡ How big does a crack have to be before it will take tow or oakum?

Generally speaking, a crack smaller than the width of a lead pencil will take caulking compound. Any crack wider than that should be filled first with tow or oakum and then caulked.

10
Inside Walls

The inside walls of your home are as important to you as your own clothes. They are the background against which your friends see you and are as vital to you as the proper shade of lipstick or the correct style of hairdo. As an integral part of your personality, they must be kept always in spic-and-span condition.

Whether your walls are of drywall construction, of wood paneling, or of plaster, they demand continual attention. Don't forget, either, that electric wires and water pipes are almost without exception installed inside these interior walls. Repairs to power or plumbing often necessitate partial or complete removal of wall coverings. You should understand this if you are planning any extensive alterations for interior decoration.

By reading the following questions and answers, you'll discover how to cope with problems of repair and maintenance which concern your walls.

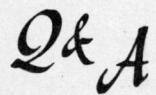

Q & A

WALL CONSTRUCTION

❪ *What holds up an interior wall surface?*
Studs, usually 2" x 4"s, hold up all interior walls.

(*Can an interior wall be composed of 2" x 3" studs?*

Yes, in certain cases. Their use depends upon building codes, and upon the weight of the walls attached to them.

(*Is an interior wall built in a manner similar to an outside wall?*

It is framed in a similar fashion. The studs are placed at 16-inch intervals, or 20- or 24-inch intervals, depending on the weight and rigidity of the surface to be attached. At the bottom, the studs are nailed to a floor plate which is attached to the subflooring. At the top, the studs are attached to 2" x 4" top plates.

(*What is the most common kind of ceiling?*

Usually, ceilings are also of drywall construction. However, they can be plaster or wood. Acoustical tile is a very popular modern-type ceiling.

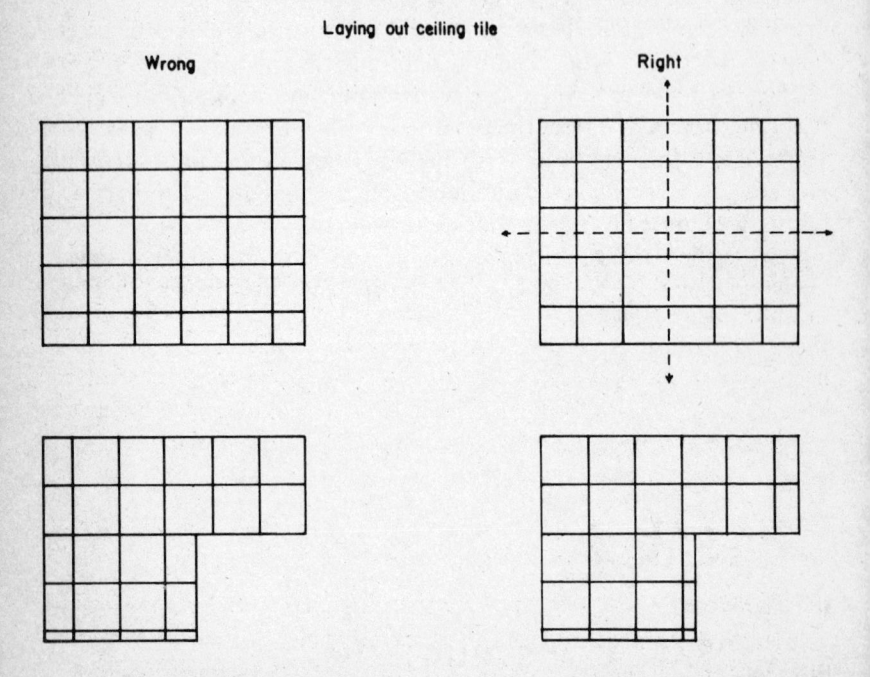

Laying out ceiling tile

Wrong Right

(*How is a ceiling applied?*

The ceiling surface is applied to the ceiling joists, which are framing timbers running across the top of the room. Generally, building paper or a vapor barrier is inserted between the rafters and the ceiling surface.

(How far apart are ceiling joists placed?

Usually, ceiling joists are spaced 16 inches apart.

(What are moldings?

Moldings are strips of wood nailed along the floor and the ceiling where each joins a wall.

(What is the purpose of a molding?

A molding tightly seals the joint between floor and wall or ceiling and wall. Also, a molding can cover any miscalculations or errors in carpentry. Molding along the floor is called baseboard molding. The molding along the ceiling, generally more ornate, is called ceiling molding. Sometimes, two or more strips of molding are put together to form the final molding. Sometimes, on a floor molding, a strip of quarter-round molding is added outside the molding over the finish floor. It is called the "shoe." A quarter-round molding is exactly that: it is a 1-inch dowel which has been cut two ways to become a quarter-circle.

(How can you sandpaper irregular surfaces, like concave curved moldings?

Oddly-curved moldings can be easily sanded by improvising a movable sanding block out of a deck of playing cards. Wrap a sheet of sandpaper around the edge of the deck, and press the edge against the surface to be sanded. Exert pressure against the surface, and the cards will slide into position as the paper touches the molding. Keep a tight grip on the deck, and you'll be able to get an accurate sanding.

INSIDE INTERIOR WALLS

(In interior walls, how are electrical outlets usually installed?

Electrical outlets are usually installed about a foot or so off the floor in positions around the room. A convenience outlet is a steel box secured to the side of a stud. When the drywall is fitted over the box, a cover plate is attached.

❡ *How are electric wires installed in walls?*

Electric cables (usually flexible steel cable called BX cable), are run through holes drilled in the studs until they reach the outlet boxes.

❡ *How are electric wall switches placed?*

Electric switches are usually placed by doorways, in such a position that they can be easily reached upon entrance into a room. The switches are actually steel boxes with toggle switches into which the BX cables run.

❡ *Why are plumbing pipes installed inside interior walls?*

Unless an outside wall is excellently insulated, it is risky to run a piece of plumbing through it, for fear of freezing in cold weather. That is the reason most plumbing runs through interior walls. Since piping is hard to work with, and since it is expensive, most builders contain piping in one or two interior walls. In many homes, one bathroom wall and one kitchen wall share the pipes. Showers, bathtubs, washbasins, and toilets can all be served by pipes run in the same wall as the kitchen water, the dishwasher, and clothes washer. Frequently, the water heater will be placed somewhere nearby.

❡ *How are the pipes put in?*

Plumbers generally do their work after the interior framing, minus the surface covering, is erected. The pipes are run through the studs and floor exactly the way the electric BX cable is run. In some cases, the studs must be braced after the pipes are put through: drilling and notching weakens them.

❡ *What is a load-bearing wall?*

A load-bearing wall is a wall whose top plates carry the load of the ceiling rafters. In other words, two walls of any room must be load-bearing walls: these are the walls at which all ceiling joists end.

❡ *Is it possible to cut into an already erected load-bearing wall?*

It is possible, but not advisable. The weight of the rafters on the top plate is distributed equally enough so that the loss of two or three studs should not affect it. In any case, if a stud is being removed and replaced, the joists above should be braced by a header —a long timber nailed to support what is above the construction.

DRYWALL CONSTRUCTION

(What is the most common kind of wall surface in homes at the present time?

Most houses now are built with drywall surfaces: gypsum or wood-paneling.

(What actually is drywall construction?

Drywall construction refers to construction of any type of plasterboard or wood. It is called "drywall" in contrast to "wetwall" construction, or actual plastering.

(What are the main types of drywall construction boards?

Gypsum board, plywood, wood pulp, wood or vegetable fiber boards, and cement-asbestos boards are the most common.

(In what sizes is drywall manufactured?

Drywall comes in 4' x 8' pieces, 4' x 10', and various other lengths. It comes in several thicknesses: from ¼ to ¾ inch.

(What is gypsum board?

Gypsum board is a common type of drywall board. It is composed of gypsum plaster, enclosed on both sides and edges by thick paper. This type of plasterboard usually comes in ⅜- to ⅝- inch thickness. It may have beveled edges, or tongue-and-groove edges. Gypsum board is also called plasterboard, sheet rock, and rock wall.

(What kind of plywood can be used for drywall use?

Plywood made of Douglas fir is the most common kind in use. It comes in thicknesses of ¼, ⅜, ½, ⅝, and ¾ inch. It can be purchased with 3, 5, or 7 plies.

(What is decorative hardwood paneling?

This is a hardwood-plywood veneered paneling, which can be attached directly to the studs to form a wall. Its best feature is that the surface—usually of carefully selected, polished and hand-rubbed perfection wood veneer—is finished. You need not worry about maintenance.

¶ What kind of plywood veneers are available for interior installation?

Teak, butternut, black walnut, heirloom cherry, golden elm, pecan, birch, elm, honeytone oak, American elm, flame gum, antique laurel, cafe laurel, Amber maple, antique amazon maple, and dove amazon maple are now available.

¶ How do you estimate the number of sheets of drywall needed to cover a room?

Measure the wall you want to cover. Assuming it is an 8-foot wall, find out how many four-foot widths of drywall you will need to reach the end. Thus: if your room is 12 feet wide, and your ceiling is 8 feet high, you'll need three sheets. If your wall is 11 feet wide, and 8 feet high, you'll need three sheets, too. Just cut the last sheet lengthwise to fit.

¶ Can you apply drywall to existing walls?

Yes. If the original wall is plastered, you'll want to find the studs first. Use nails which will cover the thickness of the drywall, the width of the plaster, the width of the lath, and on into the stud for at least an inch-and-a-half.

¶ How do you find the location of studs in a covered wall?

See Chapter One, Page 11, under question about hanging a picture on a gypsum board wall.

APPLYING DRYWALL

¶ How do you apply drywall gypsum board?

Lean the gypsum board vertically against the wall first, making sure that it will clear ceiling and floor. If it won't, cut it to fit. Push the sheet against the wall, and nail to the top plate at the ceiling first. The two side borders should end directly over studs if the wall is built correctly. With the edges parallel to the floor, ceiling and studs, nail the panel in place against the studs with 4d, 5d, or 6d flat-head nails. Drive in the nails ⅜ inch from the panel's edge, spacing the nails 5 to 7 inches apart along the edges. In the middle of the panel, space the nails 6 to 8 inches apart. Place the next board against the wall, leaving ⅛ inch between, and apply that one the same way. At electrical outlets, remove the cover of the box, and measure the distance from the floor to the top of box and then to the bottom of box. Transfer these measurements to the gypsum board. Measure the distance of both edges of the box from the end of panel, and mark it on the gypsum board. With a knife, cut out the rectangular hole so that it will fit over the open outlet box. When the panels are all up, replace the outlet's cover. Mix a small quantity of gypsum filler, and, with a putty knife, fill all the ⅛-inch openings between the panels. Sandpaper the filler when dry.

(What if the joints between the gypsum board have to be taped?

Fill the groove with prepared gypsum cement. Immediately apply the tape, pushing it firmly into the cement with a 4-inch putty knife. Force the cement through the holes in the tape. Before the cement dries, smooth it over where it has oozed through the holes. Let it dry. Apply a thin second cover of cement over the tape, feathering out the edges. Sandpaper the joint when it is dry. Fill all the holes over set nails the same way.

(What is the best way to cut gypsum wallboard?

You can use a handsaw. But it is easier to make the cut with a knife. To do so, place the board on a table, or on sawhorses, with the top surface up. Mark the cut. Score the lines with a sharp knife, using a straight edge. Cut only through the paper surface, not through the plaster inside. Let the line of the cut hang a little over the edge of the table or workbench, and snap downward. The gypsum board will break along the scored line. Merely cut the paper on the back.

(How do you apply furring strips?

A furring strip is simply a 1" x 3" strip of wood to which you nail gypsum board or paneling. Attach furring horizontally along a wall at the top, the middle, and the bottom. Or attach it vertically to an existing wall. Be sure the furring is located at the points where you will be nailing your panels.

¶ How do you apply finished plywood?

Finished plywood is a bit more difficult to apply to a wall than gypsum board, because it is harder to shape. The principles of putting up the board are the same. You should start at a corner, and work in. Be sure to check the corner to see if it is off-center. Most rooms are not exactly true. While this inaccuracy will not show up too much with plasterboard, which can be shaped easily with a knife, it will make a great difference with plywood, which is stiff and demands shaping to fit. Make the first panel fit perfectly by shaping it; then nail it to the studs.

At a window, measure the distance from the end of the hung panel to the edge of the frame. Cut the next sheet of paneling lengthwise to fit. Nail this piece. Continue on, full length, at the end of the window to the far wall. Now measure the portion above and below the window, and cut them out of a fresh panel. In some instances, depending on the circumstances, it might be easier to cut the window out of a full section. Use your own judgment. For outlet boxes, use the same method as described with plasterboard. Then drill 4 holes in the paneling at the corners of the rectangle. With a keyhole saw, cut out the marked area for a neat fit over the box.

¶ How can you cut 4' x 8' sheets of plywood by hand in the house?

Prop two lengths of 2" x 4" vertically against a wall at a sharp angle. Lean the plywood sheet against these 2" x 4"s so that it is held out from the wall. Cut down through the panel while in this position. Guide your saw by clamping a straight board onto your marked line.

PLASTER

¶ In a finished plaster wall, what causes a wet bulge?

A leak from plumbing within a wall will cause the plaster to loosen from its hold and to bulge.

¶ How can you fix a wet bulge?

If the plaster has loosened from the wall, cut out the loose portion and replace it with new. However, for a temporary measure you can use flathead screws and tin washers, and screw the bulge back into the lath.

(How do you patch a large crack in plaster?

Widen the crack by pulling out all the loose plaster. Prepare an undercut so that the patch you make will lock itself in. An undercut, incidentally, is a cut made so that the surface opening is of smaller area than the opening at the lath.

Mix patching plaster which you can procure at a hardware or paint store. Force the patching plaster into the crack, and smooth it to within 1/8 inch of the top. Let it dry. It will shrink a little. Now apply more plaster patching with a putty knife, level it with the old wall, and smooth.

(How do you fill fine hairline cracks in plaster?

Fill small cracks, called "fire cracks," by brushing them with a mixture of 3 parts boiled linseed oil and 1 part turpentine. For somewhat larger cracks, thin white lead with turpentine to a fairly thin paste. Rub this on with a cloth; then wipe off the excess. Sandpaper lightly when the paste has dried.

(How do you smooth out rough plaster?

Rub rough plaster down with carborundum black. Continue to rub down with sandpaper. Smooth that with filling: such as texture paint, ordinary paint thickened with powdered whiting to a paste, or white lead thinned with linseed oil. Brush the wall, and clean it first by washing off dust, grease, and smudges. Apply the filling with a trowel.

PANEL VENEERS

(Can an interior room be refinished by applying paneling?

Yes. There are many types of actual tongue-and-groove paneling, which can be applied board by board. Cedar and redwood, for instance, can be applied and finished in a natural state. So can oak and many other types of wood.

(How do you go about putting paneling over an old wall?

Apply horizontal furring strips at convenient intervals, and attach the paneling to the furring strips. Nail the furring solidly into the studs. Nail each panel solidly to the furring strips, working from one corner to the other. Use finish nails. Set them. Or, a more informal effect can be achieved by using boating nails, which, like flooring nails, are square cut. The advantage of using square-cut nails is that they don't split wood so much as round nails do. To be on the safe side, you can always drill holes in the wood with a hand drill. It will save you a lot of worry and effort. Do not make the drill holes too big. Cut pieces out of the wood paneling to surround electric outlets and windows and doors.

❰ *On finish wood, how is it possible to prevent hammer marks from marring the surface?*

Get a piece of scrap cardboard or thin plywood about the size of your hand. Drill a hole in one end large enough to take the head of the nail or brad you want to hammer into the finish wood. After you begin your nail, slip the cardboard or plywood mask over the nail, and hold it in place until you have the nail almost all the way in. The wood will absorb the blow and keep the hammer from damaging the paneling. Remove the guard when the nail is almost all in, and finish the job with a nail set.

HANGING THINGS

❰ *How do you hang a picture on a wall which is made of gypsum board?*

See Chapter One, Page 11.

❰ *How do you attach towel racks and the like to gypsum board walls?*

If the towels do not weigh too much, the racks can be supported by the gypsum board itself. The problem here is that even if you find one stud to which you can attach the screw, the other side of the rack probably won't hit a stud. In this case, use molly screws. A molly screw is a lead or plastic device which you insert into gypsum board after drilling a hole to accommodate it. Through this hollow device, you insert a screw after sending it through a hole in the object to be hung. The screw will push out the hollow lead sleeve hard against the inside of the drilled hole, or spread out on the far side of the gypsum board for a tight fit. Plastic devices are made which work on the same principle. In either case, the screw will stay in the wall.

(How do you mount a heavy can opener or other mechanical appliance on a gypsum board wall when the appliance is manufactured to go on a wooden wall?

Locate a stud. If the appliance is to be mounted with vertically lined screws, simply screw them into the stud. If the appliance is to be mounted with horizontally lined screws, or a rectangle of screws, attach a rectangle of tough plywood to the stud, holding it solidly with wood screws in the nearest stud. Then, secure the appliance to the plywood mounting. Paint it the same color as the wall, and you are in business.

WALLPAPER

(What is the best way to clean spotty wallpaper?

A dough-like substance available at hardware or paint stores makes a fine wallpaper cleaner. All you do is roll or knead the substance across the paper, letting the dirt and grime work into the compound. It works like an artist's kneaded eraser, and will leave your paper looking like new. In some cases, however, color will come off with the substance. Try it out in a hidden corner to see how it works.

(How can you remove grease spots, oil spots, and crayon stains from wallpaper?

Make a soft paste of fuller's earth or powdered chalk. Moisten this with carbon tetrachloride or any non-inflammable spot-removing liquid. Cover the dirty spot with about a quarter-inch thickness of the paste. Let this poultice dry, then remove it with a soft brush. If you have to, repeat the process.

(How can you fix a soiled spot which cannot be cleaned?

It's always a good idea to have extra pieces of your wallpaper on hand for emergencies. In this case, tear out a patch which matches the pattern of the soiled area, making sure you tear from the back and leave the edges feathery and fragile. Do not cut it. Apply paste to the back of the patch, and slide it exactly over the right spot so that the pattern continues.

❰ *How do you remove wallpaper from plaster walls?*

Soak it with warm water to soften the paste. Then soak it again. Add a handful of washing soda to a gallon of warm water to quicken the action. If water doesn't work, try a steam generator.

❰ *Explain how to use a steam generator to remove wallpaper.*

You can rent a steam wallpaper remover from a hardware or paintstore. Usually electric, a steam generator pushes steam through a nozzle while you run it slowly over the old wallpaper. The steam penetrates the paper and loosens the paste.

❰ *How do you pull off the paper after it is steamed and moistened?*

Tear it off from the top, nudging the sticking places with a broad putty knife or with a "wall-paper remover" knife with a slanted blade. Once the paper is off, sponge the wall with clear warm water. Then rub with a portable power sander, or sandpaper with a fine grade of paper.

❰ *Is there any way to remove wallpaper without a steam machine?*

There are several knife gadgets which will do the job. One has a head angled to ride across the plaster or wallboard, so the paper is literally planed off the wall.

❰ *What precautions must you take in removing wallpaper from plasterboard?*

Be sure you don't use too much water, or you'll take off the surface of the drywall construction underneath.

❰ *Can you re-surface drywall construction which has been torn in removing wallpaper?*

Yes. Apply a thin coat of shellac or varnish to the torn surface after it has dried. Rub lightly with fine sandpaper when it dries. The shellac will hold the fibers stiff.

❰ *How do you remove air bulges in wallpaper?*

Cut a slit in the bulge with a sharp knife. Force paste in through the slit, either with a brush or with an ear syringe. Then press down. Be sure to cut the slit along a line in the pattern, so it will not be noticeable.

Inside Walls

❨ How do you prepare a newly plastered wall for papering?

Size it first with glue size, which you can buy at a paint or hardware store. Apply the size with a large calcimine brush. Heat the glue before applying. Allow the size to dry completely before papering.

❨ How do you prepare an already-papered wall for re-papering?

It is best to remove all the old paper, scrub down the wall, and give it a new coating of glue size. However, if there are less than three layers of paper, you can put the new paper right over the old. You get a better job papering over butted-seam joints, rather than on top of overlapped joints.

❨ How do you prepare a wall painted with flat paint for papering?

Flat paint, either water-based or oil-based, must be washed thoroughly. Then it must be given a coating of thinned glue size.

❨ Is it possible to apply wallpaper to a wall with a rough texture or a sand finish?

Yes. Sand the surface down, and fill it with a thick sizing of whiting compound and linseed oil.

❨ What is the best kind of paste to use in hanging wallpaper?

Cold-water paste is the most popular adhesive for wallpaper. It comes in a powder, which you mix with water in a galvanized bucket.

❨ How can you be sure all the rolls of a shipment of wallpaper are exactly the same color?

A good trick is to check the "run" number on the selvage, or waste, edge of the paper. If the run numbers are all the same, the paper will all come out the same shade. The run number is applied at the factory for each new batch of color mixed. With a change of run number, you can tell that a new batch has been printed with a different color.

❨ Describe how to hang wallpaper.

Uncurl the paper and lay it pattern-down on a table. Coat the entire back with paste, using long, overlapping strokes. Fold the paper together, end to end, with the two pasted surfaces together, and the edges carefully aligned. Trim the edges by cutting through both layers at once. Cut into the good part of the paper at least 1/16 inch to make sure no guidelines remain to mar the design. Carry the folded paper onto the stepladder, hold the top securely against the wall, and let the paper unfold of its own weight. Adjust it to its proper position, and smooth it on with a brush in sweeping motions. Remove all bubbles. Then roll the seam roller over the first edge to press it down and attach it firmly to the wall.

¶ *Which is easier: to butt wallpaper, or to overlap it?*

For the amateur, it is much better to overlap. This means that you will trim only one edge, and lap the trimmed side over the selvage edge of the strip already hung. Only slight ridges will result. Any possible trimming slips you might make when you butt will not be noticed.

¶ *How do you hang wallpaper in corners?*

In corners, it is best to use a narrow fill-in strip about ½ or 1 foot wide. Your other strips can work out from this. Or, you can cut your strip not more than 6 inches after it reaches the corner. Hang your next strip onto this. You cannot hang a wide piece successfully around the average corner, because walls in most houses are not true.

WOOD PROJECTS

¶ *How do you make bookshelves?*

Bookshelves may be made of white pine without too much difficulty. The problem is in hanging them. A box-shaped bookcase can stand on its own legs. If, however, you wish to cover a wall with book shelving, the problem is slightly different. You can buy steel L braces, and attach these solidly to every other stud. Attach the shelving firmly to these.

If you wish a semi-permanent series of shelves, you can buy metal strips which attach to studs and have supports which can be slipped in and out under the shelving in different positions.

¶ *How do you make closet shelves?*

Find the studs in the left closet wall. With a level, mark a line for a 1" x 2" cleat. Cut the cleat to fit from front to back. Attach the cleat solidly to the studs with wood screws. Then do the same along the back of the closet, and at the right side. Cut the shelf to fit. Set it in over the cleats. You can attach it or not, as you wish.

For a shelf which will take less weight, use quarter rounds instead of 1" x 2" wood cleats for supports.

Or, you can recess the shelving into the lining of the closet by cutting a solid groove into which the board can be inserted.

11
Doors

If the doors in your house are warped, loose, or in any way imperfect, they will constantly annoy you by their squeaking and sticking. In order to keep them always working, you must check them frequently to be sure that the hinges are not loosening in the frame and that the latches are striking properly.

By following the instructions listed in the following questions and answers, you'll be able to keep yours in good order.

Q & A

DOOR PARTS

What are the various parts of a door?

Stiles are vertical pieces which run the length of the door. Rails are horizontal pieces which run across the bottom, the top, and through the middle. Panels are of wood, glass, or screen. Moldings seal the joints between the panels.

Describe the parts of a door frame.

Casings are the finish borders, or "trim," which cover the joint between the rough frame and the wall studs. The jambs are the borders which surround the interior face of the door opening. Stops are the moldings against which the door closes. The sill is the bottom tread of the door frame. A threshold is a continuation of a door sill.

❪ What kinds of door hardware are there?

Hinges, also called butts, hold the door to the frame. Locks, latches, and handles are used to open and close the door; these are mortised, or inset, into the outside stile of the door and the jamb of the door frame.

DOOR REPAIR

❪ What causes a door to stick and not close properly?

Sticking can be caused by swelling, by warping, or by any distortion in the shape of the door itself. Or it can be caused by a change in the hinge alignment.

❪ Why does a door rattle?

Warping or shrinking from dryness can cause a door to rattle.

❪ How do you correct these faults?

You must be able to take the door off its hinges in order to correct sticking, warping, and rattling.

❪ Describe the steps in removing a door from its hinges.

First, you open the door and prop up the outer corner at the bottom by using something like a thin book or a magazine. When you prop up the end, you take the weight off the hinges. Next, remove the bottom pin from the hinges. Indoor hinges are made with a pin which connects the two leaves, one of which is fastened to the door, and the other to the frame. To withdraw the pin, lift it out from the top, or hammer it up with a nail or a cold chisel laid against the underside of the top knob of the pin. Remove the top pin from the hinges the same way, and lift off the door.

❪ Explain how to put the door back.

Reverse the procedure, being sure to insert the top pin first. Then, remove the prop under the edge of the door, and put in the bottom hinge.

❪ How do you fix a door which strikes too closely against the frame?

If the door latch strikes too closely to the frame, it is probably easier to reset the hinges than it is to plane down the front of the door and reseat the lock. In resetting the hinges, simply remove them, chisel away the wood until each hinge lies deeper in the seating. Rehang, and see if the door closes properly. If the door itself is too big for the frame, plane the entire back of the door.

(If a door has shrunk so much that the latch does not catch, how can you fix it?

You reverse the process in the previous situation. Remove the hinges, and build up the seating with shims, strips of cardboard or thin wood, until the hinge is set at the proper height. Be sure you use longer wood screws when you put the hinges in again. The built-up cushion will demand more length.

(How do you fix a door which strikes on the upper or lower outer corner of the frame?

Check carefully to see exactly what is happening. It is quite possible that the door may be hanging askew; the lower edge of the door may be striking the door sill. On the other hand, the upper edge of the door may be striking the top of the frame. In the first case, build up the lower hinge by adding shims. In the second case, build up the upper hinge by adding shims. Or, you can obtain the same result in each case by setting the opposite hinge deeper into the frame.

(Is there any other cause of sticking?

Some of the screws holding the hinges may have loosened. It is a good idea to tighten all the screws in all the hinges of all your doors once or twice a year. The top hinges are usually under more strain, since they bear more weight by their position.

(What causes a door to rattle?

The latch of the door is slipping into its catch hole in the strike plate before the door closes against the stop molding. In a well-hung door, the latch should not close in the catch hole until the door is pressing firmly against the stop molding.

(How can you cure a rattling door?

Don't remove the door; shift the strike plate slightly toward the side of the door containing the stop molding. Unscrew the strike plate from the frame, removing it entirely. With a sharp chisel, dig the hole out toward the direction you want to shift the strike plate. Cut along the top to accommodate the thickness of the strike plate. Now, re-fasten the strike plate in its new position with wood screws in fresh holes. You may have to fill the old screw holes with wood pegs, glue, wood putty, or even soft solder. Test it until the latch does not catch before the door is solidly pressing the stop molding.

❡ *How do you fix a door in which the latch no longer hits the center of the strike plate?*

Check first to be sure the door is hanging correctly. If it is not, readjust your hinges. If the door is hanging correctly, remove the strike plate, and reset it.

DOOR MAINTENANCE

❡ *Why do door knobs slip and sag?*

Sometimes the knob pin is bent. The spring can be broken. With constant use, the entire door knob may be clogged with dust and rust.

❡ *How do you cure a sticking door knob?*

Use powdered graphite, not oil, to make it turn more easily. If that doesn't work, remove the knob, and clean it.

❡ *Explain how to remove a door knob.*

Unscrew the knob from its stem and remove it. Take the stem out from the opposite end. If the spring is broken, replace it. If the trouble is caused by dust and dirt, clean it out. Do not oil; use powdered graphite.

❡ *Describe how to remove a door knob which has a lock in it.*

Unfasten one knob, take it off, and remove the knob containing the knob stem. Release the lock by unscrewing the two exposed screws. One side of the lock is a loose plate. When you withdraw this loose plate, you expose the mechanism. Clean out the mechanism, using powdered graphite.

❡ *When re-setting hinges, how do you refill screw holes?*

If it is impossible to replace screws with longer ones, carve wooden pegs with a jackknife so that they are slightly larger than the screw hole in question. Use the same kind of wood which is in the door. Smear the peg and the screw hole with wood glue. Hammer the peg into the hole until it is snug. Allow the glue to dry thoroughly. Now, trim the ends of the plugs with a jackknife until flush. The wood will now take a new wood screw.

❨ Why do wooden doors creak on their hinges?

If it isn't simply because the hinges aren't oiled properly, creaking can be caused by the aging of the wood in the door. As wood ages, it tends to sag and warp. Twisted out of line, a door will not hang properly on its hinges. Because of that, the hinges begin squealing.

❨ Is there any kind of a door which does not sag, warp or crack?

A steel door is immune to rotting, swelling, warping, and sagging, regardless of climate changes or age and wear. Such a door can be bought and installed.

❨ How do you install a steel door?

There are 6 steps:

(1) Set the factory-assembled frame in place, and secure it to the studs.

(2) Fix the loose hinge leaves to the door with the sheet-metal screws provided.

(3) Drop the pins in the hinges. You'll get a perfect fit everytime because of the accurate assembly.

(4) Hang the door.

(5) Set the cylindrical lock in the door, which is already mortised, drilled, and tapped.

(6) Attach the strike plate to the pre-mortised steel frame.

HANGING A NEW DOOR

❨ How do you hang a door?

There are three basic steps in the hanging of a door.

(1) *The first step* is the reduction of the door to the proper size to fit in the frame.

(2) *The second* is the attachment of the hinges.

(3) *The third* is the installation of the lock latch and strike plate.

❰[What tools do you need for hanging a door?

You need a plane, a ripsaw, and a 1-inch chisel.

❰[Describe how to reduce the new door to the proper size to fit its frame.

Place the door with the back resting lightly against the edge of the door frame where the hinges will be attached. Mark a line down the door where it passes the opposite jamb, to show yourself the amount of material you must remove before the door will fit inside the jambs. Once you have planed the vertical sides down to the proper width, stand the door between the jambs, and mark a line along the bottom parallel to the threshold or sill. Do not take off all the material from the bottom; save some for the top. Allow 3/16 inch all around the door for easy hanging and swinging.

❰[Explain how to attach door hinges.

Make undercuts in both the edge of the door and the door jamb, so that the leaves of the hinges are recessed to set flush with the wood. Top hinges should be set about 10 to 12 inches from the top of the door; lower hinges about a foot from the floor. Remove one hinge leaf, and trace its outline on the edge of the door. On the side edge of the door, mark the thickness or depth of the leaf. With chisel and hammer, cut along the marked lines, and pare out the wood carefully. Mark the screw holes, and insert the pins. When both top and bottom hinges are attached to the door, insert the pins, and join the leaves. Place the leaves in position on the jamb, holding the door against the back jamb where it will hang. Mark the hinge positions on the jamb. Remove the door, separate the leaves, and mark the outlines of the leaves on the door jamb. With a chisel and knife, undercut as before. Drill screw holes, and secure the hinge leaves with screws of the proper size in the jamb. Place the top hinge pin, and see if the bottom hinge leaves will meet correctly. If not, adjust. Then insert the bottom pin in the hinge leaves.

❰[Name the various kinds of locks.

There are many different kinds of locks: mortise, bore-in, rim, and half-mortise.

❰[Show how to install a mortise lock.

A mortise lock, the kind which is usually used on outside doors, is called that because it is mortised or set into the door edge. Lay the lock against the side of the door, and mark in the knob spindle hole, the keyhole, and the lock edge. Mark the borders of the lock cover plate against the door edge. With a brace and bit, drill holes of the correct size for both the keyhole and the knob spindle through the side. From the door end, drill several starting holes, and then chisel out a rectangle to receive the lock part. Install the lock, securing it in place with screws. Attach the keyhole, knobs, and spindle plate to the door. Close the door, and operate the lock and latch. Mark the jamb at the proper place for installation of the plate. Mark the borders of the plate against the jamb, and then chisel the segment out for mortising. Test for the right depth by working the latch and lock. Then attach the striking plate to the jamb.

(How do you install bore-in locks?

Bore-in locks, made usually for interior doors, are installed by means of two large holes, one bored into the edge of the door, and the other bored into the stile of the door. Follow the directions on the hardware, and install the lock in a cut-out mortise. Then install the strike plate as above.

(How do you install a tubular lock?

When you buy a tubular lock, a template comes with it. The template is a piece of cardboard, which you bend around the edge of the door. The template shows you exactly where to start the centers of the two holes you must drill. When the holes are drilled, install the latchbolt, and insert the knob spindle through the connection. Secure it by fastening on the opposite knob with the screw. Install the strike plate as above.

(How can you keep your door locks from freezing in the winter when water accidentally seeps in and turns to ice?

Use a graphite lubricant, squirting a few drops inside the key hole to coat the tumblers and key openings. This will cause the water to run out before it can freeze.

(When you paint a door between two rooms of opposite color, where do you change colors?

As a rule, figure that the outside edge of the door, or the edge with the latch in it, should be the color of the room into which the door swings. The hinge edge of the door should be painted the color of the other room, so that when you see it from the room into which it opens, you will not look at the other room's color.

(How can you keep outside doors and windows from swelling or warping?

One point you may overlook is in painting them. Be sure and cover the top and bottom edges as well as the sides of each door. If you leave the end grain out in the open, you're asking for trouble. The water simply enters where the paint has not been applied, and goes about its damaging ways.

PAINTING A DOOR

(How do you paint outside doors?

You usually finish the outside of a door with an undercoat and a coat of trim paint. On front doors, however, you should use spar varnish.

(What kind of paint surface does a door take?

You'll need three coats on new wood: three of varnish, or a coat of filler-sealer followed by two coats of varnish. If you want a stain finish, apply a coat of oil stain to the bare wood before putting on two coats of varnish. Do not use shellac on door exteriors; a shellac will turn white.

(How do you finish a door?

Paint the woodwork on the door frame first, starting at the corners and brushing away from them. On the door, cross-brush the recessed panels, brushing up and down from top and bottom toward the center. Paint the door edges, top, bottom, and sides. Then paint the rails and the stiles.

(How do you refinish a door?

Clean thoroughly, and sand the surface. Apply varnish. Bleach if necessary. To bleach, use a solution of ¾ pound of oxalic acid to 1 gallon of hot water. Rinse with alcohol, and, when dry, smooth with sandpaper. Use varnish to touch up any worn spots. When dry, apply either one or two coats of varnish.

12
Windows

A window, like a door, is an integral part of any house, and must constantly be kept in proper working order. Squeaking, sticking, and rattling can cause you great annoyance if not cured.

Broken panes are not only an eye-sore to people outside, but are an obvious safety hazard to you inside. Since the greatest part of a window is composed of glass, you must handle your work carefully in repairing. And, if a pane does break, you must guard against personal injury.

By paying attention to the instructions which follow, you may save yourself much pain and discomfort—besides a lot of extra work.

Q & A

WINDOW PARTS

❮ *Describe the parts of a window.*

The two main elements of any window are the frame and the sash. The frame is built in the wall of the house; the sash is the wooden framework which holds the glass panes.

The principal parts of the rough framing which forms the window space in the wall are the sill, the jambs, and the lintel, which are respectively the bottom piece, the side pieces, and the upper piece.

Windows [157

Supporting sill, jambs, and lintel inside the wall are horizontal double headers at top and bottom, and vertical double studs at the sides. These pieces of framing timber are usually 2" x 4"s nailed together side by side, hence "double." The double headers and double studs give extra-strong support to the frame itself. The finish frame of a window is composed of the finish sill running along the bottom, the side jambs, and the head jamb along the top. In a double-hung window, the jambs are in turn composed of stops and parting strips: the stop is the edge against which the sash slides; the parting strip is the dividing strip between the two sashes. The head jamb has stops and parting strip, too. The sill has a sill stool; behind this, the lower sash slides down for a tight fit.

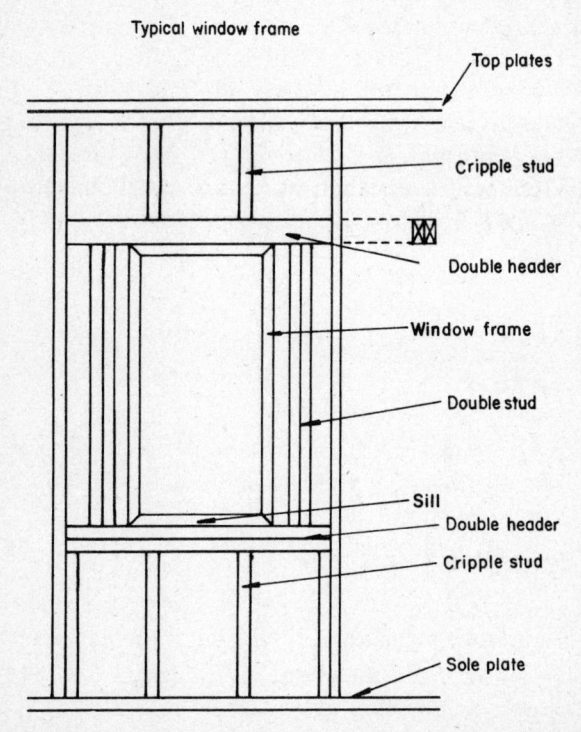

Typical window frame
- Top plates
- Cripple stud
- Double header
- Window frame
- Double stud
- Sill
- Double header
- Cripple stud
- Sole plate

The principal parts of a sash are rails and stiles, the rails being border horizontal strips, and the stiles being border vertical strips. The rail at the top of an upper double-hung window is the bottom rail; the rails on the opposite ends of each window are called the meeting rails. A rail or stile which separates the panes in the middle of the window is called a muntin.

WINDOW REPAIR

❰ How can you repair a window which rattles?

Inspect the window first to find out what makes it rattle. The rattle may be caused by a loose pane of glass or by a loose sash in the frame. You can always get temporary relief, of course, by sticking a piece of folded cardboard, rubber, or wood in the sash.

❰ If a window rattles because of a loose glass pane how do you fix it?

Rattling panes are caused by loose putty. To repair, you must reputty the pane.

❰ What materials and tools do you need to putty or reputty a window pane?

You need putty, glaziers points, linseed oil, and paint. Glaziers points are thin strips of metal, which are inserted in the stile or rail of a window to keep the glass tight against the rabbet, or outer molding.

PUTTY

❰ What is putty?

Putty is made out of whiting and boiled linseed oil, mixed to a dough-like consistency. It is used to keep water from seeping in around a pane of glass in a window. Putty does not hold a window pane in the sash; metal pieces called glazing points do. Putty can also be used to fill small cracks and nail holes. It takes paint smoothly.

❰ What are the two main kinds of putty?

Wood sash putty, and metal sash putty. Metal sash putty comes in interior and exterior forms; be sure to use them on the right side of the window.

❰ How do you prepare a window sash for a putty job?

Clean and dry the surface. Apply a quality priming paint to

Windows

keep the oil in the putty from flowing into the wood, leaving the putty dry and brittle. You should prime steel with a good steel primer to retard rust, which would loosen the bond between the putty and the steel.

❮ How do you repatch a loose putty job?

Remove all loose or crumbly putty. Prime as described. Apply the putty by making a long, thin roll and pressing it into place. Smooth it firmly against the glass with a putty knife.

❮ How do you use putty in replacing a glass pane?

Remove all old putty. Prime the sash, and let it dry. Apply an even coat of putty to the inside of the sash and on the molding against which the glass will rest. Insert the glass, and press it lightly against the bed of putty. A thin stream of "putty ribbon" will ooze up around the glass. Insert the glaziers points to hold the glass, and apply the putty. When the putty has dried, seal and protect it with a coat of paint. Apply the same number of coats to the putty as you do to the sash. The paint should be slightly lapped over the glass to insure sealing action at the critical edge.

❮ How do you keep putty from falling out of the hole it is to fill?

One good way is to use a staple gun to shoot a few staples into position at the bottom of the cavity. When you press the compound into place, you'll get a good mechanical bond with the staples.

❮ How do you putty a pane of glass in a window sash?

See Chapter One, Page 9, under the following question:

❮ How do you replace a broken pane of glass in a window?

See Chapter One, Page 9.

❮ How do you replace a broken pane of glass in a metal sash?

If the pane is held by putty, remove as described above, except that metal clips are used in steel construction, rather than glaziers points. Save these metal clips; they are hard to replace. Scrape the metal bed of the pane with a knife. Apply a thin layer of sash putty, so that it covers all the metal in the sash joint. When it is set in, the glass must never touch the metal. Press the pane into the putty. Replace the metal clips. Putty over the pane and the sash joint. Let the putty dry, and paint.

¶ Explain how to remove a sash from a casement window.

Unscrew the hinges from the sash of the frame. When lifting the sash out, do not let it drop. If it is heavy, have someone help you—one of you will hold the sash; the other will loosen the hinges.

¶ How can you lubricate the sliding parts on metal windows without slopping oil all over?

Try rubbing kitchen waxpaper briskly over the surface. This will apply a very light film, which will be just enough to ease up stiff-moving pieces.

¶ Explain how to remove the sash from a sliding window.

Simply pry out the inside window stop on one side and on the bottom. Lift the sash out.

¶ Is there any way to protect a picture window from tornado and hurricane damage?

The best way to make a shutter for a picture window is to use galvanized rib-metal lath, attached to a wooden frame built to fit into the window space. You can get the rib-metal lath at your building supplier's; it is used as a base for plaster walls. Such shutters will work for smaller windows, too, and are much lighter to handle.

¶ Explain how to repair a loose, wooden window sash.

You can tighten a loose window sash with a wood strip, or with a felt strip, by inserting it between the sash and the jamb against which it rattles. If the space between the sash and the jamb is over ⅜ inch, use a wood strip; if the space is less, use a felt strip.

PAINTING A WINDOW

¶ How do you prepare a window for painting?

Brush away all loose dirt and dust, and scrape off any peeling paint. Prime all bare wood with enamel undercoater. On metal windows, steel-wool away all traces of rust; prime bare spots with a metal primer.

❰ What kind of paint do you use on a window?

Use gloss or semigloss enamel, the same color as the walls. Paint with a narrow sash brush made especially for window jobs. The main problem in painting a window is to keep the paint off the window panes. Place either a metal shield or a shirt cardboard on the glass against the edge of the wood. Paint up to it, wipe the guard clean, and then move on. Or, you can use masking tape which is manufactured especially for easy removal.

❰ How do you proceed with the painting?

With a double-hung window, raise the bottom sash and lower the top sash, leaving a few inches clearance at both ends. Start painting the raised bottom sash. Paint its top horizontal, then paint the mullions, which are the strips separating the panes. Paint its verticals. Then switch to the upper sash, which is still lowered. Paint its mullions, working as high as you can. Do not paint between the sashes. Paint its bottom horizontal. Now, lower the bottom sash to its regular position, holding it by the unpainted bottom horizontal. Raise the upper sash by pushing its unpainted top. Leave a space between the upper sash and the top of the window opening. Paint the upper horizontal of the top sash. Next, paint the mullions which you could not reach before. Finish the unpainted verticals of the top sash. Now paint the bottom horizontal of the lower sash.

❰ Should you paint the channel in which the lower sash moves?

It is best not to. The windows might stick shut. The thickness of the enamel coats will make it hard to move. You can brush on a coat of boiled linseed oil or a penetrating sealer for protection.

❰ How do you keep windows from sticking after being freshly painted?

After painting an outside window, move each window up and down a few times after the paint is partially dry. This will keep it from caking and hardening in the grooves between the sliding sash and the window frame.

❋ How do you unstick a window sash which is completely jammed in the frame?

See Chapter One, Page 8.

VENETIAN BLINDS

❋ Is it possible to install a venetian blind if your window is not a standard width?

Most stores which sell blinds will cut unusual sizes to your special order.

❋ How are venetian blinds installed?

The blinds hang from valances above the window frame. Built-in venetian blinds are generally hung on special fixtures built in the window frame, or from hangers installed outside the frame. If you intend to install a venetian blind over a window, you will most likely install the valance type hanger. Instructions are on all blinds and valances you buy. Follow them carefully. Usually, two mountings are fastened to the top border of the window molding, and the hanger is slipped into these slotted box-like pieces.

❋ Can you correct venetian blind cords which begin to slip and slide through the pulley?

Slipping and sliding indicates that the metal gears are so worn that they no longer grip the tapes which move the slats. Replace the pulleys and gears with new ones from your hardware store.

❋ How do you install pulleys and gears?

Read the directions on the replacements and follow them carefully. A screwdriver is all you need.

❋ Can you replace worn, warped, or bent slats?

Yes. Loosen the cords running through the center of the tapes at the bottom of the blind, and remove it from the bottom bar. Do this on both sides. Slip out the ailing slat, and replace it with a new one. Run the cords back through the slats, and refasten them to the bottom bar.

❋ Should you remove the entire blind to replace several slats?

It is easier to leave the blind hanging in its place. After you remove the cords, take out one slat at a time, and replace it with new.

❬ How do you remove defective tapes?

Remove the cords, and take out all the slats, one at a time. Replace your old tapes with new. Slip the slats back into place, and replace the cords.

❬ Is it possible to keep metal slats from rusting?

Yes. Keep them painted all the time. If you do not like metal slats, replace them with plastic slats. Unlike wood or metal, plastic will neither rot nor rust. Colored tapes to match colored slats are also available.

ROLLER SHADES

❬ What kind of roller shades are in use today?

There are washable cloth shades, paper-coated with a starch solution, plastic, and wood strip roller shades.

❬ How can a hole be repaired in a regular roller shade?

You can use plastic tape to patch splits and holes.

❬ Can you replace a shade which has pulled off its roller?

Yes. Staple it back on with a staple gun.

❬ Is there any way to snap up the ragged edges on a roller shade?

Paint the surface with a thin shellac, carefully touching up the edges. It will dry wth a clean edge. Do not use it until it is completely dry.

❬ Describe how to replace a roller if the spring breaks.

Buy a whole new shade. Be sure to measure the width of your window carefully, or you will have to reset the pieces which hold it up.

WINDOW SCREENS

❬ What kinds of window screens are now available?

You can buy copper and bronze screening, aluminum, and, of course, the standard iron-wire screening.

❲ *Are there any advantages to copper and bronze screening?*

They will not rust. Because of that, they will last longer.

❲ *Are there any disadvantages to copper and bronze screening?*

If rain drips down from them, a greenish discoloration may be left on light-colored trim and walls.

❲ *Can stain from copper drip be washed away?*

Yes. Mix ½ cup of household ammonia in 1 quart of water, or ½ cup of trisodium phosphate in 1 quart of water. These solutions will remove the stain. Follow the solution immediately by rinsing with clear water.

❲ *Is there any way to keep copper and bronze screening from staining?*

Clean it; then wash it with benzene. Using a spar varnish, thin it with an equal amount of half-and-half mix of linseed oil and turpentine. Coat the screening with this thinned varnish. One coat should last for a season.

You can also use pure shellac, thinned by one-half as much denatured alcohol. You can apply it with a brush if you want, but you may find that a brush fills the mesh. Tack a piece of carpet around a block of wood, nap-side-out. Brush the varnish first onto the carpeting; then transfer it to the screening.

❲ *How do you mend window or door screens which have pulled out of their frames?*

See Chapter One, Page 10.

❲ *Is there any way to repair a hole in the middle of a screen?*

If it's a big hole, you'll have to patch it with a piece of screening, cut to fit. Use model-airplane cement to stick the patch on. If it's a small hole, fill in the gap with the same cement.

❲ *Is wire screening made of rustproof galvanized iron?*

No. If protected with varnish or screen enamel, however, it will resist rusting.

❲ *Is there any shortcut to spraying screens before storing for the winter?*

You can stack four or five of them against a sawhorse, and

spray them with a clear plastic from an aerosol can. Be sure all the mesh is covered.

CARE OF AWNINGS

❰ Can awning cloth be repainted?

If it is a single color, the entire awning can be redyed.

❰ How do you paint awning cloth?

Use house paint thinned with ¼ as much turpentine. Apply the paint in a thin coat, and brush it into the fibers. The paint must be completely dry before you fold the awning to store.

❰ Should you take any special precautions in storing your awnings for the winter?

All awning material should be sprayed with anti-mildew compound, which can be applied from an aerosol can. Be sure you do not tear the cloth when you store it.

❰ How can you waterproof awning cloth?

Canvas and awning cloth can be waterproofed by painting. Use a solution of 1 pound of shaved paraffin in a gallon of turpentine or clear kerosene. Stretch the fabric when you apply the coating. Paraffin will dissolve more quickly when heated; do not heat turpentine or kerosene over an open fire, but put the container in a pail of hot water to heat.

❰ How can you repair a tear in an awning?

Sew a patch on the underside.

There is a patching preparation on the market which you can use, too, or you might try household cement or rubber cement.

To repair, lay the awning face down on a flat surface, cut the canvas, and coat the patch and the awning separately with cement. Let this dry until it is strongly tacky; then put the patch in position, and force it into contact by hammering.

❰ Can you buy fireproof awning cloth?

Yes. However, once rain has touched it, the fireproofing will wash out.

❰ How can you repaint aluminum awnings which begin to lose their coating?

Repaint with a special paint designed for use with aluminum.

❲ How do you install aluminum awnings?

Kits are available with standard lengths of material. With a hack saw and a screwdriver, you can make your own awnings to fit your windows.

WEATHERSTRIPPING

❲ How can you close up a leaky joint around a window sash?

Weatherstrips are made which will check or stop most of the entrance of outdoor air. Caulking can help. Good weatherstripping and caulking can save 20% on your fuel bill.

❲ Is there a "best kind" of weatherstripping for a window?

A permanent type of weatherstrip is metal. It is formed into shapes that will remain tight and fit snugly into a groove cut in the edge of the sash.

❲ Is metal weatherstripping always enough to seal a window?

If it isn't, you can use a strip or a groove of felt lining. Carpenters and experts can do this complicated job better than you.

❲ In hot desert areas, what will keep out dust and dirt and sand?

The same weatherstripping as is used in winter will prevent wind-driven sand from coming inside in a hot desert area.

❲ Are there any metal weatherstrips that can be installed by non-professionals?

Yes. These are generally springy V-shaped strips. Attach them to the window frame outside the window. Once they lose their springiness, however, the air will come in.

❲ Are there any other satisfactory types of weatherstrips?

There are weatherstrips made of fabric and other flexible materials. If you apply them tightly, you will get excellent insulation. This type of weatherstripping is not permanent, however. When the material ages, you will get leaks.

❲ Is it easy to attach weatherstrips to wood-frame windows?

Yes. Simply nail them on.

❰ Is it easy to attach weatherstrips to metal-frame windows?

Snap them into the grooves around the edges of double-hung window sashes. They will be held in by their springiness. Use felt and rubber for closing the joints in a metal casement window. Scrape the metal clean of paint, rust, or corrosion along the edges of the frame, and then wipe it with benzene. Attach felt strips with plastic cement; attach rubber with rubber-to-metal adhesive. Some weatherstrips of felt come with special adhesive already on the back; you simply pull off the protective wax paper and press the strip right in.

❰ Besides windows, where else are open joints liable to occur?

You may have an open joint between the top of a wall and the underside of the roof. Winter air can move in from this point and chill an entire downstairs.

❰ How do you tighten up this joint?

Use caulking compound. Oakum or tow can also be used, if the hole is large. Or, you can purchase aerosol cans of caulking compound at most hardware stores. (See caulking, pages 130-2.)

❰ Are there any other danger areas for bad leaking joints?

Yes. You may have a leak between the top of the foundation wall and the sill. The sill is wood, and it lies on the foundation to support the wall studs. A leak here may be caused by a falling away of the mortar in which the sill is bedded. Close this leak from outside, using mortar. Mix 1 part Portland cement and 3 parts sand. Remove all old, loose mortar and pack in the new as tightly as you can. Slope the surface of the new mortar to shed rain to the outside. Then make double sure by caulking the entire area from the inside.

STORM WINDOWS

❰ What are the principal causes of heat loss by conduction?

Glass windows cause most conduction heat loss. Touch your window from the inside on a cold day, and you'll understand how quickly heat passes through it and vanishes.

❡ Is there any kind of window which does not lose heat by conduction?

Windows are manufactured with double panes separated by a thin layer of air. A strip of metal insulation keeps the windows air-tight and apart. They must be ordered to size, and installed by a professional.

❡ Can you stop heat loss through a window in any other way than complete new installation?

Storm windows are the easiest way to cut down conduction loss through windows. Two separate glass surfaces with a layer of air in between causes a great decrease in heat loss. A storm window should be close-fitted and weatherstripped.

❡ Do you need storm windows on all sides of the house or only on the exposed side?

All windows should be fitted with storm windows, not only to keep the outside cold air from coming in, but to keep the inside warm air from going out.

❡ Are storm windows needed outside metal windows?

Absolutely. Metal has a high conductivity of heat; a metal sash will grow colder faster than a wood sash.

❡ Aren't storm windows cumbersome and inconvenient to put in and take out each year?

You can buy "combination" windows, which contain both screens for summer and glass for winter. Screen and storm panes are contained in one frame, sliding in separate channels. These sections need never be removed; you merely slide them up during summer. Many of these storm window combinations have aluminum or wood frames.

❡ What are the main points to look out for when shopping for a combination storm window?

(1) Be sure you know your dealer. Look over his shop and estimate whether he'll still be in business six months from now when you may need servicing. (2) Be sure the storm windows have good weatherseal insulation. (3) Be sure your storm windows

are compatible with the present windows in your home. (4) Be sure the price is right. Don't shop for price alone; you usually get what you pay for. (5) Be sure your storm windows have good separation between the glass inserts. When the separate glass panes and screen elements are slid by each other, there should be no metal-on-metal sounds. Push your finger gently but firmly against the outside glass pane. If the weatherseal is doing its job, the window glass insert should not give against the pressure of your finger. If it does give, you'll have to expect noisy rattling. (6) Be sure your storm windows can be repaired easily. It's much more practical to take a single insert to your dealer to have the glazing replaced than it is to wait for a home-service call. (7) Be sure your aluminum is quality material. Cheap aluminum can become an eyesore after a season of exposure to the elements. (8) Be sure you can raise the insert part-way for partial or "controlled" ventilation. Check to see how easy it is to clean the window elements. Another most important test is how quickly you can open the window to its widest position or remove inserts completely. (9) Be sure you read your contract carefully and understand it. Be sure there is a clause written in to the effect that the windows must be installed "to the satisfaction of the purchaser" before the contract is considered fulfilled. (10) Be sure you get a good national brand name. Generally speaking, you'll do better with them than with products no one has ever heard of.

13
Concrete

Ever since concrete was first devised by the Romans to build the Appian Way, it has been used in construction of all kinds: sidewalks, roads, buildings, swimming pools, and so on. You may find it in your driveway, in the walls of your basement, or in the floor of your porch.

Concrete is the most permanent of materials: the Pantheon in Rome was built 1800 years ago; its dome is made of cast concrete. Concrete has strength, density, and permanence. However, it must be carefully mixed and carefully cast to be at its best.

Don't be afraid of concrete; it isn't that difficult to handle. By mixing and pouring a small portion at a time, you can do a large job slowly. If you hire a ready-mix batch, you can have the heavy work done by the men who pour the concrete for you.

What you should know is how to use it, where it serves best, and where it will afford strength and durability. And, you should know something about it, even if you hire someone else to do the job for you.

Q & A

PORTLAND CEMENT

What is the difference between cement and concrete?

Although used interchangeably, the two terms are actually not

Concrete [171]

similar. Cement refers to Portland cement, a binding material developed by calcining limestone and clay. Portland cement is the basic material used to make concrete.

❮ What is concrete?

Concrete is a mixture of Portland cement, sand, gravel or crushed stone, and water.

❮ What is mortar?

Mortar is a mixture of Portland cement, 10% by volume of hydrated lime, sand, and water. This mortar is used to lay concrete bricks, clay bricks, and also to plaster walls.

❮ What is grout?

Grout is a mixture of Portland cement and fine sand, sometimes with 5 to 10% of lime added. Grout is used to lay tile: in that case, the mix is sometimes Portland cement, lime and water, mixed to a thin paste about the consistency of toothpaste.

❮ How is Portland cement bought?

It is marketed in sacks which usually hold a cubic foot, and is also available in bulk for large uses. It is a whitish-gray powder. Cement is measured in sacks or barrels — four sacks to a barrel. In the United States, 1 sack weighs 94 pounds; in Canada, 1 sack weighs 87 pounds. Concrete is measured in cubic feet.

❮ Does 1 cubic foot of cement and 1 cubic foot of sand make 2 cubic feet of concrete?

No. Sand and cement fill in, and the mixture chemically bonds together as it dries. A concrete mixture of 1 cubic foot of cement, 2 cubic feet of sand, and 4 cubic feet of broken stone or pebbles — 7 cubic feet in all — will combine as concrete and eventually occupy a space of only 4 cubic feet.

❮ How do you purchase cement?

You can buy Portland cement, sand and gravel, and hydrated lime separately and mix it yourself. You can also buy the dry materials already mixed in various ratios, and simply add the water. Or, you can hire a contractor to bring concrete to your site in a mixer truck. This is usually the best way to operate if the area you want to fill is large, say for a concrete driveway, a garage slab, walkways, or foundations. For smaller jobs, the mixed dry materials should work.

❮[*What is aggregate?*

Aggregate is a combination of gravel and small pebbles or crushed stone which, added to sand, cement, and water, make concrete. Aggregate is generally measured in relation to the maximum size of the stones composing it.

❮[*How is concrete mix proportioned?*

It is figured generally by the weight of the various ingredients. The difference in character will depend on the proportion of cement in relation to the sand and stone.

❮[*What proportion of cement gives strength and watertightness?*

The more Portland cement used in relation to sand and aggregate, the stronger and more watertight the concrete.

❮[*Can concrete of a high cement ratio be used for almost any purpose?*

Yes.

❮[*Why is the proportion of cement lower in some mixes?*

When great quantities of concrete must be used and high strength is not required, increasing the amount of aggregate will increase the total volume and save on the cement, which costs more than the aggregate; in large masses, it would be wasteful to use too much.

❮[*How do you figure the amount of water to use in a mix?*

Water should be used in proportion to the cement to be mixed.

❮[*Will more water in a mix cause greater strength later?*

No. Just the opposite. When concrete for important work is mixed, a trial batch should be made, using the correctly estimated amount of water. If there is too much water, you must add stone and sand to bring the mixture to a necessary stiffness. If the mix is too stiff, you must reduce the quantity of sand and gravel.

❮[*What is the best kind of sand to use in concrete?*

Always use dry well-graded sand, if possible. However, most sand carries some moisture; you have to allow for this. Use less water for wet sand than for damp sand.

❮ How can you tell "damp" sand from "wet" sand and "moist" sand?

"Damp" sand feels moist to the touch, but leaves no moisture on the fingers. "Moist" sand leaves moisture. "Wet" sand drips.

❮ What are the main advantages to using concrete as a building material?

Concrete can be formed into any shape you want. Since it is mixed and cast in semi-liquid form, it is easy to handle. It tends to smooth itself out, once cast; gravity pulls the surface almost flat. In building a form, you must remember that concrete, after it is cast, will tend to seek its own level. Once it sets, you merely remove the wood forms (which do not stick to the concrete if properly oiled), and the formed concrete will be rigid and strong for a long time.

❮ For what purposes is concrete used around the home?

It can be used for sidewalks, for driveways, for basement floors, or for patio slabs.

MIXING CONCRETE

❮ On what surface should you mix concrete?

For work around the home, you should mix concrete on a tight floor or on a platform made of tightly fitting boards. A platform 6 feet square should be adequate for work you might want to do around the house.

❮ Describe the steps in hand-mixing a batch of concrete.

Measure out the amount of sand first. Add the amount of measured cement. Shovel and hoe the pile until the mixture is of an even color. Cover that mixture with the correct measure of stone and pebbles, and continue mixing until evenly distributed. Hollow out a circle in the middle. Pour part of the water into the circle. Shovel or hoe this until sand, pebbles, and cement are thoroughly and evenly combined. Take it easy on the water. It spreads faster than you think.

PRACTICAL HOME REPAIR FOR WOMEN

❊ How long can you let mixed concrete sit before pouring it?

Mixed concrete should be used within 30 minutes of mixing, possibly sooner in hot, dry weather.

❊ Is there any way to mix concrete other than by hand?

Electric or gasoline mixers are usually available at building supply houses. You can rent one which will hold about ½ to 1 cubic yard of concrete mix. You can also rent wheelbarrows for moving it.

❊ How can sand and aggregate be measured?

You can make "bottomless boxes" to measure sand and aggregate. A bottomless box 12 inches square and 12 inches deep will have a capacity of 1 cubic foot. A box 18 inches square and 10⅝ inches deep will hold 2 cubic feet. A box 18 inches square and 16 inches deep will hold 3 cubic feet.

TOOLS

❊ Name and describe the tools you need to work with concrete.

(1) *Strike board.* A strike board is merely a long, straight 2" x 4", long enough to reach entirely across the part of the form being poured. You run the strike board across the unformed concrete, "striking" off the higher levels, and forcing the mixture into a flat form.

(2) *Tamp.* A tamp is a square piece of wood mounted at right angles to a long pole. It is used to compact the concrete into a dense mass after striking off a level surface.

(3) *Wood float.* A box-like "float," usually 3 or 4 feet long by 6 to 8 inches wide, is operated on a long handle. It is used to make the surface of the concrete smooth.

(4) *Steel trowels.* A steel trowel is used to give the concrete a dense, smooth finish. A small steel trowel is used for smaller repair and replacement jobs.

(5) *Edger.* An edger is like a steel trowel, but it has a curved edge which helps round off the work corners.

(6) *Wheelbarrow.* A wheelbarrow is used as a carrier to move concrete from its mixing location to the casting site.

(7) *Shovel.* You'll need a shovel to move the concrete, either from the mixer to the carrier, or from the carrier to the casting site.

Concrete [175

(8) *Hoe.* You'll need a flat-edged hoe to mix the concrete.

(9) *Broom.* You'll need an old broom, or an old paint brush lashed to a long handle, to texture the concrete before it dries.

TOOLS YOU'LL NEED

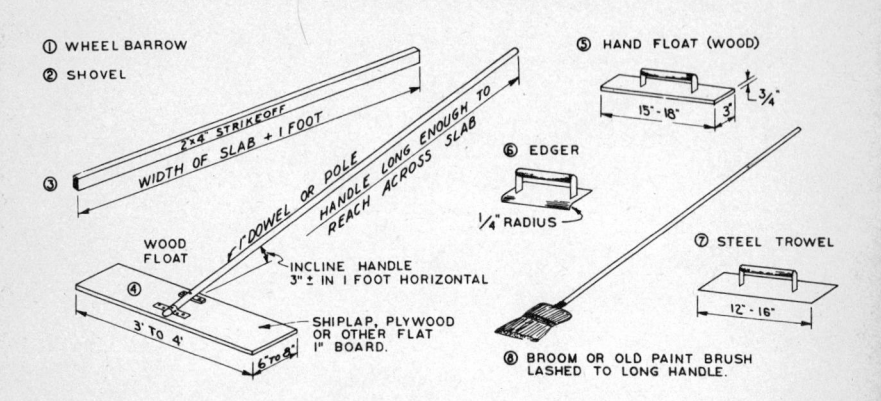

① WHEEL BARROW
② SHOVEL
③ 2"x4" STRIKEOFF — WIDTH OF SLAB + 1 FOOT
④ WOOD FLOAT — 3' TO 4', 6" TO 4", SHIPLAP, PLYWOOD OR OTHER FLAT 1" BOARD. 1" DOWEL OR POLE HANDLE LONG ENOUGH TO REACH ACROSS SLAB. INCLINE HANDLE 3" ± IN 1 FOOT HORIZONTAL
⑤ HAND FLOAT (WOOD) — 15"-18", 3", ¾"
⑥ EDGER — ¼" RADIUS
⑦ STEEL TROWEL — 12"-16"
⑧ BROOM OR OLD PAINT BRUSH LASHED TO LONG HANDLE.

(What kind of aggregate can you buy?

Any commercial sand and gravel or crushed stone prepared for use in concrete work is satisfactory.

(For improvements around the house, what is a recommended mix?

Use 1 part Portland cement, 2¼ parts sand, 3 parts gravel or crushed stone (1 inch maximum size), and ⅔ parts water (5 gallons of water per sack of cement).

(Can this mix be revised?

Do not change the proportions of cement to water; the key to quality concrete is the ratio of cement to water.

(What if the concrete is too stiff after mixing?

Use less sand and coarse aggregate in subsequent batches. If the mix is too soupy, adjust the amount of sand and coarse aggregate.

(How much is needed to make 1 cubic yard of concrete?

You'll need 6¼ bags of Portland cement, 14 cubic feet of sand (1,260 pounds), 19 cubic feet of gravel or crushed stone (1,900 pounds), and 31½ gallons of water.

PRACTICAL HOME REPAIR FOR WOMEN

(What about wastage?

It is wise to figure 10% over your total for wastage.

(How do you order ready-mixed concrete?

Ready-mixed concrete is sold by the cubic yard (27 cubic feet). For normal wastage, order 10% more than you calculate.

(Will concrete hold up under freezing and thawing conditions?

If you are worried about freezing, thawing, or salt action, buy Type 1A Portland cement. It has an added chemical agent, called an "air-entrained" agent, which causes the formation of millions of microscopic air bubbles in the concrete. It resists scaling and the action of salts used to melt snow and ice. Air-entrained concrete should be used for all exterior work.

PATIO CONSTRUCTION DETAILS

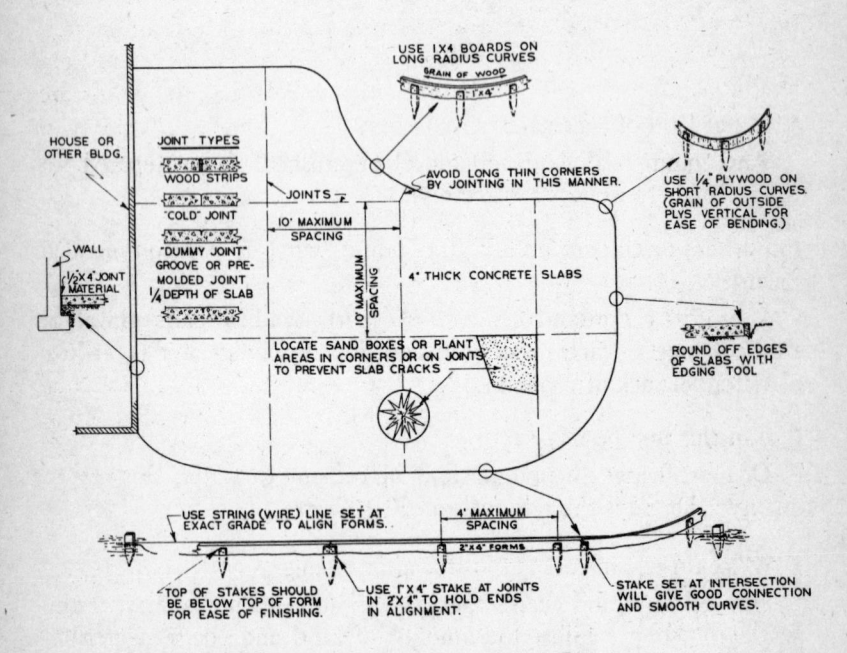

BUILDING A PATIO SLAB

(Outline the main steps in pouring a concrete patio slab.

(1) *Preparation of subgrade and grading.* After planning where you want your patio slab, your first step is to remove the soil to a

Concrete

depth of about 4 inches below the desired surface level of the concrete slab. Smooth the dirt out to approximately the correct grade, and compact it thoroughly. The slab should drain quickly after a rain or washing, so it should be built with a slight slope (⅛ inch per foot) away from the house. Fill low spots or pockets. Remove all black dirt, vegetation, wood, bricks, and large rocks from the soil. Level and compact the loose soil with a tamper or heavy roller. If the soil is clay, the subgrade should be soaked several days before placing the concrete.

(2) *Forming.* Design the patio any way you wish: in a square, a diamond, a rectangle, or a circle. Use 2" x 4" boards for side forms, and nail them securely to 1" x 2" or 2" x 2" stakes driven firmly into the ground. The stakes should be no more than 4 feet apart. You will need them at every joint in the form lumber. A 1" x 4" stake can be used to lap the joints in the 2" x 4" to help hold both ends in alignment. For flat, horizontal curves, use ¼" x 4" plywood strips. Cut the strips so that the exterior grain will be vertical when they are in place. You will need stakes closer together on curves to hold the forms at the proper grade and curvature. When the forms are set, smooth the subgrade to accommodate the desired thickness of the slab. Pull a templet, riding on top of the forms, across the subgrade to get a smooth, uniform depth.

(3) *Estimating concrete needed.* Except for very small jobs or for work at inaccessible locations, you should use ready-mixed concrete for the easiest and most satisfactory job. Order no more concrete than you can place and finish in three hours, if you do the work yourself. About 3 cubic yards of concrete is the most you should order at one time. You will need the help of at least one person. Estimating the amount of concrete is your next step. First, find the area in square feet; then use the following table:

Area in square feet (width × length)						
10	25	50	100	200	300	
0.12	0.31	0.62	1.23	2.47	3.70	at 4-inch thickness

Say you want to lay a slab 4 inches thick and 20 feet by 12½ feet. This gives a total of 250 square feet. From the table, 200 sq. ft. = 2.47 cu. yd.; 50 sq. ft. = 0.62 cu. yd.; 250 sq. ft. = 3.09 cu. yds. To be safe, order 3½ cubic yards.

(4) *How to Order:* There are several things you must do when

you order ready-mixed concrete. Here they are:

(A) Order the quantity of concrete in cubic yards, making allowance for uneven subgrade, spillage, and so on.

(B) Specify at least 6 sacks of cement per cubic yard.

(C) Ask for not more than a 4-inch slump, or not over 5½ gallons of water per sack of cement. "Slump" refers to a measure of consistency of concrete. A 4-inch slump will give you a good, workable mix. Stiffer mixes are harder to finish by hand. Very wet, soupy mixes will not give durable concrete.

(D) Specify a coarse aggregate (gravel) with a maximum size between ¾ inch and 1½ inch. A maximum size of 1 inch is recommended.

(E) Ask for 6% air entrainment to obtain good durability in concrete on all outside work.

(F) Specify where and when to deliver the concrete, and if possible, place your concrete order at least one day ahead of time.

(5) *Placing.* Be ready to place the concrete and finish it off when the ready-mix truck arrives. Wet the ground and the forms with a hose just before placing the concrete. Have a good wheelbarrow on hand to transport the concrete from the truck chute to the job site. Many ready-mix producers have construction wheelbarrows to rent if you need one. Place the concrete in the forms to the full depth, spading along the sides to ensure complete filling. "Strike off" the concrete with a length of 2" x 4" board, drawn in a sawlike motion across the slab. This will smooth the surface of the concrete while cutting it off to the proper elevation. Go over the concrete twice to take out any bumps that remain after the first pass. This will make your finishing easier. Fill in any low spots before the second pass to provide a uniform surface. Immediately after striking off, work a big wood float back and forth across the slab to smooth it and remove irregularities. Work a slight amount of cement paste to the surface. For areas with curves, use a small wood hand float for smoothing. Next, do some preliminary edging. You will do final edging near the end of finishing and before brooming.

(6) *Finishing.* The rough texture produced by the wood float can be your final finish. Or, you can use the wooden hand float in a swirl pattern; do this after the concrete has begun to stiffen. You can get out on the slab by kneeling on pieces of wide flat boards laid on the surface of the concrete. If you want a roughened texture,

draw a fiber brush across the surface; wait until the concrete is hard enough to retain the grooves or marks. You can use a stiff broom or a very soft brush, as you prefer. If you want a very smooth surface, finish it off with a steel trowel. Delay steel-troweling until the concrete is quite stiff; otherwise, excessive water will be worked to the surface. Too much water on the surface will weaken the slab. Work the trowel in sweeping arcs. For the final finish, use the steel trowel again when the concrete is almost hard. The trowel should make a ringing noise as it is worked over the slab. Little or no mortar should cling to it. Clean all tools with water as soon as you finish with them.

(7) *Curing.* You must cure concrete to make it strong and durable. The best curing is done by keeping the concrete continuously wet for at least 5 days in warm weather and 7 days in cool weather. When the concrete is hard, moisten with a hose, and cover with a plastic sheet weighted down around the edges. This will prevent rapid evaporation of the moisture. You can also cure it by keeping the slab wet with a sprinkler, or by covering the slab with burlap or other material and keeping the burlap moist by spraying it often with water.

TIPS ON CONCRETE

How can you repair a concrete slab or floor which has patched or cracked?

Thoroughly roughen the surface with a chisel, and then clean it. Remove all dust and loose particles with a wire brush; then flush the surface with water. Cracks to be patched should be slightly undercut. Dampen the surface that is to be patched. The old concrete should be no more than damp; no excess water should be present on the surface. Make a thick, creamy mixture of Portland cement and water, and brush it onto the prepared surface. Place the patch before this creamy mixture dries. Make a stiff mix of 1 part of Portland cement, 2 parts sand, and 2 parts pea gravel. Tamp this mixture firmly into the cavity, and lightly smooth it off with a wood float. After the concrete begins to stiffen, finish it with a steel trowel or wood float. For narrow cracks where pea gravel cannot be used, use mortar made of 1 part Portland cement to 3 parts sand. Keep the freshly placed patch damp for a minimum of 5 days.

❰ *How do you mix colored concrete?*

You must mix the limeproof coloring matter into the cement during mixing. You must mix thoroughly to avoid streakiness. Actually, you should pass the dry cement and the coloring powder many times through a screen with 1/8 inch meshes for a good mix.

❰ *What kind of coloring agents can be used in concrete?*

Use only commercially pure mineral oxides. Mix no more than 10% pigment per total weight of cement. Pigment and aggregate should be mixed dry until the color is right. Try a test sample first.

❰ *What are the best pigments to use?*

Use the following:

Blues	Cobalt oxide
Browns	Brown oxide of iron
Buffs	Synthetic yellow oxide of iron
Greens	Chromium oxide
Reds	Red oxide of iron
Black, gray, slate	Black iron oxide
Clear white	White cement and white sand

There are commercial mixtures also available. Follow directions.

❰ *Is it necessary to have color all the way through the thick slab for a concrete driveway?*

No. The best thing to do with a driveway or a walk is to place all the walk up to 1 inch of the top surface in regular uncolored concrete. Let the concrete stiffen; then apply the colored top.

❰ *What is the usual mixture for colored concrete?*

1 part cement to 1 part sand. After mixing dry, add water, but not more than 5 gallons, to a sack of cement. Try to get the sand as nearly the color of the mixture as possible.

CONCRETE MAINTENANCE

❰ *How do you remove stains in concrete and cement?*

Since concrete is porous, stains do sink in. Removal of stains usually takes some time; you must allow the agent to act on the stains inside the cement.

How do you remove oil or grease from concrete?

Cover them with an inch or more of dry Portland cement and hydrated lime. Moisten the powder with benzene, and cover it with canvas. You can buy special absorbing materials, or you can scrub the surface with trisodium phosphate or washing soda—2 pounds to the gallon of water, followed by ample flushing with water.

How do you remove rust from cement?

Dissolve 1 part of sodium citrate in 6 parts of water and 6 parts of commercial glycerin. Mix a portion of this with enough powdered whiting, hydrated lime, or other absorbing powder to form a paste. Spread the paste on the stain in a thick coat. When dry, replace with fresh paste, or moisten it with the remaining liquid. This may take a week or more.

How do you remove copper and bronze stains from concrete?

Make a poultice of 1 part sal ammoniac and 4 parts whiting or some other absorbing powder. Moisten the surface with household ammonia. You will need several applications of this poultice to remove the stains.

How do you remove ink from concrete?

Make a poultice of sodium perborate, sodium hypochlorite, and household ammonia. Soak it into cotton batting or thick flannel, and put the cloth on the stain.

How do you remove soot or smut, as on the outside of a stucco chimney?

Make a solution of trisodium phosphate, ½ pound to the gallon of water, and apply it with a stiff scrubbing brush. Rinse. The solution will soften the paint and the stain. It should be kept away from all woodwork, however. Wash it off immediately.

14
Masonry

There is a special technique for laying a good brick wall, just as there is a best way for laying a good concrete block foundation. All masonry must be placed properly for maximum strength and permanence.

Tiles and flooring are frequently made of masonry. Since you sometimes find it expedient to re-lay a kitchen floor, or to re-tile a bathroom, you must know all the do's and don'ts of working with this kind of material.

If this seems to be man's work specifically, it doesn't have to be. A mason does not lift an entire wall of bricks: he lays them one at a time. You can easily handle one brick, and you'll be able to adjust and manipulate the brick easily before the mortar has set.

Plus which, if you know about brick-laying and masonry, you will be able to supervise a hired man at the job that much more confidently.

Masonry is not really as difficult as it seems. Try it and see.

Q & A

⟨ What are the main kinds of brick used in home construction?

The most common is the salmon-red brick which comes in three grades:

(1) Grade H (for hard) common brick is designed for extra weathering.

(2) Grade M (medium-hard) brick is usually referred to as "run-of-the-kiln" and consists of brick ranging from medium red to dark brownish red. Medium-hard brick is the kind mostly used in house construction. It withstands normal weathering very well.

(3) Grade S (soft) brick is light red in color and is quickly affected by severe weathering. Soft brick should never be used for outside construction unless covered with stucco or plaster. It is used mostly in interior work.

LAYING BRICK

❮ *Describe "face" brick.*

"Face" brick is another kind of brick. It has a facing color, or texture, highly resistant to weathering. It is similar enough to present an even and matched appearance when used for exterior facing, such as brick walls, fences, and so on. That is why it is called "face" brick.

❮ *What is the common size of bricks?*

Bricks are usually 3¾ inches wide, 2¼ inches thick, and 8 inches long.

❮ *What is fire brick?*

Fire brick is made from special high-temperature clay. It is used in chimneys, furnace fireboxes, fireplace linings, and wherever else fire resistance is needed. These bricks are 4½ inches wide, 2½ inches thick and 9 inches long. You must use special mortar in building up a masonry that withstands extreme heat and flame.

❮ *With bricks, what kind of mortar is generally used?*

Brick-laying mortar consists of 1 part Portland cement and 3 parts sand. This mix is used for underground masonry and for other work where dampness is present. It sets quickly.

❮ *What is cement-lime mortar?*

Cement-lime mortar sets slowly. It will not, however, contract in setting. It bonds more completely to brick, tile, and stone. The difference between cement-lime mortar and straight mortar is the proportion of lime; in cement-lime, lime comprises from 10 to 20 per cent of the cement.

❧ *What is straight-lime mortar?*

Straight-lime mortar is 1 part slaked or hydrated lime to 2½ parts sand.

❧ *How much mortar is needed to lay a brick?*

Using a ⅜-inch mortar joint, you will need 6 sacks, 6 cubic feet of cement, and 18 cubic feet of sand to lay 1000 bricks. If you wish, you can add 50 to 60 pounds of hydrated lime for a better bond.

❧ *For laying brick, what tools are necessary?*

(1) The *brick trowel* is used for laying work.

(2) The *buttering trowel* is small, and is used in cramped quarters where small areas must be mortared.

(3) The *pointing trowel* is the smallest of all, and is used for shaping joints between the brick and for cleaning off extra mortar.

(4) A brick hammer and a blocking chisel are used to break and split bricks that must be used to fit small spots.

(5) *Levels*, measuring tapes, and straight edges are also needed.

(6) A zig-zag rule should be available.

(7) You will also need a heavy piece of cord with two long metal spikes at each end to stick into the work to provide a horizontal guide.

❧ *How do you estimate the number of bricks needed for a particular wall?*

Figure the area of the wall in square feet. 22 bricks per square foot will be needed for a wall 12 inches thick. A handy rule-of-thumb is this: multiply the number of square feet by 21 in order to find out the number required.

❧ *Is it an easy job to lay brick?*

No. It is best to have a professional do your brick work. Many building codes will not permit you to lay brick. But you can build fences, outdoor barbecues, gateways, walks, and so on, using brick.

❧ *Describe the basic steps in laying brick.*

Wet down the bricks thoroughly. Soak them on all sides with water. Stretch a string straight along the line of the wall to guide you. "Butter" the footing or foundation for the brickwork with ¾ inch of mortar. Lay each brick in place, with the end that fits against the previous one well-buttered with the same thickness of mortar. The mortar should cover the end of the brick and overlap the edges. After you lay one full course, place the straight edge along it, with the level on top to judge whether the work is started correctly. If one brick is high, tap it into place. Lift out all low bricks, apply more mortar, and replace. If you are laying bricks in hot weather, be sure the bricks are periodically soaked in water. Cover the pile of wet bricks with a tarpaulin in order to slow down evaporation.

REPAIRING BRICK

❰ *How do you repair crumbling mortar in brickwork?*

Repair on brickwork is called "repointing." To repoint, first remove the old mortar. Chip it out to a depth of at least ¾ inch, but do not chip any of the brick. Clean the joint. Brush it off. Clean it with a stream of hose water. Now mix mortar in small quantities so that it is about as thick as caulking compound. Use Portland cement with 2 parts of fine sand, or use a prepared, pre-mixed mortar. Start at one end, and force the new mortar sideways into the joints with a pointing trowel. Hold a piece of wet burlap over the new joint, braced with a board. This will keep the mortar from drying out too fast. It should be protected from the sun's rays.

❰ *How do you fix a brick which is broken?*

If a brick is damaged, remove the whole brick by chipping it apart and pulling it out with a hammer. Wear goggles for your protection. Flush out the dust and debris with a stream of water. Soak a new brick in a bucket for 15 minutes, and then place it in the empty spot. Force ¾ inch of mortar around the space with a small trowel. Then push the new brick into the cavity. Even off all the mortar which is forced out. Cover the area with a wet piece of burlap to protect it from the sun.

CONCRETE BLOCK

❰ *Describe concrete block.*

Concrete block is 8 inches wide, 8 inches thick and 16 inches long. It is made out of concrete; it is hollowed out in places; and it is generally used for foundations.

❮ *How do you lay concrete block?*

You will need more mortar to lay concrete blocks than you do to lay bricks. Concrete block material is more porous. Never wet concrete blocks before laying them.

❮ *Do you need footings for concrete block as you do for bricks?*

No. Level the ground, and start the first course of block on the ground. Put mortar in between the blocks, and not on the bottom where the blocks touch the soil. Build up the foundation at the corners after the first course is laid; then fill in the center, one course at a time. Use a standard-mix mortar.

CLEANING BRICK

❮ *What is the best way to clean regular brick?*

Rent a portable sandblaster from a building supply dealer.

❮ *Is a sandblaster safe?*

You have to watch out for the fine dust which may blow into your eyes.

❮ *Can brick be waterproofed?*

Yes. Commercial waterproofing compound can be put on in two coats. If the first coat disappears immediately, apply a second coat until you get a slight luster on the surface of the brick. Do not apply so much that the brick becomes shiny.

CLEANING MASONRY

❮ *How can you clean a smoked and sooty brick fireplace surface?*

Use a stiff brush or steel wool and a scrubbing powder or paste containing grit. You can take off any traces of the cleaner with a rinsing of clear water.

❮ *How can you clean off a surface which won't respond?*

If the soiling is too deep, you will have to remove part of the brick surface with a carborundum block. This grinding will expose a brand new fresh and smooth surface. It's a rough job, however.

❰ Is there anything with which you can enrich a layer of brick?
Yes. Apply a soaking coat of raw linseed oil. It will improve the appearance and help keep the brickwork clean.

❰ What are the two kinds of ceramic tile used in homes?
Wall tile and floor tile.

❰ What distinguishes a wall tile from a floor tile?
A wall tile has a soft base. The color lies only on the surface and is usually protected with a glaze. Floor tiles are hard and colored throughout.

❰ For setting tile, what kind of a base must be used?
For floor tile, use a Portland cement mixture, 1 part cement, and 3 parts sand. For wall tile, use metal lath, with the cement mixture over that.

❰ How do you set wall tile?
Soak the tiles with water, and attach them one at a time with cement mortar spread on the backs. You can make any kind of pattern you want with different colors.

❰ How do you set inch-square floor tile?
(1) Inch-square floor tiles come pasted on sheets of paper. You must lay these groups on fresh cement with the paper up. You strip off the paper when the cement has hardened. After the tiles are set, you fill the joints by wiping the surface with cement mixed with water to the consistency of thick cream. Once the mixture settles into the joints, you wipe off the face of the tile while it is still wet. (2) Commercially inlaid tiles come now in foot-square sections. They are set in vinyl grout, and can be laid very simply on floors and on walls with mastic supplied by the manufacturer.

❰ What is crazing?
Crazing is a malady of tile distinguished by the development of a network of fine cracks in the surface. It is caused by a difference in the expansion of the tile and of its glaze.

❰ What causes wall tiles to fall out?

Faulty workmanship will do it, or the failure of the setter to soak the tiles before applying them. Or, there might have been too little cement on, or poor cement. Vibration and a weak foundation could also cause a tile to fall out.

❰ How do you replace a tile which has fallen out?

In replacing a tile which comes out, use a paste or a glue, not mortar. You can buy all sorts of adhesives for this purpose.

❰ How do you clean weathered spots off tile?

If the trouble comes from cement between the tiles, you can clean that by wiping with a bleaching liquid containing chlorine. You can also scrape out the cement with a thin-bladed tool, and fill the joints with a paste made of powdered zinc white and a little glycerin.

❰ In glazed tile, how can you change an unsatisfactory color?

It is impossible to change glazed tile. Paint or similar finish will not adhere.

❰ Can you change unglazed tile?

Sometimes you can change an unglazed floor tile to black or to a darker color by staining it with an aniline dye. One such dye is called "water-soluble nigrosine," and it will produce a very dark blue. Tannic chloride in tincture of iron will make a tile black. Test out these effects in an obscure corner before you try it on the whole floor.

REPAIRING MASONRY

❰ What causes tiles to shrink and draw away from fixtures?

Tiles cannot shrink. What happens is that wall tiling may draw away from a built-in bathtub or other fixture, because the wood beams at the end of the wall shrink or warp. This will leave large cracks at the end of the fixture near the tiles.

❰ Is it possible to remedy cracks in tiling?

You can get a waterproof cement that will adhere to enamel as well as to tiling. It is made of powdered litharge. Mix this with glycerin, and apply to the joint. Or, you can fill a broken or empty joint with caulking compound. First, clean out the crack. Then fill with oakum, and seal with caulking compound. Dust with talcum powder to take away the stickiness.

**(Can you lay tile to protect the floor under a kitchen range?*

Yes. Cover the area to be tiled with heavy tar paper or thin plywood. Secure the tiles to this, using tile cement. Protect the margins by quarterround molding nailed to the baseboard.

**(Is there any simple way to lay wall tile?*

There are several brands of ceramic tile now on the market which are made with an adhesive backing. All you do is pull off the wax paper, and apply the tile directly to the wall. Be sure you know exactly where to place the tile, however. It will stick for good when it goes up. Just follow the instructions.

**(How are steel tiles laid?*

A relatively new product on the market is a steel tile which comes with a permanent color and surface. These tiles are produced in standard sizes, and can be used for walls or floors. Steel tiles weigh more than ceramic tiles, however; be sure that your wall can support the load before you apply them. Steel tiles for the floor are laid over plywood or any other flat surface. Mastic is provided by the manufacturers; the tiles are laid over the mastic.

**(Describe how to lay aluminum tiles.*

Aluminum tiles are similar to steel tiles, except that they weigh less and can be applied to any wall or floor. These are laid with a mastic. Several brands are obtainable with adhesive already applied to the back. You pull off the wax paper, and stick it right onto the wall or floor.

15
Insulation

The key to good heating, good air conditioning, good sound conditioning, and good living is insulation. No matter how expensive your finishings are or how much money you put into materials, if your house isn't properly insulated, it won't be worth living in.

Bad insulation can cost you money, too, by raising your winter heat bills. It can cause you discomfort in the summer when your house becomes too steamy.

Where comfort and health are concerned, insulation is one of the most important things about your house. You should be sure that you have the best, and if you don't have the best, get the best. With electricity becoming more and more the chief source of power in the home, year-round electric heating and electric air conditioning will soon be the common thing. You should look ahead, and be sure that your insulation conforms to present standards, so you can enjoy the house of tomorrow.

Q & A

AIR MOVEMENT

⁋ *In what three main ways does heat escape from a house?*

By simple leakage of warmed air out; by conduction, which is the

Insulation

movement of heat through solid substances; and by air movement, in which warm air in circulation cools as it touches colder surfaces.

❪ Is it possible to stop this heat loss?
Yes. By insulation.

❪ In what manner does insulation material prevent the movement of heat through walls?
Air in repose is the best of all insulators. Most commercial insulating manufacturers make use of this fact and confine particles of air to small spaces: for instance, in wood fiber, in cork, in spongy material, and between matted fibers. Thus insulating arrests the flow of heat by conduction.

❪ Most insulation for the home is made of what kind of material?
Insulation is usually "mineral wool," made from rock, slag, or glass fibers.

❪ What happens when cold leaks into a warm home?
Once inside, cold air displaces the warm air, and forces the warm air to the sheltered side of the house. There, the warm air touches the cold wall surface and escapes by conduction or through joints and crevices.

❪ Most cold air leaks in through what points?
Cold air may blow in through joints and crevices near doors and windows, and near roof and floor joints.

"R" FACTOR

❪ Is it possible to measure the amount of resistance to heat flow in an insulating material?
Insulation engineers have devised a system of measuring by which an "R" number indicates the "installed resistance" of a given material. The greater the "R" number, the greater its insulating power.

❪ How much insulation is recommended in various parts of the modern home?
According to the National Mineral Wool Insulation Association,

the following ratings are excellent for a modern home, and can be used with electric heating: ceilings, R-19; walls, R-11; floors, R-13.

Can the "R" factor be translated into thickness in inches by a homeowner in order to find out the "R" rating of his own home?

Yes. For instance, tests have been made which show the following results. On the left is the type of insulation; in columns under the special "R" ratings is the thickness of each material by inches.

HOW TO TRANSLATE INCHES INTO NEW RESISTANCE ("R") FACTOR RATINGS

Installed Resistance Ratings

Type of material	R19	R13	R7
Mineral Wool Blanket	6"	3⅝"	2"
Mineral Wool Batting	6–6¼"	3⅝–4"	2–2⅜"
Balsam Wool Batting	5½"	3½"	2"
Glass Fiber Blowing Wool	6–6.7"	3⅝–4½"	2–2½"

WALL INSULATION

Can heat be lost directly through the walls of a house by conduction?

Yes. A frame house wall usually is built of two-by-four studs covered on the inside by dry-wall and on the outside by sheathing, building paper, and clapboards, shingles, brick, or stucco. Often cold wind blows through the outside cracks and conduction then pulls heat out through the drywall.

Is there any way to cut down this heat loss?

You can put on an outside "overcoat" of wood shingles, clapboards, masonry, or an extra layer of roofing felt.

How can you cut down heat loss by repairs from the inside?

Line the inside walls of your house with stiff sheets of insulating material, nailing it to the original surface.

Insulation

❰ When a space of wall becomes unlivable because of persistent cold, what can you do?

Hang a rug or a heavy curtain over it. The thickness of the fabric and the layer of air behind it will keep the chill from the rest of the room.

❰ Does heat loss through the roof constitute much of the total loss in a home?

About one-fifth of the heat lost in a home will be through the roof.

❰ Explain how to correct this condition.

Adequate insulation in the roof rafters or in the floor of the attic should correct this condition.

BUILDING INSULATION

❰ In what forms does insulation come?

It can be bought in the form of paper-covered batts and blankets; in the form of blowing and pouring wools; and in the form of rigid perimeter insulation.

❰ Where are batts and blankets usually used?

They are designed for use between floor joists, or beneath ceiling rafters. They can also be used for wall insulation, if they are installed during construction.

❰ Where is blowing and pouring wool usually used?

These mineral and wool pellets can be blown through a hose or poured from a bag into outside walls after construction, or they can be poured in crawl spaces or in unfinished attics between the ceiling joists.

❰ If the attic is open, how do you insulate?

Use batts, blankets, or pouring wools. Batts and blankets come in widths to fit a standard rafter space, which is usually 16 inches. You can staple them to the rafters with a staple gun; nail them with big-headed roofing nails; or suspend them by wires from one rafter to the next. Follow the instructions which come with the batts or blankets. A professional insulator can pour wool into your open attic spaces for you.

❲ Can blowing or pouring wools be used in an attic?

Certainly. Simply pour the wool into the spaces between the ceiling rafters of the room below. If you want the insulation in the roof rafters, nail plasterboard or wallboard to the underedges of the roof rafters and pour the loose insulation inside. Professionals can do this job for you.

❲ If the attic is only a crawl space, how do you insulate?

Use stiff sheets, nailing them to the upstairs ceiling and to the walls. Use two layers, giving you a thickness of ¾ to 1 inch.

❲ Can you insulate an unfinished attic which has no flooring?

Yes. Pour blowing insulation between the attic floor joists. You can also use batts or blankets, fastening them to the tops of the joists.

❲ Is it possible to insulate a completely sealed attic?

Yes. Blowing insulation may be forced in by professionals, in much the same way loose insulation can be blown into finished downstairs walls.

❲ Can a cement slab floor be insulated?

The best way to insulate a slab floor is to include a layer of insulating material when the floor is being poured. You can insulate an already laid floor by putting a damp-proof coating and a single or double thickness of insulating sheets on top, and covering it with flooring.

❲ Is it easy to insulate a wooden floor?

If the floor has a space beneath it, simply attach insulation batts between the floor joists. Or, nail stiff sheets of insulation under the joists. Cover the insulation with tarred or asphalted paper, or with felt, to protect it from dampness.

❲ Can the amount of moisture rising from underneath the floor be cut down?

Cover the ground with building paper, overlapping the strips by 6 inches or more. Or, lay plastic sheets on the ground in the crawl space beneath the floor.

Insulation

❨ Is it possible to insulate against dampness around the lower edges of a concrete floor?

Use perimeter insulation which is construction-type insulation. Lay planks of water-repellent plastic around the base of the concrete slab as a moisture preventive.

VAPOR BARRIERS

❨ What sometimes causes moisture to form on the inside of a wall?

Condensation occurs on the inside walls and the ceiling of a house when the warm moist air inside comes in contact with the cooler surface of the wall or the ceiling. Any water vapor in a house will condense on a cold surface; without proper insulation, an interior wall can be cooled by conduction.

❨ Is condensation on walls and ceiling dangerous?

Condensed vapor may freeze in wintertime. When ice melts, it will run into the insulation, which becomes damp and loses its insulating power. You may even have dripping on the attic floor as you might with an open leak.

❨ Do batts and blankets have vapor barriers attached?

Yes. Most have a vapor barrier on one side and a vapor-permeable material on the other.

❨ On which side of the wall should a vapor barrier be placed?

It should be placed on the warm (heated-in-winter) side of walls, ceilings, and floors.

❨ If vapor barriers are not provided with insulation, what kind of material on the other.

You can use: waterproofed laminated asphalt coated paper; polyethylene sheeting 2 mil or thicker in walls and ceiling, and 4 mil or thicker as ground moisture seals under slabs or over crawl space earth; foil-backed gypsum board; or similar films, sheets, or materials.

❨ Does blown insulation need a vapor barrier?

Yes. Apply continuous vapor barriers to the underside of ceiling joists and to the inside of wall studs. Bring the barrier up tight against electrical outlets, registers, door and window frames, and other similar openings.

❮❮ *If it is impossible to install a vapor barrier, can one be painted on an existing wall?*

Yes. Use two coats of good vapor-resistant paint.

VENTILATION

❮❮ *Do any structural situations contribute to condensation?*

Yes. Completely airtight construction in the roof sheathing causes condensation. A looser construction with small holes would allow vapor to escape to the outside.

❮❮ *Can a roof of wood shingles built on open-shingle lath cause condensation?*

No. In this case, there is enough porousness in the materials to allow the moisture-laden air to escape.

❮❮ *Is it advisable to seal off an attic air space at the top to prevent condensation?*

Absolutely not. You should thoroughly ventilate that air space the year round by louvers at each end and as near the peak of the roof as possible.

❮❮ *What size should the louvers be?*

Have at least 1 square foot of louver opening for each 300 square feet of insulated floor space.

❮❮ *Can vapor be prevented from entering through a wall?*

Apply two coats of aluminum paint to the plaster or drywall material. Conceal this aluminum paint by house paint or wallpaper. This aluminum barrier will prevent moisture from coming through the wall.

❮❮ *Is it possible to control the humidity inside a house?*

You can if you use a humidifier and a de-humidifier. Indoor humidities should be kept within certain limits: with the outside temperature below 0, the inside relative humidity should not be more than 20%; with the outside temperature 0-20 above, the relative humidity should not be more than 30%; with outside 20 above and over, the relative humidity should not be more than 40%.

(For what reason is metal-foil insulation used?

Metal foil checks the passage of heat by reflecting heat waves back to the source.

(How is metal foil usually applied to walls?

You can obtain stiff insulating boards with one side covered by foil. Or you can obtain building felt with a foil backing. You can also obtain insulating batts, covered with foil on both sides.

(In what direction should the metal foil be placed?

You should place the metal foil so that the foil side faces in the direction of the heat to be reflected across an air space.

(How are stiff sheets of insulation usually used?

You use them as sheathing boards or in place of lath. These sheets are usually 4 feet by 8 feet and are sawed, nailed, and handled as lumber.

(What is the value of building paper and building felt?

Because of their thinness, paper and felt have no value as insulation. They are, however, useful when added to insulation in order to provide a vapor barrier.

16

Air Conditioning

With comfort and health becoming more and more a must in the modern home, air conditioning has come into its own for use in private dwellings. At one time confined to large industrial plants, to hotels and motels and motion picture theaters, air conditioning has become as much a necessity in the home as a television set or a refrigerator.

There are many different kinds of household air conditioning units. Some are small, and can be installed in a room window in a matter of hours for use during the summer months. Others are large enough to air condition the second floor of a two-story house. Still others can air condition an entire house.

There are problems involved with the use of air-conditioners, and these problems should be understood before the homeowner decides to put in a unit. A fundamental comprehension of exactly how an air-conditioning unit works and what kind of maintenance is expected will make you more sure of yourself when you begin shopping around.

Q & A

COOLING THEORY

❰ *What effects does a well-functioning air-conditioning unit perform?*
It maintains a desired air temperature; it holds the amount of

humidity in the air to a comfortable ratio; it provides proper air motion and distribution of air; it gives sufficient outside air for ventilation purposes; and it removes by filter all dust particles and lint which are suspended in the air.

❰ *How does an air-conditioning unit perform these functions?*

It contains a cooling coil which cools the air; it removes excess humidity from the air with a condenser; it has a fan to circulate the air; it uses outside air to carry away heat drawn from the inside air; and it has a filter to remove dust and filth.

❰ *Are there heater-air-conditioner setups which warm the house in the winter and cool it in the summer?*

A genuine heater-air-conditioner plant will do both. A house must be completely insulated to use a heater-air-conditioner plant efficiently.

❰ *What is a British Thermal Unit?*

A British Thermal Unit, or BTU, is a unit of heat used by air-conditioning engineers to measure amounts of heat moved by a refrigeration unit. A BTU is the amount of heat to be added or removed in order to raise or lower the temperature of one pound of water by one degree Fahrenheit. It is roughly equivalent to the amount of heat given off by an old-fashioned wooden kitchen match.

❰ *About how many BTU's of heat can a 1-ton air-conditioning unit remove from a room?*

One ton of cooling capacity will move roughly 12,000 BTU's per hour. Two tons of cooling capacity will move roughly 24,000 BTU's per hour.

❰ *How much insulation is required to keep an air-conditioner working at efficient capacity?*

A good combination is 6 inches of insulation in the ceiling, and 3 or 4 inches in the walls, with a vapor barrier of aluminum foil or other suitable material to keep out the moisture. You should have 2 inches of insulation under the floor, unless your house is built on a slab. Storm windows or double-glazing in glass areas can be quite helpful.

❨ For cutting down radiant heat gain through windows and glass areas, what is the best thing to do?

Use draperies and venetian blinds. Awnings are even better. A generous overhang on southern exposures can help, as can a well-ventilated attic space and a light-colored roof.

❨ Is it possible to cut down on air leakage through door jambs, cracks and window sashes?

Yes. Use weatherstripping and caulking to tighten your house.

❨ Can air-conditioning units be installed independently of hot water, steam, or other types of heating systems?

Yes. You can install either an independent duct system, or a single package unit which feeds directly into existing ductwork.

❨ What size of air-conditioning unit can take care of a 6-room house?

Figure that 12,000 BTU's per hour can handle anything up to 600 square feet of home space. A one-story, 6-room house, 28 by 40 feet, would probably require a 24,000 BTU rated system under normal conditions. For 12,000 BTU's that would be a 1-ton unit, which would be rated at about 1200 watts, and would use a 1⅕-horsepower motor.

❨ Can you equate horsepower, tonnage, watts, amperes, and BTU's?

Yes. Tonnage is a measure of air-conditioning capacity, in the same way that horsepower is a measure of motor capacity. A 1-horsepower air-conditioning motor draws about 1000 watts of power. A 1-horsepower compressor motor will produce roughly 5/6 ton of cooling capacity; it will take 1/5 horsepower to produce 1 ton. On a 120-volt circuit, 1200 watts (1/5 x 1000) would be roughly equivalent to 10 amperes of current. So a compressor motor 1/5 horsepower in capacity is needed to perform 1 ton of air-conditioning capacity, or to remove 12,000 BTU's of heat an hour; it would draw 10 amperes of current and consume 1200 watts, or use 1.2 KWH of power in so doing.

AIR-CONDITIONERS

❨ Name the two types of air-conditioning equipment available.

Air-cooled, and water-cooled. Air-cooled conditioners are the ones

Air Conditioning

generally used in homes today; water-cooled conditioners are used for larger buildings and in commercial establishments.

❰ Are there two main sizes of air-conditioners available?

Yes. There are single-room units and full-house units.

❰ Of what does a full-house air-conditioning unit consist?

A full-house unit consists of a condenser coil, a compressor, a fan, refrigerant lines, a cooling coil, and a duct system carrying the cool air to each room.

❰ How much voltage does a full-house air-conditioning unit require?

Usually a 240-volt line will operate the 230-volt rated motor that runs the compressor and fan. In an older house, a special electric circuit must be installed to carry the air-conditioning unit.

❰ Is it possible to add an air-conditioning unit to a forced hot-air system in a house?

Yes. The conversion unit is installed to include condenser coil, compressor, and blower fan. The furnace may also be removed, and new ductwork and a combustion heater-cooler package installed. You may install a new conversion unit to dispense cool air above the jacket area of a warm-air furnace.

❰ How does an air-conditioner work?

Freon gas, similar to the freezing gas in a refrigerator, is forced under compression into a series of pipes. Air circulates about the pipes at room temperature. Because the Freon under pressure is hotter than the outdoor air, the heat escapes from the Freon into the outer air. When the Freon travels to a condensation chamber, the air pressure becomes much less, and the Freon cools considerably. Air from the room to be cooled moves over the outside of the condensation chamber, losing its heat to the Freon in the condensation chamber. Moisture from the wet indoor air condenses on the outside of the condensation chamber as it cools. A fan blows the cooled, de-humidified air back into the room from which it came, through a filter. The warmed-up decompressed Freon gas is pushed back into the compression chamber, where it heats to travel through the same cycle again.

❡ *Will all air-conditioners work on the regular 120-volt AC household current?*

Not all. Most ½- and some ¾-ton units will operate on a 120-volt AC current, but the air-conditioner should be on a separate 15 ampere circuit all by itself.

❡ *How are the bigger units handled?*

Most ¾-, 1-, and 2-ton units operate on 240 volts only. An air-conditioner that size needs a special wiring circuit which must be installed by a licensed electrician.

❡ *Is it best to place the air-conditioning unit in a sunny window?*

No. To be completely successful, a window air-conditioning unit should be placed on the shady side of the house. Direct sunlight makes the unit less efficient. You can always shade the unit with an awning, or plant a tree nearby to cut off the sun's rays.

❡ *Where should the air-conditioning unit be placed in relation to the room which it cools?*

It should be as far from a door or other entrance to the room as possible. Drafts and cross ventilation carry away good, clean, cool air before it has a chance to circulate in the room. Place no obstructions in front of the unit. Hang drapes and curtains away from the outlet vents.

❡ *Which way should the vents of the air-conditioner be placed?*

They should be placed so that the cool air blows up, and does not come directly out into the room. Cool air descends; if it is forced high, it cools more area as it falls.

❡ *Must special attention be paid to doors and windows in a room with an air-conditioner in it?*

All doors and other windows must be weatherstripped to insure a tight seal. Otherwise, excess humidity and heat will enter and cut down the air-conditioning machine's efficiency.

❡ *Is it necessary to curtain off windows which are exposed to the sun in a room being air-conditioned?*

Yes. Drapes should be placed not only to cut off the sunlight,

Air Conditioning [203

which will warm the room, but also to halt conduction of heat from outside-in through the glass windows.

❴ In the circuit supplying power to an air-conditioner, what size wire should be used?

The Electric Code requires that air-conditioners be wired with No. 12 wire. Most houses are wired with No. 14. If you are planning to have a large air-conditioner installed, you should consult an electrical engineer and have him suggest changes in your wiring circuits. Then a professional electrician should install the circuit.

❴ For air-conditioners, what kind of fuses are necessary?

At the moment an air-conditioner starts up, the electric motor often draws three times the current it uses later. This quick large drain may burn out an ordinary fuse before the motor settles down to a normal running load. Because of this, it is suggested you use Fustat, Therm-a-Trip, or Temre fuses, which you can get at your hardware store. This type of fuse is a special time-delay fuse. It will permit an overload for a certain specified time, which will be too short a time to allow the wires to heat too much, but will permit the motor to start. If there is an actual short circuit or a malfunctioning motor, the fuse will burn out after the delay.

MOUNTING AIR-CONDITIONERS

❴ In what kind of windows is it easiest to install an air-conditioner?

Double-hung are the most common windows in the average home. Most air-conditioning units are made to fit them. But casement windows can be used too. Units are specially built for casements.

❴ Is there anything to be especially careful about when shopping for an air-conditioner?

Yes. First you should measure your window carefully. You should know the measurement across the window from stop to stop. Some air-conditioning machines are larger than others. You should know your window width to insure buying the right sized unit.

❴ How do you mount an air-conditioner in a double-hung window?

Many units come with mounting kits. Others are constructed in such a way that mounting kits are unnecessary. Some have mounting boards which must be fitted around the unit. Others supply rubber channel strips. And, some come with accordion-type sides which stretch out to be bolted to the window stops on the two sides.

❊ Can a window air-conditioner be used to cool more than one room?

Yes. If the capacity of the unit, usually measured in square feet of area, is enough to cool the area of two adjacent rooms, all you have to do is to be sure the two rooms are sealed off from the rest of the house. The unit will condition air from both rooms.

❊ What is a console-type air-conditioner?

A console is a window-type unit. It stands on the floor in front of the window, and draws air from the window. It exhausts the hot air from its condenser coils into the outside air.

❊ How do you store an air-conditioner for the winter?

Store it in a storage room or basement. First, remove it from the window and tighten down the shipping bolts — if there are any — to keep the compressor from damage. Thoroughly clean the unit, removing all dust with a brush, and taking out debris from the motor, the frame, the compressor, and the coil. Remove the filter, and clean it. Cover the case with plastic or canvas, and strap it up.

❊ Explain how you ready it up for use again in the summer.

Check it for worn belts, broken or leaking joints, bent fan blades, and loose bolts. Oil the fan motor according to directions. Start the unit, and run it at the lowest thermostat setting for an hour before putting a full load on the compressor.

❊ For how long are most compressor units guaranteed?

Most air-conditioners are guaranteed for five years, in much the same way a refrigerator is guaranteed. But it is a good idea to check the fan motor occasionally, and to see that the coils are not being overheated or damaged by excessive vibration.

17

Sound Conditioning

Apart from the purely unpleasant effect of excessive noise, psychologists claim that strident sounds can give headaches, can make babies cry, and can cause animals to run. The clangor of traffic drives people away from huge urban complexes to quiet suburban areas in our day.

And yet, once in your own private home in the suburbs, you may find as much noise present as in a city apartment. Traffic sounds, airplanes overhead, dogs barking, babies crying, children screaming at play: all these things follow you wherever you go.

In the modern world, with its ever-present tensions and anxieties, your home should be as quiet and as remote from the hustle-bustle of the world as possible. You deserve a quiet home, or at least an isolated room to which you can retire for relaxation, shut off from the cacophony and strife of living.

While mainly theoretical, the following chapter outlines some of the advantages you can get from a partial acoustical repair job on your present home. If you plan to build a place of your own, it will give you invaluable tips to follow in cutting down noise.

Q & A

QUIET, PLEASE

(*How can you build a house which cuts out all outside noise?*
The best way is to build a completely insulated home.

❲ *In noise control, what is the main problem?*

The main problem is in selecting a system that will reduce all sound to a level where it can be tolerated by the human ear.

❲ *List the three primary sound control problems.*

(1) You must have complete acoustical control inside a room. In other words, you must be able to absorb and contain all the noise which originates in a room. (2) You must have air-borne sound control. In other words, you must be able to stop noise from being transmitted from room to room through walls, floors, or ceilings. (3) You must have impact sound control. In other words, you must be able to eliminate all structurally-borne sound like tappings through floors and ceilings.

❲ *Sound is measured in what way by sound engineers?*

In decibels. The more decibels you have, the louder the sound being measured.

❲ *How do sound engineers measure the amount of sound stoppage achieved by insulated walls, floors, or ceilings?*

Sound stoppage is called transmission loss, or decibel loss, by sound engineers.

❲ *Can resistance to sound be measured in units?*

Sound engineers have devised a unit to measure resistance to sound in a given material. It is called STC, or Sound Transmission Class.

❲ *For the sake of practical comparison, what is a high decibel rating?*

130 is a high decibel rating. For instance, you get 130 decibels when you are listening to a bass drum being pounded three feet from your ear. Thunder achieves about 120 decibels. A symphony orchestra, a stereo set, a cocktail party, or a washer-dryer, will rate about 80 or 90 decibels.

❲ *What is a low decibel rating?*

A private office, or a quiet home in which a quiet conversation can be held, will run between 20 to 35 decibels. Rustling leaves, and a truly sound-proof room, will give about 10 to 20 decibels.

"STC" RATINGS

◖ A loud STC rating would be about how high?

In a noisy house in which you can hear conversation clearly through a wall, the STC is about 25. In a house in which you can hear loud speech through a wall, the STC is about 30. At STC 35, you can hear the speech, but it is not intelligible. At STC 42, you hear only a murmur.

◖ What do sound engineers consider a quiet STC rating?

At STC 45, you have to strain to hear loud speech through a wall. At STC 48, loud speech is barely audible. And finally, at STC 50, it is really quiet, and you can hear nothing but the faintest sound from the outside world.

◖ Which sounds are easier to stop — high frequency sounds or low frequency sounds?

It is easier to stop low frequency sounds. One wall might blot out human voices, which are of low frequency—but not stop sounds made by a passing truck, which is a high frequency squeal.

◖ How do decibel ratings and STC affect each other?

If you improve the decibel rating of a room by 3, you reduce its sound transmission by 50%. If you reduce the decibel rating by 3, the noise transmission goes up 50%.

◖ In accomplishing acoustical control, that is, in absorbing noise within a room, what are the main kinds of materials used?

You can use acoustical ceiling tile made either of wood or of mineral-fiber composition. Rugs, draperies, and upholstered furniture will also help.

◖ How much sound does the average acoustical tile ceiling blot up?

About 70% of the noise in a room can be controlled by an acoustical tile ceiling. By dropping the tiles a little lower, you will quiet the room proportionately that much more.

◖ Can you control the sound flowing between rooms?

You must use special wall, ceiling, and floor construction.

❡ Will acoustical tile keep sound from traveling out of one room into another?

No. Acoustical tile is effective only in the room where it is used. It does not keep sound from going into another room.

❡ What kind of acoustical control materials are used in wall construction?

Acoustical plaster can be used. Its rate of absorption is about the same as acoustical tile. But it is usually more expensive than tile.

❡ How is air-borne sound between rooms controlled?

Sound between rooms can be deadened by special materials in the wall, used in combination with gypsum wallboard. Noise transmission between walls, floors, and ceilings can be cut down in the same manner.

❡ What is the sound transmission of the average gypsum plaster on lath wall built with 2" x 4" studs?

The STC is about 38. You can hear loud speech through a wall of this consistency, but it is not particularly distinguishable.

❡ In wall construction, how can an acceptable rating in STC be achieved?

Sound engineers deem an STC of 46 or thereabouts "acceptable," in wall construction. Such a wall can be built with 2" x 4" studs and plates, with a ½-inch thickness of gypsum wallboard.

❡ Is there any other way to achieve a better STC rate?

If the studs are staggered — in other words, if the west wall is attached to studs 1, 3, 5, 7, and so on, and the east wall is attached to studs 2, 4, 6, 8, and so on — the STC is reduced considerably with sound deadening board also used. Glass fiber insulation inside the wall will reduce the STC.

❡ How is impact sound control improved?

The amount of noise transmitted through floors and through the house itself can be reduced by the wall-building techniques mentioned above, and also by the use of insulation on floors and ceilings. The addition of a 5/8-inch thick plywood subfloor can help. On the ceiling side, the addition of resilient ceiling clips to which wallboard is applied can help.

❨ *In an already existant house, can many of these improvements be made?*

It is economically impractical to tear out walls and floors in order to soundproof them. The best thing to do is to install ceiling acoustical tile wherever you think it will cut down the inside noise of a room.

TROUBLE SPOTS

❨ *In the average house, what are the basic trouble spots?*

Kitchens, utility rooms, and laundries are real trouble spots. These rooms all should have acoustical ceiling tile and sound-deadening insulation board in the walls; they should be closed off by means of solid-core doors with gaskets at the edges. In a kitchen, you should apply tile to the underside of the overhead cabinets. All kitchen equipment should be purchased with sound-control devices incorporated in the working parts.

❨ *In furnace rooms and laundries, what should be done with the equipment?*

All washing machines and furnaces should be mounted on sound-isolating pads. Line the room with acoustical material, and close it off with a tight-fitting door. Sound-trap furnace ducts to keep noise from filtering up through the heat registers. The same precautions should be taken with the plumbing.

❨ *What should be done to cut down noise from electric switches and wiring?*

They should be padded with resilient material to reduce noise. Never place switches back-to-back in a wall or in the same stud space.

❨ *For a bathroom, what is the "ideal" acoustical control?*

The bathroom ceiling should have plastic-coated acoustical tile or luminous lay-in panels. The ball and valve assembly in a toilet tank should be quiet.

❮ *For a basement stairway, what is the "ideal" acoustical control?*

The underside of the stairway should be covered with sound-deadening board. The wall from ceiling to stair should be covered with sound-deadening board.

❮ *Is there an "ideal" acoustical control for a bedroom?*

A bedroom should have sound-deadening board on its walls.

❮ *How about the average kitchen?*

The walls should be covered with sound-deadening board. The ceiling should be covered with acoustical tile. The dishwasher should be "quiet." The disposal should be double-trapped. The air chamber in the cold-water supply should be deadened to stop the hammering. All kitchen exhaust fans should be controlled from outside.

❮ *Is there an "ideal" acoustical control for a garage?*

The garage door should be mounted on nylon rollers. The ceiling and duct work in the garage should be covered with sound-deadening board and gypsum wallboard.

❮ *What is the ideal acoustical control for a utility room?*

All inside frame walls and the ceiling should be covered with sound-deadening board. The main ducts of the furnace should be insulated. The lavatory and the basement should have sound-deadening boards on walls and ceiling.

❮ *For a basement room, what is the "ideal" acoustical control?*

Ceiling tile could be installed for sound control.

❮ *Can added quiet be achieved between levels?*

You can get an STC of 53 (superior) by suspending flooring with resilient clips and placing carpeting over the plywood subfloor.

❮ *Are there any rules to follow in selecting materials for general construction?*

Wood, hollow block, and concrete all have inherent acoustical properties which are desirable. Use them as much as possible.

❮ *How do these materials compare when used in a walls?*

A wall made of 2" x 4" studs with a ½-inch gypsum wallboard on both sides has an STC rating of 37. A wall made of ¾-inch plaster on both sides of 3¼-inch steel studs has an STC rating of 34. A wall made of 8-inch dense aggregate hollow block (concrete blocks) has an STC rating of 49.

❊ *How do these materials compare when used in floors?*

A floor made of 6-inch reinforced concrete slab, with two coats of plaster, and a ⅝-inch mastic asphalt surface, has an STC rating of 50. A floor made of 2" x 8" wood joists, a ¾-inch subfloor, building paper, a ¾-inch finish floor, and a ½-inch GWB ceiling, has an STC rating of 36.

INSTALLING CEILING

❊ *How do you install an acoustical ceiling?*

There are many different types. Generally, the system involves using lightweight metal furring and edge strips to which squares of various sizes can be attached. Some tiles snap into place, requiring no stapling, nailing, or gluing. Without furring, plastic tile can simply be stapled, nailed, or glued. There are also large ceiling planks which can be applied with adhesives of various kinds.

❊ *How effective is acoustical ceiling?*

It will absorb 70% of the room noise in which it is installed. It will not, however, take care of air-borne sound or impact sound.

❊ *Is it possible to apply acoustical ceiling tile to open framing?*

Yes. Open framing requires furring-strip application, both in remodeling and in new construction. You can apply tiles to wood furring strips with staples, with nails, with special clips, or sometimes just snap them on.

❊ *What is the best way to apply acoustical tiles to a ceiling which is in poor condition?*

Use wood furring strips, nailing the furring through the ceiling finish into the ceiling joists.

❊ *If a ceiling is in good shape, what kind of hanging do you use?*

Where a continuous ceiling is sound and in good condition, you may apply your tile with adhesive. However, if in any spot in the ceiling is not level, you should use furring-strip application.

❮ When using square individual tiles for a ceiling, how do you start to lay out your ceiling?

You must plan the entire ceiling before you start, making sure that off-size tile borders are of equal widths on opposite sides of the ceiling. Draw your ceiling design on a piece of graph paper with one square indicating a square foot: it will give you a good idea of how the finished ceiling will look.

❮ Is there any way to make an irregularly-shaped ceiling come out right?

Plan your tiles so that their best appearance occurs in the largest ceiling area; let the smaller areas come out the way they will. See the pictures on page 134.

❮ Describe in step-by-step terms the hanging of a ceiling with tile clips.

Locate the center of the ceiling, the spot equidistant from east and west walls and from north and south walls. Apply furring strips to the framing or the old ceiling surface. At right angles to these strips, nail 1" x 3" wood furring strips from which to hang the tiles. If 12-inch tiles are used, locate the furring strips 12 inches apart from center to center; for 16-inch tiles, 8 inches on center. Draw a chalk line on the center furring strip to guide application of the first tile row. Nail a straight-edged board along the chalk line over the furring strip, leaving a crack between the straight edge and the furring strip. The straight edge will guide your first row of tile. Place clips on all four edges of one tile. After the first row is hung, only two clips will be used on each tile. To apply the first tile, butt the grooved edge of the tile against the straight-edged board. Nail the exposed clips in place, using 2d box or blued lath nails. Start application in the center of the room, according to your lay-out plan. Complete one row of tile against the straight edge. After the last tile of the first row, the positioning of the other tiles will be automatic. Remove the straight edge, and tile the rest of the ceiling, working out from the laid row. Where the tile rows meet the wall edge, allow a ¼-inch space between the last tile and the wall for expansion purposes. Face-nail the tiles along this edge, and later cover the face-nailing and expansion space with molding. (When cutting tile at the border or around light fixtures, use a handcutter. Always make cuts with the decorated tile surface facing up.)

❡ *What is the procedure for hanging acoustical tiles with nails or staples?*

Mark out the ceiling and apply the furring as before. Do not start applying tile in the center of the ceiling, but measure the strips and cut your border tiles to fit. Start hanging tiles in the corner. Only in this way can you get the proper room to staple corner tiles. Then work out from the corner, following a chalk line.

❡ *What are the special requirements for use of adhesive on acoustical tile?*

To use adhesive to hang ceiling tile, you must have a solid plaster base in the ceiling; your ceiling must be completely level; and wallpaper or calcimine must be removed.

❡ *Explain how to hang a ceiling using adhesive on acoustical tile.*

Lay out your ceiling as before, planning the location of each tile. Nail a straight edge in the center of the ceiling. The first row of tiles will go against this straight edge. Remove tiles from the cartons the day before you work with them in order to let them adjust to the atmosphere. Open the can of adhesive. Apply dabs of adhesive to the back side of an adhesive tile in its four corner spots. Dabs should be placed about 1½ inches from the tile edge at the corners. Each dab should be big enough to cover about a 2½-inch diameter when flattened out to a ⅛-inch thickness. A dab of adhesive 1 cubic inch in size is recommended. A gallon of adhesive will cover 40 to 45 square feet of ceiling of 12" x 12" tile. Use 6 dabs for a 12" x 24" tile, and 8 for a 16" x 16" tile. To determine if the adhesive bonds well, apply one tile, and slide it back and forth slightly under uniform pressure to obtain a good contact. Then pull it down. The adhesive should separate, leaving part on the tile and part on the ceiling base. Now attach your first tile, with the groove edge butting the straight edge. Apply with a slight weaving motion, using uniform pressure. Then apply the tiles adjacent, one by one, until you have finished the ceiling. Leave the usual ¼-inch expansion space at the wall's edge and cover it with cove molding.

18

New Developments in Home Repair

Advances in technology are being made every day and many of these developments are incorporated in products marketed to help the homeowner perform household repairs. Since the first edition of this book was published, many products have appeared that will speed up and simplify some of the repairs discussed in the previous chapters.

New products appear in the sections ahead in a sequence which corresponds to the earlier chapters of this book. For instance, new products in painting appear first, followed by new products in hardware fasteners, wood, plumbing, and so on.

Q & A

PAINTING

❮ How can you paint a ceiling without dripping and dribbling paint all over yourself?

Use a dripless paint roller. The handle of the roller is hollow, acting as a reservoir which will hold enough paint to coat seventy

New Developments in Home Repair [215

square feet of ceiling before refilling. Light pressure on the handle forces paint through the roller's perforated core and flows it onto the surface.

❴ Is there any way to remove paint without using liquid remover?

There is available an electrically operated heating unit that works on ordinary house current. The unit generates intense heat and concentrates it on a small painted area, softening up the coating so you can scrape it off easily.

❴ How can you keep paint from chipping off a radiator in the winter?

Get heat-resistant paint that will withstand temperatures up to 1,000° F. You can buy it in an aerosal can. Apply it to radiators, furnaces, heat ducts, and barbecue grills; heat will not cause it to peel.

❴ Is there any kind of paintbrush made that won't tire your hand?

A new design in paint brushes features a "pistol-grip," developed to fit the hand in a natural way and to avoid the fatigue and the so-called "painter's cramp." These brushes come in 3- and 4-inch widths.

❴ How can you repaint an old kitchen appliance to make it look new?

Try spray-on epoxy enamel that has been developed to afford more adhesion to metal and porcelain surfaces than normal enamel. Epoxy enamel resists detergents, chemicals, alkalis, and bleaching agents such as chlorox; it is waterproof and peel-proof, and can be applied from an aerosol can.

HARDWARE

❴ How do you keep nuts and bolts from loosening in a home appliance?

Simply tighten the nut or bolt firmly with a wrench and apply two or three drops of shellac onto the threads that protrude from the nut. The nut will never shake loose from vibration. When you want to take it off, simply use a little extra pressure on the wrench or screwdriver.

TOOLS

❪ Is there any kind of measuring tape that doesn't break your back when you try to get accurate measurements on the floor or in some out-of-the-way place?

A new tape-less rule has been made to avoid stooping fatigue. It is a device with a wheel on the end of a long telescopic handle capable of extending to 44 inches. You roll the wheel over linear, curved, and irregular surfaces to get accurate readings on an odometer-type dial in the wheel.

ADHESIVES

❪ What's the quickest way to repair a burst, frozen water pipe?

Use an "instant" epoxy cement that has been developed; it takes only five minutes to set and will harden even at 0° F. It will adhere to iron, steel, aluminum, bronze, brass, porcelain, glass, wood, and cement. To use: squeeze the two separate components out, mix them thoroughly, and apply to the object to be repaired.

❪ Is there a special kind of adhesive that holds down carpeting?

There are adhesives for every kind of carpet application: rubber-backed carpeting; indoor/outdoor carpeting; sponge-bonded or foam-backed carpeting; foam-, sponge-, or urethane foam-backed carpeting; carpet tiles; and so on. These adhesives will fasten carpeting to wooden floors, concrete floors, sub-surfaces, or tile floors.

PLUMBING

❪ Is there any quick way to thaw out a frozen pipe?

Use a handy little infra-red heat bulb that operates on regular house current in an ordinary heat-lamp fixture. It is only 3¾ inches in diameter, is rated at 200 watts, and has a built-in silver reflector. You can use it for drying paint, too, and for defrosting the refrigerator.

❪ What's the best way to repair a leaky pipe instantly?

A self-sticking all-purpose tape is now available. The flexible, foamed-plastic material has a smooth-surface finish. You remove the release backing when the tape is applied. And the tape is so treated that condensation of moisture is prevented from forming on the tape.

❮ How can you stop excessive toilet noise?

If the noise is caused by a leaky float, either replace it or try a newly developed ball cock that works by hydraulic water pressure rather than by leverage. This unit is made of plastic and stainless steel and won't corrode.

HEATING

❮ How can you install permanent electric heating in a room without breaking the walls or floors which is required by the conventional radiant heating?

A new single-layer, radiant-heat, dry-wall ceiling system has been developed to be installed with conventional wallboard hanging techniques—from the ceiling. Each panel is self-enclosed, with a separate heating unit, yet all panels are controlled by a single thermostat. Panels come in several models and sizes.

FLOORS

❮ Can you change a light-colored wood floor to a darker color without removing the finish and repainting?

Yes. Use a new penetrating finish-and-wax developed for just this purpose. You simply sand the floor and apply two coats of the finish, then, twenty-four hours later, apply a paste-finishing wax that goes with the wood finish. You'll have a darker color and a more durable surface.

❮ Is it possible to get an "instant" floor cleaner?

The nearest thing to it is a type of foam cleaner available in an aerosol can. You shoot it onto the floor and then wipe up the foam with a sponge, mop, or cloth. Five minutes after you have cleaned the floor you can walk on it. This foam can be used on vinyl, vinyl asbestos, asphalt tile, rubber tile, or linoleum.

❮ What do you do to snap up a tile surface that has worn away?

Use an epoxy-type coating, which comes as a two-component mix. Use it on wood, metal, masonry, or plastic surfaces. When it hardens, it duplicates the original tile surface and is resistant to acids, alkalis, chemical fumes, and salt water.

❬ How do you clean the grout between ceramic tiles when that dirty gray film comes on and won't scrub off with powders or detergents?

A paste-form tile cleaner will do the trick. Apply the paste with a sponge, let it stay on a few minutes, and then rinse it off. It won't discolor porcelain enamel, and you can use it in the kitchen, the bathroom, and even in an outdoor swimming pool.

❬ Is there any kind of waterproof house carpeting that you can lay in a simple manner?

Many firms make carpet "tiles"—usually 12-inch-square pieces—that can be laid square by square. This type of carpeting usually has a latex foam-rubber base, is mildew-proof, stain-resistant, and moisture-proof. The tiles can be laid in kitchen, bathroom, and even in the basement, in addition to the livingroom, bedroom, and hallway.

You lay all the tiles down, starting from the center of the room, and then cut them at the wall joints to fit. Afterward, install the tiles in one quarter of the room, using either adhesive or double-faced tape. You can lay these pieces without the complicated kind of tools you would need in a conventional carpet-laying situation. A carpet tile can be replaced easily in case one is permanently damaged in any way.

❬ Are "outdoor" carpets any good?

The "outdoor" carpet is a new development that has proved itself in the long run. It is made from synthetic materials that are impervious to moisture, sunlight, and rotting. It is for use around swimming pools, on terraces, patios, and sun decks. Many outdoor carpets have backings of embossed foam rubber; this backing adds to resiliency and makes the carpeting "non-skiddable." It also gives it "dimensional stability" so that it will not expand and contract as temperature and humidity vary. Also, seams will not open up, and you won't get ripples or puckers. The backing keeps the unbound edges from unraveling. The backing of the carpet should be made of material that will resist mildew—something like polypropylene. Some outdoor carpets are needle-bonded, a process that makes the surface look like felt. Others are tufted to look like ordinary carpets.

New Developments in Home Repair [219

❰ Can you use an "outdoor" carpet indoors?

Many "outdoor" carpets are now used indoors in tough-wear situations, for basements, playrooms, kitchens, and bathrooms. In fact, you can usually get special high-density foam-rubber backings on outdoor carpets for use indoors. This 3/16-inch backing gives you greater resilience and comfort, but you cannot use this type outdoors because it will hold water if saturated. So, carpeting for outdoor use should be outdoor/outdoor carpeting, not indoor-use/outdoor carpeting.

❰ When concrete floors crack, how can you fill in the holes?

To fill cracks in concrete slabs and basement floors, usually caused by settling, apply an ordinary patching cement. Mix the patching cement with water to the proper consistency, and then push the mixture down into the crack, leveling the surface with a wooden spatula or regular mason's trowel.

❰ Is there any way to remove rust from concrete or stone?

There is a mustard-like paste that you can buy for use in removing grease and rust stains from concrete, cement, terrazzo, stone, tile, or paint surfaces. It will take rust spots from window sills or from concrete stained by the rust of iron railings. A similar product will also remove rust from steel; you apply the paste, then rinse it off a few minutes later with plain water.

WALLS

❰ What's a simple way to replace a wall tile that has suddenly fallen out?

Use double-faced tape, the kind mentioned above under carpeting. Double-faced adhesive tape is designated for use in laying carpet strips or any kind of permanent carpeting. The tape comes rolled up with one side protected by waxed paper. To reset the wall tile, cut the double-faced tape to the proper length and width, place the tape on the wall surface, and press the tile into position over it. You can use double-faced tape to fasten fabric on surfaces, too, or even to refasten loose wallpaper or repair furniture upholstering.

❡ Is there such a thing as "instant" wall tile?

Vinyl floor- and wall-tile now comes especially prepared for the do-it-yourselfer. Each tile is marketed with a self-stick backing, protected by a special covering. You peel off the covering, place the tile in position, and firmly press it down. For small spaces, you cut a foot-square tile to size with a pair of household scissors and apply.

❡ How can you remove wallpaper without using a steamer or paint scraper?

A liquid product has been marketed that soaks through the wallpaper and breaks down the adhesive that holds the paper onto the wall. Mix the remover with water, then apply the mixture with a sponge, brush, or sprayer. The solution is stainless and does not harm the paint on the wall. Nor will it in any way affect the surface of the wall beneath.

❡ If you don't like wallpaper, paneling, tile, or paint as a wall surface, is there anything else you can use?

There is a new vinyl wall covering that can be used on any kind of surface. It is the next thing to textured cloth and will give beauty and warmth to an otherwise dull room. Vinyl wallcover is also a good answer to a wallpaper surface that is damaged, or a wall surface that has cracks or holes in it.

❡ Is there a wall tile that can be put up quickly?

A type of aluminum wall tile, with a vulcanized polyester outer film, is marketed in 1-foot squares, although the pattern of the tile is smaller than that. You simply pull off the protective layer covering the pressure-sensitive adhesive on the back of the tile, and apply the tile to the wall.

❡ What is the easiest way to repair a broken or scratched baseboard?

A snap-on baseboard made of rigid vinyl is now being sold for instant repair to faulty floor moulding. You simply attach clips to the wall and then snap the moulding into place on the clips and over the old baseboard. The vinyl has a smooth, nail-free surface that does not need painting and can be cleaned off with soap and water. The baseboard sections can be cut to any length.

New Developments in Home Repair

❲ Is it possible to hang shelves without complicated carpentry work?

Yes. Use a peg board and steel-shelving kit. Peg board can be fastened to any wall space by screws or nails. The steel shelving framework can be installed on the peg board by means of the fastenings provided with the kit. The work can be done with a wrench and screwdriver.

❲ Can shelves be hung on paneling without permanently damaging the surface?

Get prefinished wood-grain paneling that comes with pre-slotted grooves already provided. The grooves are random-spaced to avoid stud locations. You insert shelf brackets into the grooves and lay on walnut grained wood shelves wherever you want them.

❲ Is it possible to remove scratches and scuff from wood paneling?

There are products available that will fill in any gaps caused by scratches; if these products don't work, simply add a layer of clear varnish squeezed from an aerosol can.

EXTERIOR

❲ How do you fix a leaky downspout?

There is a "downspout repair kit" available that will repair anything from a pinhole to a large leak and a rusted-out area. The kit provides a special rubber coating and some "instant" patch material. Once the material is applied, paint over it with aluminum paint.

❲ Is there a simple tape for metal gutter repairs?

Yes. You can repair downspouts and metal gutters with an easy-to-apply, aluminum, pressure-sensitive tape. The adhesive will give a permanent bond to any clean, dry surface and will conform to any shape without breaking. It makes an airtight, watertight seal in seconds. You can also paint over it or use patching compounds on it after application.

❲ How do you patch a torn awning?

A canvas adhesive is available that comes in a self-applicator squeeze bottle. It will repair worn spots and rips in canvas and is flexible when dry to conform to the shape of the canvas.

❊ *How do you get rid of ice on the driveway or sidewalk?*

Calcium chloride is a fast, dependable de-icer, one that will work at all temperatures down to −59° F. It will not permanently harm vegetation or trees, nor will it leave that powdery white dust on sidewalk or pavement.

DOORS

❊ *How do you unstick a sticking doorknob?*

There are three kinds of graphite lubricants you can use for such a situation: dry graphite, graphite oil, and lock lubricant. Dry graphite will work for locks, wood, or plastic window channels. Graphite oil will work for casters, hinges, locks, and springs. Lock lubricant, which is unaffected by heat or cold, will work for locks, latches, and hinges on cars.

❊ *Is there any easy way to patch holes in door and window screens?*

If the rips are big, but less than an inch in diameter, use a type of snap patch that you can buy, ready to push into place over the hole. The patch has a row of hooks at the borders; these fit into the screening and hold in the square. If you can't buy the product, improvise some patches yourself.

WINDOWS

❊ *Is there any way to make a sticking window slide more easily?*

Use a dry lubricant that is a combination of cleaning fluid and teflon. You spray on the lubricant from an aerosol can; the solvent quickly evaporates and leaves behind the teflon which then acts as a dry lubricant. It will work on anything that sticks: drawers, windows, doors, or whatever.

❊ *What can you use temporarily to seal off cracks near windows, doors, and baseboards before tackling a permanent job of caulking or weatherstripping?*

There is a tough polyethylene tape made especially for sealing out weather and dirt. You just apply it around windows and over cracks with your fingertips. It sticks tightly, and yet you can always remove it cleanly and easily when you get ready to do a permanent job. It's almost invisible.

❧ How can you give temporary repair to a broken window pane?

If the break isn't too bad, use transparent pressure-sensitive tape. You'll have to replace the pane when the weather improves, of course.

❧ Is there any way to install bang-proof shutters?

Get prefinished, durable, permanent, lightweight nylon shutters that resemble the real thing but simply clip on to the outside of the house. They need no maintenance, they do not move in the wind, and they can be lifted off easily when you're painting the outside of the house. You can affix them to any kind of house surface. Heavy-duty spring clips come with the shutters.

FURNITURE

❧ What's the best way to repair dinette chair upholstering?

Buy a repair kit containing vinyl on an elastic-knit fabric backing. It can be used for making covers for chair backs, seats, card-table tops, and auto-top carrier covers.

❧ Is there anything you can do with an old piece of wooden furniture that has been around the house for generations?

Save it. Then give the piece an antique finish. There are many kits available for antiquing hand-me-downs. Most include three or four stages: a sanding or smoothing stage, a base-coat stage, an antiquing-toner stage, and a finish coat. When you've finished, the piece of furniture looks like a real, honest antique.

❧ How do you snap up sagging furniture upholstery?

Use foam rubber to replace the deadened upholstering. You can get it in thicknesses from half an inch to eight inches which you can cut to any length, width, or shape necessary. If your cushion covers are zippered, all you need to do is cut a latex foam cushion to the proper size and thickness and insert it into the cushion. You will have a resilient, comfortable cushion that is fully reversible, mildewproof, dustfree, non-allergenic, and lightweight, and that recovers its shape instantly and will not mat down, hollow out, or sag.

❮ Can you repair wooden chairs covered with vinyl?

Wooden chairs that are covered with vinyl or plastic upholstery can be repaired by buying any covering material of your choice and following the size and shape of the original in cutting out your own foam-rubber filler. Fit the foam-rubber filler and plastic covering tightly to the chair seat and fasten it with tacks.

❮ How do you replace broken springs in upholstered chairs and couches?

Don't bother. First of all, replace the material that is used for bulking out the cushions with foam rubber, as described above. Then replace the broken base of the chair with a board or a section of plywood. Drill a half dozen holes in the board or plywood in order to permit the latex foam cushion to "breathe." If the foam rubber is thick enough, you can use it directly on any flat, hard surface.

❮ Is there any way to fix a broken spring assembly in a couch?

As above, don't bother. Remake the couch yourself in the following two steps. First, replace the upholstered cushion material with latex foam rubber, as described above. Second, lay a honeycomb-construction interior flush door across the couch's base and fasten it to the frame. Then simply place the upholstered cushion material on the door. If you have a thickness of 6 to 8 inches, you will find it quite comfortable.

❮ What's the easiest way to tighten loose chair legs, rungs that don't fit, and loose backs?

The best way to make these furniture repairs is to use a kind of furniture adhesive that can be introduced into the holes with a hypodermic-type syringe. There is a furniture-repair kit that contains exactly these materials: adhesive, hypodermic syringe, and clamps. You shoot the glue into the loose portion where the leg fits, clamp it, and let it dry.

EMERGENCY

❮ How can you protect yourself against fire in the home?

Use a type of fire alarm that can be hung on the wall and plugged into a household outlet. A unit of this type will go off if the temperature around it exceeds 136° F. It will give a distinctive shriek that cannot fail to be heard.

❰ *How can you put out a fire in the home?*

Always keep some kind of foam fire extinguisher in the house, garage, or attic. There is an aerosol-type extinguisher on the market which works exactly like any pressurized aerosol can.

❰ *Is there any way to take care of accident emergencies when they arise in the home?*

Buy a marketed kit that contains the following emergency equipment: dry-powder fire extinguisher, first-aid kit, poison-antidote kit, airway resuscitator, aerosol spray, emergency bar, magnetic flashlight and heavy-duty batteries, candles, and safety matches.

INDEX

Acrylic paint, 16
Acoustical ceiling, 212
Acoustical tile, 207-208
Adhesives, 62-65, 216; (chart) 63; animal glue, 62; casein glue, 62; contact cement, 63; epoxy cement, 62, 216; fish glue, 62; for carpeting, 216; library paste, 62; liquid vinyl cement, 63; mucilage, 62; plastic aluminum cement, 63; plastic rubber cement, 62; polystyrene cement, 64; silicone rubber sealant, 63; steel paste, 63; synthetic thermoplastic resin glue, 62; synthetic thermosetting resin glue, 62
Adjustable wrench, 41, 53
Aggregate, 172
Air conditioner, types, 198-199; air-cooled, 201; amperage, 200; fuses, 203; horsepower, 200; mounting, 203; tonnage, 200; water cooled, 201; wattage, 200; where to place, 202; where to store, 204; wiring, 203
Air conditioning, 198-204; theory, 201; air leakage control, 200; British Thermal Unit, 199, 200
Alkyd paint, 16, 25
Alkyd resin paint, 15
Aluminum cement, 63
Aluminum tile, 189
Amperes, 91, 200
Animal glue, 62
Appliance motors, 104-105

Appliances, electric, 3, 101-107 (and see under Electricity)
Auger, 6, 79
Awnings, 165-166; torn, 221

Baseboard repair, 220
Batts, insulating, 193
Bits, 40, 49-50
Blanket, electric, 104
Blowing wool, 193
Boiler, 84
Broken glass, 9; (picture), 9
Bolts, 60-62
Bookshelves, 146
Box nails, 57
Brace, 40, 49
Brace & bit, 49-50; (picture), 49
Brads, 57, 60
Brick, 182-185 (and see under Masonry)
Brick hammer, 184
Brick mortar, 183
Brick wall, 127; (picture), 126
British Thermal Unit, 199, 200
Broom, concrete, 175; (picture), 175
Brushes, paint, 33-36; (picture), 34
BTU, 199, 200
Buffing, 28
Buttering trowel, 184
Building felt, 197
Building paper, 197
Butadiene styrene paint, 16
BX cable, 94, 136

"C" clamp, 65
Calcimine, 16
Carpeting, waterproof, 218; outdoor, 218
Carriage bolts, 61
Casein glue, 62
Casein paint, 16
Casing nails, 57
Caulking, 130-131
Ceilings, 134-135
Ceiling tile, how to hang, 212; (picture), 134
Cement, Portland, 171 (see Concrete)
Cement-coated nails, 57, 113
Cement-lime mortar, 183
Ceramic tile, 187, 189 (and see under Masonry)
Cesspool, 81; clogged, 82
Chair, broken, 224; legs loose, 224; upholstery repair, 223; vinyl-covered, 224
Chimneys, 87-88; flue, 88
Chisel, 40, 46-47; (picture), 46
Circuit breaker, 4, 94
Circuit, electric, 95, 97; (picture), 96
Clamps, 40, 65
Claw hammer, 40, 41-42
Closet auger, 6, 79
Cold chisel, 47-48; (picture), 47
Colored concrete, 180
Combination square, 40, 51
Common nails, 57
Compass saw, 40, 45
Concrete, 170-181; aggregate, 172; components, 171; cracked, 179, 219; cubic yard of, 175; grout, 171; how to color, 180; how to mix, 172-173; maintenance, 180-181; mixing tools, 174-175 (and see under Tools); mortar, 171 (and see under Masonry); patio slab, 176-179; Portland cement, 171; purchasing, 171; sand, 172-173; strength, 172
Concrete block, 185-186 (and see under Masonry)
Conduction, 85, 190
Convenience outlet, 2, 135
Convection, 85

Convectors, 85
Contact cement, 63
Coping saw, 40, 45
Cord, electric, 2, 94
Corrugated fastener, 61
Couch, broken, 224
Cover of paint (chart), 24
Cracked plaster, 141
Cracked stucco, 127
Crazing, 187
Curling iron, electric, 104
Current, electric (AC, DC), 92

Decibels, 206
Detergents in septic tank, 82
Doorbell, 3-4
Doorknob, sticky, 222
Door screens, 10, 164
Doors, 148-155, 222; frame, 148; how to hang, 152-153; how to paint, 155; how to remove, 149; lock installation, 153-155; maintenance, 151-152; rattling, 149-150; screen doors, 10; steel doors, 152; scraping, 10; sticking, 149-150
Downspout, leaky, 221
Draftsman's symbols, 55-56; (picture), 56
Drain cleaners, 82
Drainage pipe, 6
Drill, hand, 50
Dripless paint, 16
Driveway, icy, 222
Drywall, 137-139

Edger, 174; (picture), 175
Electric appliances, 3, 101-107; blankets, 104; curling iron, 104; electric heater, 103; electric iron, 103, 104; electric roaster, 104; fan, 106; heating element, 102; heating pad, 104; hotplate, 103; motors, 101; percolator, 104; refrigerator, 106-107; steam iron, 103; toaster, 102, 103; wattage (chart) 98; vacuum cleaner, 105-106; waffle iron, 104

Index

Electric circuits (picture) 96
Electric fuse, 4, 94-95
Electric heat, 80, 88; (picture), 89
Electric lights, 2, 3, 100-101; incandescent, 2; fluorescent, 3, 100-101
Electric meter, 92
Electric outlets, 2; convenience-type, 93, 135-136; fixed-light, 93; three-prong, 100
Electric wall switch, 3, 136
Electric wiring, 2, 93-94; BX cable, 94; circuit breaker, 4, 94; color of wire, 93; cord, 3; fuses, 4, 94-95; insulation, 94; lights, 2; outlets, 2, 92, 93, 99, 100, 135-136 (and see under Electric outlets); plugs, 99-100; sockets, 93; wall switches, 3, 136
Electricity, 90-107; amperes, 91; circuit, 95, 97, (picture), 96; current (AC, DC), 92; cycles, 92; horsepower & wattage, 97; kilowatt hours, 91; theory, 90; volts, 91; watts, 91, 94, 97
Elevation (architectural), 56
Emergencies, accident, 225
Emulsion paint, 15, 16, 25
Enamel, 17, 19, 29, 31
Enamel undercoat, 17
Epoxy cement, 62; "instant," 216
Epoxy resin paint, 17
Exterior enamel, 17
Exterior paints (chart), 21

Face brick, 183
Fan, electric, 106
Fasteners, nails, nuts & bolts, screws, 56-62
Fat fire, 12
Faucet, leaky, 5, 77, 78; thumping, 80; (picture), 6
Faucet seat dresser, 78
File, wood, 41
Filler, 28
Finish, 29
Finish nails, 57
Fire, alarm, 224; extinguisher, 225
Fire brick, 183

Fireplace, 87
Fireproof awning, 165
Fish glue, 62
Flashing, 131
Flat paint, 14
Floor cleaner, 217; tile surface, 217
Floor wax, 118; finish-and-wax, 217
Floors, 108-122; basement, 121-122; bathroom, 120; finish, 110; finish-and-wax, 217; flooded, 121-122; how to power-sand, 118-120; how to tile, 114; joists, 108, 109; kitchen, 121; maintenance, 114, 120; nails, 113; repair, 110; sub-floor, 109; wax, 118; (picture), 109, 111
Floor surfaces, 113-114; asphalt tile, 113; ceramic tile, 113; cork, 114; hardwood, 113, 117; linoleum, 113, 115-116; rubber tile, 113; softwood, 113, 117; terrazzo, 113, 116-117; vinyl, 113; vinyl asbestos tile, 113
Floor tile, 114, 187
Fluorescent light, 3, 100-101
Folding rule, 54-55
Forced-air heat, 86
Framing timber, 67
Framing square, 51
Fuels, heating, 85
Fungus paint, 23
Furniture repair, 223-224; antiquing, 223; chair, broken, 224; chair leg, loose, 224; chair upholstery, repair, 223; chair, vinyl-covered, 224; couch, broken, 224; upholstery, sagging, 223; upholstery springs, broken, 224
Furring strips, 139
Fuse, blown, 4
Fuse box, (picture), 96

Garbage can lid, 12
Garden hose, leaky, 7
Gas heat, 80
Glass, broken, 9; (picture), 9
Glass-cutter, 40, 51-52
Glaziers points, 9
Glossy paint, 14

Glue (chart), 63; see Adhesives
Glues, 62-65; how to glue, 64
Grease trap, 82
Grout, 171; cleaner, 218
Gutter repairs, 221
Gypsum board, 137, 138-139

Hammer, 40, 41, 42; (picture), 41
Hand drill, 41, 50
Handsaw, 40, 43-46; (picture), 44
Hardwood, 67
Header, 124, 137
Heat loss, 191
Heat, types of, 84-89; electric, 80, 88; forced-air, 86; hot-water, 85, 86; radiant, 85, 217; steam, 85; gas, 85
Heater, electric, 103; (picture), 89; ceiling, 217
Heating, 84-89; chimneys, 87, 88; coal, 85; electricity, 85; fireplaces, 87; natural gas, 85, oil, 85; theory, 84-86
Heating pad, 104
Hoe, 175; (picture), 175
Horsepower & wattage, 97, 200
Hotplate, 103
Hot-water heat, 80, 85-86
Hot-water tank, 81
House paint, 15
House-paint undercoat, 15
How to hang things, 11-12; 142-143

Inside flat paint, 15
Insulating materials, 191-197; batts & blankets, 193; blowing wool, 193; metal-foil, 197; mineral wool, 191; pouring wool, 193; (chart), 192
Insulation, 190-197; attic, 193, 196; building felt, 197; building paper, 197; cement slab floor, 194; cold leaks, 192; crawl space, 194; heat loss, 191; humidity, 196; moisture, 194; "R" factor, 191; roof, 193; vapor barrier, 195, 196; ventilation, 196; wall, 192; wooden floor, 194
Insulation (chart), 192

Insulation, electric, 94
Interior enamel, 17
Interior paints (chart), 18
Iron, electric, 103-104
Iron, steam, 103

Kilowatt hours, 91

Lacquer, 16, 30
Lamp, flickering, 4
Latex paint, 15, 25, 31, 32
Laying out jobs, 54
Leaks, basement, 121, 122; roofs, 10; walls, 128, 130-132
Level, 40, 51, 184
Library paste, 62
Light bulb, electric, 2
Light, fluorescent, 3, 100-101
Light socket, 93
Linoleum, 113; how to paint, 31
Linseed oil, 14, 15, 16
Liquid vinyl cement, 63
Locks, 153-155
Lumber, 67-76 (see Wood)
Lumber, defects, 70; sizes, 69

Machine bolts, 61
Masonry, 182-189; repair, 188-189
Masonry, bricks, 182-185; face brick, 183; fire brick, 183; Grade H brick, 183; Grade M Brick, 183; Grade S brick, 183; how to clean brick, 186; how to enrich brick, 187; how to lay brick, 184-186; brick mortar, 183
Masonry, ceramic tile, 187-189; crazing, 187; floor tile, 187; how to lay tile, 189; repair, 188; wall tile, 187
Masonry, concrete block, 185-186; footings, 186; how to lay, 186
Masonry, mortar, 171, 183-184; brick mortar, 183; cement-lime mortar, 183; crumbling, 185; repair, 185; straight-lime mortar, 184; tools, 184
Masonry paint, 17, 31
Marking gauge, 40

Index

Metal-foil insulation, 197
Meter, electric, 92
Mildew paint, 23
Millwork, 68
Mineral wool, 191
Mineral spirits, 15, 16
Miter box, 41
Moisture control, 194
Molding, 135
Monkey wrench, 53
Mortar, 171, 183-184; (and see under Masonry)
Motors, electric, 101
Mucilage, 62

Nail set, 40, 52
Nails, 56-59; (chart), 58; box nails, 57; brads, 57, 60; casing nails, 57; cement-coated nails, 57; common nails, 57; finish nails, 57; wire nails, 57
Nails, popping, 11
Nut, 12, 61-62
Nut and bolt, 61-62; anti-loosening, 215

Oil heat, 85
Oil paint, 15, 19
Oil, penetrating, 62
Oilstone, 41
Outlet, convenience, 2, 135
Outlet, electric, 2, 92, 93, 99, 100, 135-136
Overload, 99

Packing, faucet, 78
Paint, 13-39, 214-215; types, 15; acrylic, 16; alkyd, 16, 25; alkyd resin, 15; butadiene styrene, 16; calcimine, 16; casein, 16; dripless, 16; emulsion, 15, 16, 25; enamel, 17, 19, 29, 31; enamel undercoat, 17; epoxy enamel, 215; epoxy resin, 17; exterior (chart), 21; exterior enamel, 17; flat, 14; glossy, 14; heat-resistant, 215; house, 15; house-paint undercoat, 15; inside flat paint, 15; interior (chart), 18; interior enamel, 17; lacquer, 16, 30; latex, 15, 25, 31, 32; masonry, 17, 31; mildew, 23; oil, 15, 19; polyvinyl-acetate, 16; primer, 15; rubber, 17, 25; screening enamel, 17; sealer, 16, 28; semi-gloss, 14; shellac, 16, 29; stain, 28; texture, 16; undercoat, 15; varnish, 16, 19, 29, 30; waterproofing sealer, 17; water-thinned, 16, 19; whitewash, 16
Paint, accessories for, 33-38
Paint brushes, 33-36; cleaning, 35; parts, 33; pistol-grip, 215; preconditioning, 35; reclaiming, 36; shapes, 34; sizes, 33; special types, 34; storing, 35; (chart), 34
Paint, components, 14
Paint, interior, 17; basement, 31, 32; basement floors, 20; basement walls, 20, 31; bathroom, 31; bathroom woodwork, 31; bathroom color, 31; ceiling, 17, 27, 214; doors, 155; drywall, 18; floor, 20, 28; floor buffing, 28; floor enamel, 29, 31; floor filler, 28; floor finish, 29; floor lacquer, 30; floor sealer, 28; floor shellac, 29; floor stain, 28; floor varnish, 29; kitchen, 30, 31; kitchen cabinets 30; kitchen ceiling, 30; kitchen colors, 30; kitchen drawers, 30; kitchen linoleum, 31; kitchen walls, 30; molding, 19; plaster wall, 17; radiators, 20; trim, 19; vinyl-covered wall, 18; walls, 17, 25, 26; windows, 160-161; woodwork, 25
Paint, exterior, 20-32; coats, 21; cost, 20; aluminum, 33; brick, 22; bronze, 33; copper, 33; fresh plaster, 17, 22; galvanized iron, 32; gutters, 32; masonry, 22; metal, 32; new wood, 21; old plaster, 22; old wood, 22; painted wood, 23; porch floors, 22; screening, 32; shingles, 22; stain for knotty pine, 25; trim, 22; unpainted wood, 23
Paint, preparation of, 19, 23; enamel, 19; mildewcide, 23; oil, 19; varnish, 19; water-thinned, 19

Paint remover, electric, 215
Paint rollers, 36-37; cleaning, 37; dripless, 214; how to use, 36; parts, 36; sizes, 36; types, 36
Paint sprayers, 37; aerosol type, 38; cleaning, 38; how to use, 37; parts, 37; p.s.i., 37; (picture), 37, 38
Paint thinner, 14
Paint, wet, 11
Paneling, 137-138, 141-142, removing scratches, 221; shelving on, 221
Patio slab, contruction, 176-179; (picture), 176
Pennyweight (of nails), 58; (chart), 58
Penetrating oil, 62
Percolator, electric, 104
Picture hanging, 11
Pipe, frozen, 216; leaky, 8, 216
Pipe wrench, 41
Pipes, drainage, 79
Pipes, hammering, 79; rumbling, 80
Plane, 40, 48-49; (picture), 48
Plans, how to read, 55-56; (picture), 56
Plasterboard, 137, 138-139
Plaster, cracked, 141
Plastic aluminum cement, 63
Plastic rubber cement, 62, 63
Pliers, 41, 52
Plugs, electric, 99-100
Plumbing, 77-83, 216; drain trap, 6; leak, 5
Plumbing solvent, 6
Plunger, 6; (picture), 7
Plywood, 73-76, 137
Pointing trowel, 184
Putty, 9, 158-159; (picture), 9
Polystyrene cement, 64
Polyvinyl-acetate paint, 16
Portland cement, 171
Pouring wool, 193
Primer, 15

Rabbet, 9; (picture), 9
Radiant heat, 85
Radiation, 85
Radiators, 86-87

Rasp, 41
Ready-mix concrete, 176
Refrigerator, 106-107
Resin emulsion, 14
"R" factor (in insulation), 191
Riveting, 54
Rive-tool, 41, 54
Roaster, electric, 104
Rockwall, 137, 138-139
Rollers, paint, 36
Roof, (picture), 129
Roof leaks, 11
Rubber cement, 62
Rubber paint, 17, 25
Rule, measuring, 40; folding, 54-55; tapeless, 216
Rust remover, 219

Saw, hand, 40, 43-46; (picture), 44
Scissors, how to sharpen, 12
Scorch spots, 12
Screen door, 10
Screening enamel, 17
Screens, broken, 10, 222
Screens, window, 163-165
Screw jack, 110-111; (picture), 111
Screws, 12, 56, 59-61; (chart), 59
Screwdriver, 40, 42-43; (picture), 42
Screwdriver bit, 40, 50
Sealer, 16, 28
Seasoning (of lumber), 68
Seat, faucet, 79
Semi-gloss paint, 14
Septic tank, 82
Sewage disposal, 82
Sewer line, 83
Shades, roller, 163
Sheathing, 67; (picture), 125
Sheetrock, 137, 138-139
Shellac, 16, 29
Shelving, instant, 221; on paneling, 221
Shingles, 68; side, 128
Short circuit, 2, 4
Shovel, 174
Shutter, bangproof, 223
Sidewalk, icy, 222

Index

Siding, 126; (picture), 125
Silicone rubber sealant, 63
Sink, detergents, 82
Sizing, 145
Smooth plane, 40
Sockets, electric, 93
Socket wrench, 53
Softwood, 67
Sound conditioning, 205-213; acoustical ceiling, 212; acoustical tile, 207-208; decibels, 206; how to hang tile ceiling, 212; (picture), 134
Sound proofing, 205-213; (and see Sound conditioning)
Spark box, 87-88
Spokeshave, 41
Sprayers, paint, 37; (picture), 37, 38
Square, 40, 51
Starter, flourescent light, 3
Stain, paint, 28
Steam heat, 85
Steel paste, 63
Steel tile, 189
Steel trowel, 174; (picture), 175
Stillson wrench, 54
Storm windows, 160, 167-169
Straight-lime mortar, 184
Strike board, 174; (picture), 175
Stucco wall, 126-127; (picture), 126
Studs, 123; how to locate, 11
"Surform" tool, 40, 51
Synthetic thermoplastic resin glue, 62
Synthetic thermosetting resin glue, 62

Tamp, 174; (picture), 175
Tank, expansion, 7
Tape, measuring, 40
Taping gypsum board, 139
Texture paint, 16
Tile, 187-189; carpet, 218; ceramic, 187-189; steel, 189; aluminum, 189; (and see under Masonry)
Tile, ceiling, how to hang, (picture), 134
Tile cleaner, 217, 218
Toaster, electric, 102-103
Toggle bolts, 61

Toilet, faulty, 5; noisy, 217
Tonnage, 200
Tools, 39-54, 216; adjustable wrench, 41, 53; bits, 40, 49-50; brace, 40, 49-50; chisel, 40, 46-47; clamps, 40, 65; claw hammer, 40, 41-42; cold chisel, 47-48; compass saw, 40; coping saw, 40; glass-cutter, 40, 51-52; hand drill, 41, 50; hand saw, 40, 43-46; level, 40, 51; marking gauge, 40; miter box, 41; monkey wrench, 53; nail set, 40, 52; oilstone, 41; pipe wrench, 41, 54; plane, 40, 48-49; pliers, 41, 52; rasp, 41; Rive-tool, 41, 54; rule, 40; screwdrivers, 40, 42-43; screwdriver bit, 40, 50; smooth plane, 40; socket wrench, 53; spokeshave, 41; square, 40, 51; Stillson wrench, 54; "Surform," 40, 51; tapeless rule, 216; vise, 41, 52; wrenches, 53-54
Tools, for brick, 184; brick trowel, 184; brick hammer, 184; buttering trowel, 184; cord, 184; level, 184; pointing trowel, 184; zig-zag rule, 184
Tools, for concrete, 174-175; broom, 175; edger, 174; hoe, 175; shovel, 174; steel trowel, 174; strike board, 174; tamp, 174; wheelbarrow, 174; wood float, 174; (picture), 175
Trim, 68
Turpentine, 14, 15, 16

Undercoat, 15
Upholstery, sagging, 223; springs, broken, 224

Vacuum cleaner, 105-106
Valve, main supply, 5
Valve washer, 5, 78
Vapor barrier, 195-196
Varnish, 16, 19, 29, 30
Veneered panels, 141-142
Venetian blinds, 162-163
Ventilation, 196

Vise, 41, 52
Voltage drop, 91, 97
Volts, 91

Waffle iron, 104
Wallcover, vinyl, 220
Wallpaper, 143-146; removal, 220
Wall switches, 3, 136
Walls, inside, 133-147; bookshelves, 146; ceilings, 134; closet shelves, 146-147; drywall, 137-139; furring strips, 139; how to hang things, 142-143; molding, 135; outlets, electric, 135-136; paneling, 137-138, 141-142; plaster, 140-141; plumbing pipes, 136; plywood, 137; wallpaper, 143-146; wall switches, electric, 3, 136
Walls, outside, 123-132; brick, 127; caulking, 130-131; leaks, 128-132; shingles, 130; siding types, 125-126; stucco, 126-127; studs, 123; tow & oakum, 132; windows, 124; (picture), 124, 125, 126
Wall tile, 187; aluminum, 220; "instant," 220; replacing, 219
Washers, construction, 61; faucet, 5-6, 78
Water heater, 80-81
Waterproof awning, 165
Waterproofing sealer, 17
Water supply valve, 5
Water table, 121
Water-thinned paint, 16, 19
Wattage of appliances (chart), 98-99
Wax, floor, 118
Watts, 91, 94, 200
Weatherstripping, 166-169
Web clamp, 52

Wheelbarrow, 174
Whitewash, 16
Wigglenail, 61
Window glass, broken, 9; (picture), 9; 223
Window, how to paint, 160-161
Window, leaky, 10, 130, 222; sticky, 222
Window sash, frozen, 8
Window screens, 10, 164, 222
Window, storm, metal, 8
Windows, 156-169, 222; awnings, 165-166; frame, 156; how to paint, 160-161; leaks, 10, 130; lubrication, 160; protection, 160; putty, 9, 158-159; repair, 9, 158, 159; roller shades, 163; sash, 157; storm windows, 167-169; Venetian blinds, 162-163; weatherstripping, 166-167; window screens, 163-165; (picture), 157
Wire nails, 57
Wiring, electric, 2, 93-94 (and see under Electric wiring)
Wood, 67-76; board feet, 72; boards, 69; defects, 70; flooring, 67, 71; hardwood, 67; interior trim, 68, 72; millwork, 68; plywood, 73-76; purchase of, 72; quality grades, 70; running feet, 73; seasoning, 68; sheathing, 67; shingles, 68, 71; siding, 67, 71; softwood, 67; strips, 69; timbers, 69; cuts, (picture), 71
Wood filler, 23, 64
Wood float, 174; (picture), 175
Wood screws (chart), 59; 59-61
Wrench, adjustable, 41, 53; monkey, 53, socket, 53; Stillson, 54, (picture), 53

Zig-zag rule, 54-55; 184

THE FIRST IN LANCER'S NEW
CRAFT BOOK SERIES

THE COMPLETE BOOK OF DECOUPAGE

by
Frances S. Wing

#76305 $1.95

Discover the pleasures of decorating almost any object you wish with paper cut-outs easily obtained from magazines, newspapers, even wallpaper

THE COMPLETE BOOK OF DECOUPAGE

is filled with helpful hints, the latest innovations and techniques, and simple, step-by-step, fully illustrated instructions.

If this book is not on sale at your local newsstand send 10¢ for mailing costs to Lancer Books, Inc., 1560 Broadway, New York, N.Y. 10036. On orders of 4 or more books we pay the postage.
Write for free catalog, too!

Lancer Larchmont Craft Books

— now available —

- 76305 THE COMPLETE BOOK OF DECOUPAGE
  Frances S. Wing—$1.95
- 76308 STITCH IT IN
  Arden J. Newsome—$1.95
- 76309 NEEDLEPOINT FROM START TO FINISH
  Joan Scobey—$1.95
- 76311 THE COMPLETE BOOK OF TIE-DYEING
  Astrith Deyrup—$1.95
- 76312 CONTEMPORARY CROCHET
  Susan Morrow and Mark Dittrick—$1.95
- 76320 TOYS: A STEP-BY-STEP GUIDE TO CREATIVE TOYMAKING
  Charlene Davis Roth with Jerome Roth—$1.95
- 76318 CANDLES: A STEP-BY-STEP GUIDE TO CREATIVE CANDLEMAKING
  Arden J. Newsome—$1.95
- 76313 RUGMAKING FROM START TO FINISH
  Joan Scobey—$1.95

— and soon to be published —
books on
hand-stitched leather, patchwork and making silver jewelry.

All in digest size easy-to-read type.

If these books are not available at your local newsstand, send price indicated plus 10¢ to cover mailing costs. On orders of four or more books, Lancer will pay postage. If you wish a complete free catalogue, write to LANCER BOOKS, INC., 1560 Broadway, New York, New York 10036.

HEALTH BOOKS FROM LANCER

#71-310	YOGA AND COMMON SENSE by Ina Marx	$1.50
#75-162	HERBS: THE MAGIC HEALERS Paul Twitchell	95¢
#75-167	BIO-ORGANICS: YOUR FOOD AND YOUR HEALTH by James Rorty and N. Philip Norman, M.D.	95¢
#75-183	GET YOUR HEALTH TOGETHER by Joan Weiner	95¢
#78-620	FUNDAMENTALS OF YOGA Rammurti Mishra, M.D.	$1.25
#78-666	THE HUNZA-YOGA WAY TO HEALTH & LONGER LIFE by Renee Taylor	$1.25
#38-100	BACK TO EDEN by Jethro Kloss	$2.00

If these books are not available at your local newsstand, send price indicated plus 10¢ to cover mailing costs. On orders of four or more books, Lancer will pay postage. If you wish a complete free catalogue, write to LANCER BOOKS, INC., 1560 Broadway, New York, N.Y. 10036